CARE AND MANAGEMENT OF PATIENTS WITH HIV INFECTION

Medical Editor:
John A. Bartlett, MD
Assistant Professor of Medicine
Principal Investigator, AIDS Clinical Trials Unit
Duke University Medical Center

Developed and produced
in cooperation with

Executive Office Park, Suite 310
1920 Highway 54 East, Durham, N.C. 27713
Phone (919) 544-8752 FAX (919) 544-8558

ISBN: 1-881011-01-1

CONTENTS

Page No.

HOW TO OBTAIN CONTINUING EDUCATION CREDIT v

CHAPTER 1: OVERVIEW OF HIV INFECTION 1
    Anthony Adinolfi, RN, MSN (Candidate)
    Harry A. Gallis, MD
CHAPTER 2: BASIC CONCEPTS OF THE IMMUNE RESPONSE AND
    THE IMMUNOLOGY OF HIV INFECTION 63
    Kent J. Weinhold, PhD
CHAPTER 3: DIAGNOSIS AND TREATMENT OF THE PATIENT
    WITH HIV INFECTION 103
    John A. Bartlett, MD
    Harry A. Gallis, MD
    Kenneth W. Shipp, BS Pharm
    Karen L. Nabors, PharmD
CHAPTER 4: LEGAL ISSUES IN THE TREATMENT OF PATIENTS
    WITH HIV INFECTION 137
    Janet B. Seifert, JD
    Frank T. Flannery, MD, JD
    James G. Zimmerly, MD, JD, MPH
CHAPTER 5: THE ROLE OF THE PHYSICIAN IN THE CARE OF PATIENTS
    WITH HIV INFECTION 177
    Ross E. McKinney, Jr, MD
    Harry A. Gallis, MD
CHAPTER 6: THE ROLE OF THE PHARMACIST IN THE CARE OF PATIENTS
    WITH HIV INFECTION 225
    Kenneth W. Shipp, BS Pharm
    Karen L. Nabors, PharmD
FLORIDA LAW ON AIDS: A SUPPLEMENT TO *CARE AND MANAGEMENT
OF PATIENTS WITH HIV INFECTION* 309
    David B. Brushwood, BS Pharm, JD
CHAPTER 7: THE ROLE OF THE NURSE IN THE CARE OF PATIENTS
    WITH HIV INFECTION 331
    Anthony Adinolfi, RN, MSN (Candidate)

HOW TO OBTAIN
CONTINUING EDUCATION CREDIT

This book is designed to provide continuing education credit to pharmacists, physicians, and nurses. There are actually three continuing education programs in the book. The first four chapters contain material essential for all health professionals. Chapters 5, 6, and 7 are written specifically for physicians, pharmacists, and nurses, respectively.

PHARMACISTS:

Pharmacists who wish to obtain continuing education credit for successful completion of the pharmacy CE program (chapters 1, 2, 3, 4, and 6) should follow the instructions given in the Test Grading Options section located at the end of chapter 6. The pharmacy continuing education program contained in this book meets the requirements for and is recognized as being appropriate for the mandatory AIDS education legislated in the following states: Kansas, Kentucky, New Jersey, and Washington.

 Glaxo Inc. is approved by the American Council on Pharmaceutical Education as a provider of continuing pharmaceutical education.

Program ID No.: 686-342-92-041, 7 Contact Hours, 0.7 CEU

FLORIDA REGISTERED PHARMACISTS:

In order to meet the Florida mandatory AIDS education requirements, pharmacists registered in Florida must complete the seven-hour program (chapters 1, 2, 3, 4, and 6) *and* the supplemental one-hour program "Florida Law on AIDS," which follows chapter 6 in this book. The combination of the seven-hour course and the one-hour supplement constitutes an eight-hour program (Florida program number PSA-94-006, expiration date December 31, 1994).

Pharmacists who wish to meet the mandatory Florida AIDS education requirement *must* use the posttest answer sheet located on page 329. This answer sheet is comprehensive of the posttest questions at the end of chapter 6 and the posttest questions at the end of the supplement "Florida Law on AIDS."

 Florida Program ID No.: PSA-94-006, 8 Contact Hours, 0.8 CEU

ACPE ID No.: 686-342-92-041, 7 Contact Hours, 0.7 CEU
ACPE ID No.: 686-342-92-016, 1 Contact Hour, 0.1 CEU

PHYSICIANS:

Physicians who wish to obtain continuing education credit for successful completion of the CME program (chapters 1, 2, 3, 4, and 5) should follow the instructions on the Continuing Medical Education Posttest Answer Sheet located at the end of chapter 5.

 The Duke University School of Medicine is accredited by the Accreditation Council for Continuing Medical Education to sponsor continuing medical education.

This activity is approved for 7 credit hours (0.7 CEU) in Category 1 of the Physician's Recognition Award of the AMA provided the activity is completed as directed.

NURSES:

Nurses who wish to obtain continuing education credit for successful completion of this provider-directed independent study activity (chapters 1, 2, 3, 4, and 7) should follow the instructions in the Test Grading Options section located at the end of chapter 7.

Nurses in all states except California, Florida, Kansas, and Iowa:

Glaxo Inc. provides 7 hours of continuing education credit for *Care and Management of Patients with HIV Infection* as a provider-directed independent study activity. This provider-directed independent study activity has been approved (approval number 6574) by the North Carolina Nurses Association. The North Carolina Nurses Association is accredited as an approver of continuing education in nursing by the American Nurses' Credentialing Centers Commission on Accreditation.

Nurses in California, Florida, Kansas, and Iowa:

You may submit the program to your state board for approval as a continuing education nursing activity.

CARE AND MANAGEMENT OF PATIENTS WITH HIV INFECTION

Chapter 1: Overview of HIV Infection

Anthony Adinolfi, RN, MSN (Candidate)
Nurse Clinician, Division of Infectious Diseases
AIDS Clinical Trials Unit
Duke University Medical Center

Harry A. Gallis, MD
Associate Professor of Medicine
Duke University Medical Center

CONTENTS

Introduction 5
Objectives 5
   I.   Issues for Persons with AIDS 6
        A. Perspective of a Health Care Worker 6
        B. Typical Patient Feelings about Having AIDS 8
   II.   Overview of AIDS 10
Glossary 12
AIDS-related Organizations and Hotlines 19
AIDS Resources 21
Recommended Follow-up 22
Recommendations for Prevention of HIV Transmission in
    Health-Care Settings 25
Update: Universal Precautions for Prevention of Transmission of
    Human Immunodeficiency Virus, Hepatitis B Virus, and
    Other Bloodborne Pathogens in Health-Care Settings 43
Recommendations for Preventing Transmission of Human
    Immunodeficiency Virus and Hepatitis B Virus to Patients
    During Exposure-Prone Invasive Procedures 51

INTRODUCTION

Care and Management of Patients with HIV Infection is designed for health professionals from pharmacy, nursing, and medicine who wish to broaden their knowledge and improve their skills in taking care of patients with HIV infection. This chapter provides an overview of the problem and some resources for patients, families, and health care team members. Chapter 2 reviews the function of the immune system and the immunology of AIDS. Chapter 3 presents the diagnosis and treatment of HIV infection and the opportunistic infections and malignancies that accompany it. Chapter 4 presents some of the legal issues surrounding diagnosis and treatment of AIDS. These four chapters constitute the core curriculum of the three continuing education programs contained in this book.

Chapters 5, 6, and 7 are aimed at particular groups of health care professionals. Chapter 5 presents issues of particular interest to physicians; chapter 6 addresses issues for pharmacists; and chapter 7 presents the use of the nursing process in the care of a patient with AIDS.

CE credit will be based on a posttest that covers the core curriculum and the material in chapters 5, 6, or 7 that is germane to your particular profession. However, you may find it helpful to read the material in the chapters aimed at other health care professionals.

OBJECTIVES

Objectives presented here are intended to focus the reader's attention on expected learning outcomes.

On completion of this chapter, the reader should be able to:

1. Explain the personal impact of AIDS on the patient.

2. Describe approaches to the person with HIV infection that promote feelings of control, safety, and optimism.

3. Explain the methods of transmission of the HIV virus.

4. Recognize methods to prevent or control transmission of AIDS.

5. Identify national information resources available for the care of individuals with AIDS.

I. ISSUES FOR PERSONS WITH AIDS

As an introduction to the topic of HIV infection and AIDS, it is important to focus on the needs of the person with AIDS (PWA) that come from the reality of living with HIV infection on a daily basis.

A. PERSPECTIVE OF A HEALTH CARE WORKER

There are many issues facing people who are diagnosed as being HIV positive, including those with symptoms and those with AIDS. Some of the issues are discussed below.

   1. Control. Persons with HIV and AIDS need to develop a partnership with their health care providers (HCPs). If PWAs feel that they are the passive recipients of health care, they feel powerless in dealing with the many decisions that have to be made. By including PWAs in care planning and decision making, a sense of control is afforded to them.

   The HCP needs to be educated about HIV and its sequelae. This knowledge better prepares the HCP to provide counseling and information, thus providing the PWA with access to the most up-to-date therapies and treatments. The HCP should also have information regarding other community resources so that the PWA is not dependent on the health care system for total care. A goal for the HCP working with a PWA is to help the PWA be comfortable with decisions after all options have been examined.

   Many PWAs keep flowcharts of their own laboratory test results to monitor their trends. Even though it may take a few extra minutes for HCPs to help PWAs fill out their personal flowcharts, this activity affords PWAs a sense of control.

   Helping a PWA decide whether or not to enter a clinical trial is a role that the clinician can play. Clinical trials provide the person who is infected with HIV or has AIDS the opportunity to try new, unlicensed treatments and, at the same time, to contribute something to society.

   2. Confidentiality. The stigma that accompanies an HIV-positive diagnosis or having HIV is real. Horror stories exist that illustrate lost jobs, canceled insurance, ruined family relationships, and rejection by family and community. PWAs are very sensitive to the issues of confidentiality and may request that the HCP protect their records. It is the HCP's responsibility to keep records confidential and to demand from all those who come in contact with the patient's medical records that the information be guarded and treated sensitively. Health care delivery systems (e.g., health departments, hospitals, clinics) must assure that information contained in the charts and records is accessible only to those people delivering care, not to curious workers or prying friends of friends.

3. Knowledge of HIV. The person with HIV disease is much better educated about HIV than the average recipient of health care is about his or her medical condition. The PWA is bombarded with information from the media and has access to information through AIDS information networks. Frequently, the PWA hears or reads about an exciting new drug or experimental therapy and provides the HCP with this information, thus sharing knowledge and encouraging the HCP to keep up-to-date. The most effective HCP is one who does not feel threatened by new information coming from the patient and who openly encourages the patient to seek new information.

4. Coping Strategies and Optimism. If PWAs are told that they have three months to live and should get ready to die, that is exactly what they will do. On the other hand, telling PWAs that they have an unknown time to live, that advances in HIV treatment are being made every day, and that it is important to focus on living, not dying, affords some hope to people with many odds against them. It is unrealistic to deny that those with AIDS will die; but persons with HIV and AIDS must be taught new strategies for using available resources and focusing on living. While there is a time and a place to discuss death and dying issues, it is also important to invest time in helping PWAs develop coping skills that will enable them to maintain hope and improve their quality of life.

Maintaining hope is a primary task, and probably the most difficult one, for every person infected with HIV. The following are some strategies for the PWA to remain optimistic in the face of negative comments and grim statistics:

- participating in clinical trials, either community based or through medical centers;

- pursuing complementary therapies and treatments (those that are not considered traditional by Western medicine);

- changing life-style or modifying social and environmental milieu;

- planning for the future, such as buying next year's model of car, going back to school, or taking the cruise or vacation they have always wanted;

- developing new relationships, both primary and secondary;

- getting involved with other people in support groups who have similar concerns and issues;

- getting involved in political work (feeling that the PWA can make a difference and effect change); and

- maintaining a spiritual connection, perhaps by finding a church, synagogue, or specific member of the clergy to confide in.

5. Self-care Issues. The PWA should not believe unrealistically that medicine can or must provide all the necessary components of care. There are many guidelines available to PWAs to assist them in their everyday maintenance and care.

Many PWAs find that the traditional medical community often lacks adequate information on issues such as nutrition. Many local AIDS service organizations can help the PWA and the HCP obtain information about nutrition and other self-care issues.

6. Legal and Financial Issues. The PWA must have access to information regarding power of attorney, wills, Social Security, Medicaid, and other insurance, and be able to use this information without barriers. Many times obstacles that seem insurmountable to the PWA because of health concerns are easily overcome with assistance from an appropriate member of the health care team (e.g., social worker, nurse, pharmacist, physician).

In summary, the issues that the person with HIV disease confronts are important issues that can be managed through a partnership between the PWA and the health care team. Those of us providing care must realize that we cannot provide all the answers and solutions to the PWA's concerns. There needs to be an interdisciplinary approach that includes the PWA in all decisions that are made.

B. TYPICAL PATIENT FEELINGS ABOUT HAVING AIDS

Typically, patients have many emotions about having and living with AIDS. Most resent not being understood, and they are fearful about their future. Many are angry that the government, health care system, and others have acted so slowly. Patients also suffer a lot of pain and anguish and often poverty. Nevertheless, they respect the knowledge of the researchers who have shed light on what causes AIDS and how we might be able to treat it. They feel encouraged about some of the knowledge that has developed, and want to believe that AIDS research will have many positive spin-offs.

To confront this illness, it is critical that patients with AIDS be given support and assistance in developing a positive attitude. A positive attitude is a major weapon in fighting HIV infection. PWAs have the choice between denial and despair, and many choose denial. PWAs need our understanding of their varied and changing feelings. Many also know how difficult it must be for health care workers to see so much suffering and despair.

II. OVERVIEW OF AIDS

The illness that we now call the acquired immunodeficiency syndrome (AIDS) first came to medical attention in 1981, following the description by a group of physicians in Los Angeles, California, of *Pneumocystis carinii* pneumonia and Kaposi's sarcoma in previously healthy homosexual men. During the next few years, it became apparent that the same syndrome could occur in intravenous drug users and hemophiliacs, suggesting bloodborne as well as sexual transmission. In 1984, groups led by doctors Gallo and Montagnier discovered a pathogenic retrovirus (HTLV-III or LAV), now known as human immuno-deficiency virus type 1, to be the etiologic agent of AIDS. Shortly thereafter, a serologic test was developed and the worldwide prevalence of HIV-1 was determined.

HIV is transmitted sexually, by blood or blood products, or by infected mothers to their fetuses or neonates in the perinatal period. Transmission by casual contact does not occur. Transmission of HIV to health care workers by needle-stick injury or blood contact is very rare and considerably less hazardous than for the hepatitis B virus. In the developing world, HIV is primarily transmitted by heterosexual intercourse. In the United States, this is the major mode of transmission from bisexual males and IV drug users to their sexual partners, and, presumably, more heterosexual spread will occur as the prevalence of HIV infection increases. Transmission by blood or factor VIII products has markedly diminished with serologic testing of blood and heat treatment of factor VIII.

Three drugs are currently available for the treatment of HIV infection: zidovudine, didanosine, and zalcitabine. These drugs are nucleoside analogues that act as chain terminators of DNA replication in the HIV virus. Zidovudine has been shown to delay the onset of AIDS in HIV-infected patients and is used for both symptomatic and asymptomatic HIV-infected patients. Didanosine and zalcitabine (when used in combination with zidovudine) can be used to treat progressive HIV infection. Earlier diagnosis and more effective therapy of the opportunistic infections in AIDS has also improved the treatment of persons with AIDS. Many vaccines are in clinical trials with the hope that they will induce vigorous immune responses to protect both HIV-infected and HIV-negative patients. So far, education of the general public with regard to mechanisms of transmission and risk reduction is at the forefront of the current approach to the control of the HIV epidemic.

AIDS is having an impact on all health care systems. In areas of high prevalence, a substantial number of hospital beds and other health care resources are expended on AIDS. In many of these locales, an efficient system of using outpatient resources has evolved. It is estimated that the medical costs of treating people with AIDS and HIV infection in the United States will reach $5.8 billion in 1992 and will almost double to $10.4 billion in 1994. It is also estimated that outpatient costs will make up 25 percent of the total cost of care for a patient with AIDS. Studies have shown that the annual costs of drug therapy for HIV infection include $2,700 a year for zidovudine, $500 a year for other drugs, $700 for visits to medical offices and clinics, $800 for laboratory tests, $200 for other outpatient expenses, and $1,240 for inpatient hospital stays. These estimates are conservative and may represent a small fraction of the actual costs of treating a person with AIDS.

The care of AIDS patients will have an impact on all health care providers in virtually all areas of the United States. Knowledge of the basic epidemiology, clinical presentation, drug therapy, and management of these patients is basic to all health education. It is hoped that this book will provide a starting point for a sound knowledge base in AIDS for health care providers in the fields of pharmacy, nursing, and medicine.

The following glossary contains terms relevant to all seven chapters in this book. You are encouraged to familiarize yourself with these terms before proceeding with the other chapters. Included also are lists of resources for PWAs and for health care professionals as they carry out their care.

GLOSSARY

Absolute CD4 count: calculated by multiplying the white blood cell count by the percentage of lymphocytes, then multiplying that number by the percentage of CD4 cells.
For example:
WBC = 4,500
Lymphocyte Percentage = 30% (.30)
CD4 Percentage = 15% (.15)
Absolute CD4 Count = (4,500) × (.3) × (.15) = 202.5
CD4 count normal ranges are age dependent.

AIDS (acquired immunodeficiency syndrome): the consequence of infection with the human immunodeficiency virus type 1, which results in broad suppression of cell-mediated immunity. This results in an increased incidence of infection by a variety of opportunistic bacterial, fungal, protozoan, and viral pathogens, as well as of malignancies such as Kaposi's sarcoma and lymphomas.

AIDS service organization: a volunteer group facilitating support services and advocacy for PWAs and education for the community.

Antibody: a protein (immunoglobulin) that is produced by the immune system in response to specific antigens. The presence of antibodies indicates previous exposure to the organism it is responding to, but not necessarily active infection.

Antibody positive (HIV positive): a test that indicates that antibody to the virus is found in the blood. It indicates active HIV infection and the potential for transmission to sexual or needle-sharing contacts and mother-to-infant transmission.

Antigen: a substance that the body recognizes as foreign and that stimulates the immune system to make antibodies. One antigen is the protein found in the core of the HIV particle; it can often be detected and quantitated in the bloodstream, and has some prognostic significance.

ARC (AIDS-related complex, also called "pre-AIDS"): This syndrome refers to general systemic symptoms (e.g., fever, weight loss, diarrhea) and signs (e.g., mucosal candidiasis, hairy leukoplakia) that occur in HIV-infected individuals prior to the development of the opportunistic infections or malignancies characteristic of AIDS.

Casual contagion: the ability to transmit a pathogen through casual daily activities such as coughing, sneezing, and sharing dishes, telephones, or toilet facilities. The virus that causes AIDS is *not* transmitted by casual contagion.

Chemotaxis: the movement of cells along a chemical gradient.

Complement: a group of serum proteins, produced by the liver, that enhances phagocytosis and chemotaxis.

Cytotoxic: possessing a property destructive to cells.

Dementia: deterioration of intellectual function.

Dideoxynucleosides: compounds such as zidovudine, didanosine, or zalcitabine, consisting of modified nucleosides (DNA or RNA building blocks), that inhibit synthesis of genetic material when inserted into viral genetic material.

DNA polymerase: an enzyme that catalyzes the synthesis of DNA.

Encephalitis: inflammation of the brain.

Epidemic: affecting many individuals within a population, community, or region at the same time; an outbreak of sudden, rapid spread.

Epidemiology: the study of the frequency and distribution of disease in a population over time.

Epitope: the smallest segment of an antigen capable of eliciting an antibody response.

False positive/false negative: an inaccurate result of the HIV antibody test most frequently used. A small percentage of people tested may be told that they have been infected by the virus when in fact they have not. In addition, a small percentage of people will receive a negative test result when in fact they have been infected with the virus. The chances of receiving a false negative result are extremely low.

Glycoprotein: a protein that possesses a sugar component.

Guanosine: one of the nucleoside building blocks of DNA.

Hemophilia: an inherited disorder of the blood-clotting process that causes excessive and sometimes spontaneous bleeding; requires numerous transfusions of clotting factors, some of which may be contaminated with the HIV virus.

Homophobia: a group of responses, including fear, discomfort, and repugnance, that one may have towards homosexuals.

HTLV-III, LAV, HIV-1: names for the virus that can cause AIDS. The different names result from different research teams finding the virus independently.

Humoral: pertaining to the liquid phase of blood.

Idiopathic thrombocytopenic purpura (ITP): a term usually used to designate instances of thrombocytopenia (low number of platelets, involved in blood clotting) associated with no apparent external causes.

Immune system: mechanism by which an organism protects itself from infection, toxins, and malignancy.

Immunocompromised: denoting a person whose immunologic defenses are impaired, either because of an immunodeficiency disorder or because of therapy with immunosuppressive agents. See also *Immunosuppression*.

Immunoglobulin: see *Antibody*.

Immunosuppression: suppression of natural immune responses. The immune system may be slightly depressed temporarily due to illnesses such as influenza, or due to drug use and other factors. It may be suppressed by drugs in patients undergoing organ transplants or for other medical reasons. Certain congenital factors may suppress the immune system. With AIDS, the immune system is suppressed by the activity of a transmissible virus.

Incubation period: the time between infection of an individual by a pathogen and the manifestation of the disease it causes. With AIDS, this period is usually five to fifteen years, but may be shorter or longer in some cases.

Inguinal: pertaining to the groin.

Interferon: a lymphokine produced in response to infection by viruses and other intracellular parasites; there are different types of interferon:

- One type is produced by the virus-infected cells and, in turn, induces the production of an antiviral protein.

- Another type is produced by lymphocytes and helps activate killer T cells.

- A third type, also produced by lymphocytes, plays a regulatory role in antibody production.

Kaposi's sarcoma: a neoplasm of the lining of small blood vessels; occurs in the skin and sometimes in the lymph nodes or viscera.

Leukocytes: white blood cells, including granulocytes (also called polymorphonuclear leukocytes or PMNs), lymphocytes, and monocytes.

Leukopenia: reduction in the number of circulating white blood cells (usually less than 5,000/mm³).

Lymphadenopathy: any disease process affecting lymph nodes, characterized by enlargement of the nodes.

Lymphocyte: a white blood cell formed in lymphoid tissue (e.g., lymph nodes, spleen, thymus, tonsils, and sometimes in bone marrow); lymphocytes comprise about one-quarter of the total number of circulating leukocytes:

- B cell: lymphocyte responsible for humoral immunity (it produces antibodies).

- T cell: lymphocyte responsible for cell-mediated immunity.

  - Helper T cell: identifies invaders and stimulates the production of other cells to fight infection.

  - Killer T cell: kills infected and cancerous body cells by "puncturing" their membranes.

  - Suppressor T cell: signals B cells and other T cells to slow down or stop their activity once the infection is under control.

  - Memory T cell: circulates in the blood and lymph after an initial infection, ready to respond quickly to subsequent infection by the same organism.

Lymphokines: proteins released by certain immune cells to stimulate activity of other immune cells; the "chemical messages" by which immune cells communicate.

Lymphopenia: reduction in the number of circulating lymphocytes (usually less than 1,000/mm³).

Lymphotropic: the tendency to seek out lymphatic tissue—lymph nodes or lymphocytes.

Macrophage: a large mononuclear (having one nucleus) phagocyte; a scavenger cell that ingests dead tissue and degenerated cells; also summons helper T cells when a foreign organism is encountered.

Malaise: overall feeling of unwellness.

Meningitis: inflammation of the meninges (membranes covering the brain and spinal cord).

Multidermal herpes zoster: HIV-infected individuals are prone to multiple attacks of herpes zoster infection (shingles), which is not necessarily localized to a single nerve root or dermatome.

Neurotropic: the tendency to seek out tissue in the nervous system.

Nocardiosis: infection due to *Nocardia* spp. (nontuberculosis, acid-fast bacteria), which is prone to involve the lung and brain.

Opportunistic diseases/infections: diseases/infections caused by agents that are frequently present in our bodies or environment, but that cause disease/infection only when there is an alteration from normal, healthy conditions, such as when the immune system becomes depressed. Examples of these opportunistic diseases/infections include the following:

- **Candidiasis:** a yeast infection caused by *Candida albicans* that affects membranes, skin, and internal organs. Oral infections are called thrush and exhibit creamy white patches of exudate on inflamed and painful mucosa. Common sites are the nailbeds, axilla, umbilicus, around the anus, the esophagus, and the vaginal area. This infection has become a common problem in immunosuppressed people.

- **Cryptococcosis:** a fungus (yeast) infection often seen in AIDS patients that is acquired through the respiratory tract, with a primary focus on the lungs. It characteristically spreads to the meninges, but may also spread to the kidneys and skin. It is caused by the fungus *Cryptococcus neoformans*.

- **Cryptosporidiosis:** an infection caused by a protozoan parasite found in the intestines of animals. Acquired in some people by direct contact with the infected animal, it lodges in the intestines and causes severe diarrhea. It may be transmitted from person to person. This infection seems to be occurring more frequently in immunosuppressed people and can lead to prolonged symptoms that do not respond to most medications. One study reports a more short-lived illness in healthy persons that resolves spontaneously.

- **Cytomegalovirus (CMV):** a virus in the herpes family. CMV infections may occur without any symptoms or result in mild flu-like symptoms of aching, fever, mild sore throat, weakness, and enlarged lymph nodes. Serologic evidence of CMV is common, with evidence of past infection found in as many as 54% of healthy heterosexual men and 94% of healthy gay men studied. CMV is an opportunistic infection only when it is severe and disseminated. It may cause infections of the eye (retinitis) and blindness.

- **Herpes simplex virus type 1 (HSV-1) and Herpes simplex virus type 2 (HSV-2):** HSV-1 results in cold sores or fever blisters on the mouth or around the eyes. HSV-2 causes painful sores on the anus or genitals. Like all herpes viruses, the virus may lie dormant for months or years in nerve or lymph tissue and flare up again under stress, trauma, infection, or immunosuppression. HSV-1 and HSV-2 are opportunistic infections only when they are severe and disseminated. HSV infections can usually be controlled with acyclovir (Zovirax®).

- **Herpes zoster:** this virus of the herpes family causes chickenpox. The virus may lie dormant for years and reemerge as a localized infection of peripheral nerves (shingles), disseminate to all of the skin, or cause encephalitis.

- **Histoplasmosis:** a yeast infection caused by *Histoplasma capsulatum*; usually asymptomatic but may cause acute pneumonia, or disseminated reticuloendothelial hyperplasia with hepatosplenomegaly and anemia, or a flu-like illness with joint effusion and erythema nodosum. Reactivated infections involve the lungs, meninges, heart, peritoneum, and adrenals.

- **Kaposi's sarcoma (KS):** a tumor of the walls of blood vessels. Usually appears as pink to purple, painless spots on the skin, but may also occur internally in addition to or independent of the skin lesions. Death may occur from major organ involvement.

- **Lymphoma:** a general term for growth of new tissue in the lymphatic system. Included in this general group are Hodgkin's disease, lymphosarcoma, and malignant lymphoma.

- *Mycobacterium avium-intracellulare*: although *Mycobacterium tuberculosis* is the most common mycobacterium causing human disease, *Mycobacterium avium-intracellulare* is being increasingly recognized in persons with AIDS. It is usually a complication of late-stage HIV infection, and disseminates widely throughout the body to involve the bloodstream, lungs, gastrointestinal tract, bone marrow, liver, and spleen. It is commonly found in the environment and is not contagious to immunocompetent persons.

- *Pneumocystis carinii* **pneumonia (PCP):** a lung infection seen in immunosuppressed people. It is caused by a common protozoa that is normally controlled by healthy immune systems. People who develop PCP are susceptible to reoccurrence of the disease, and the outcome may be fatal.

- **Toxoplasmosis:** a systemic infection caused by a protozoan parasite. Primary infection is usually mild or symptomatic but can sometimes cause fever, lymphadenopathy, and lymphocytosis. Congenital infections may be severe. Disseminated disease (involving multiple organs), including meningoencephalitis, has been recognized in immunosuppressed individuals. Only cats have been shown to excrete organisms in the infectious oocyst state, but disease may also occur through ingestion of raw or undercooked meat from infected animals.

Oral hairy leukoplakia: whitish plaques, usually on the dorsum of the tongue, which are thought to be associated with Epstein-Barr virus (mononucleosis virus) infection.

PCP: *Pneumocystis carinii* pneumonia. See also *Opportunistic infections*.

Phagocyte: a cell that ingests foreign material.

Pleocytosis: the presence of cells in a normally acellular fluid, such as cerebrospinal fluid.

Polymerase chain reaction (PCR): a means of amplifying the amount of a given genetic sequence in a sample material. After the desired sequence is amplified, it can be detected more easily using one of several techniques, most typically a specific radiolabeled probe. PCR is useful in determining at an early date whether a patient is or is not infected.

PWA: abbreviation for "person with AIDS."

Recombinant DNA technology: the process of synthesizing foreign proteins or peptides by inserting mammalian or viral DNA segments into common organisms such as *Escherichia coli* or yeasts.

Retrovirus: any virus of the family Retroviridae; characterized by the presence of reverse transcriptase.

Reverse transcriptase: the enzyme of HIV and other retroviruses that converts RNA to DNA and begins the process leading to synthesis of viral proteins.

Seropositive: term denoting an individual whose serum contains antibody to a specific agent (e.g., "seropositive for HIV").

Shingles: see *Opportunistic infections: Herpes zoster*.

Thrombocytopenia: reduction in the number of circulating platelets (usually less than 200,000/mm^3).

AIDS-RELATED ORGANIZATIONS
AND HOTLINES

AIDS Hotline: US Public Health Service. (24 hours daily), (800) 342-AIDS or (800) 342-2437.

AIDS Hotline: SIDA; Spanish Speaking. (24 hours daily), (800) 344-7432.

AIDS Hotline: Hearing Impaired, TDD/TTY. (24 hours daily), (800) 243-7889.

AIDS Project Los Angeles, (213) 962-1600.

American Association of Physicians for Human Rights, (415) 255-4547; Medical Expertise Program for HIV Infected Physicians, (415) 864-0408.

American Civil Liberties Union—AIDS Project, 132 West 43rd Street, New York, NY 10036, (212) 944-9800.

American College Health Association, 15879 Crabbs Branch Way, Rockville, MD 20855.

American Foundation for AIDS Research, 733 Third Avenue, New York, NY 10017, (212) 682-7440.

American Psychological Association, 750 First Avenue, Washington, DC 20002, (202) 336-5500.

American Red Cross, AIDS Education Office, 1730 D Street, NW, Washington, DC 20006, (202) 434-4074.

ANAC: Association of Nurses in AIDS Care, 704 Stony Hill Road, Suite 106, Yardley, PA 19067.

Centers for Disease Control, AIDS Activity Office, 1600 Clifton Road, Atlanta, GA 30333, (800) 342-2437.

Gay Men's Health Crisis, Medical Information, 129 West 20th Street, New York, NY 10011, (212) 807-6655.

Health Education Resource Organization (HERO), 101 West Read Street, Suite 812, Baltimore, MD 21201, (301) 685-1180.

Hispanic AIDS Forum, 853 Broadway, Suite 2007, New York, NY 10003, (212) 523-4000.

Lambda Legal Defense and Education Fund, 666 Broadway, New York, NY 10012, (212) 995-8585.

Minority Task Force on AIDS, 475 Riverside Drive, New York, NY 10015, (212) 563-8340.

Mothers of AIDS Patients, (MAP), Los Angeles, CA, (310) 542-3019.

National AIDS Hotline, (800) 342-AIDS.

National Association of People with AIDS (NAPWA), 1413 K Street, NW, 10th Floor, Washington, DC 20005, (202) 898-0414.

National Gay and Lesbian Task Force, 1734 14th Street, NW, Washington, DC 20009, (202) 332-6483.

National Hemophilia Foundation, National Resource and Consultation Center, The Soho Building, 110 Greene Street, Room 303A, New York, NY 10012, (212) 219-8180.

National Institute of Allergy and Infectious Disease, 9000 Rockville Pike, Bethesda, MD 20892, (301) 496-4000.

National Institute of Mental Health, 5600 Fishers Lane, Rockville, MD 20857, (301) 443-4515.

National Institute on Drug Abuse, 5600 Fishers Lane, Rockville, MD 20857.

Planned Parenthood Federation of America, 810 Seventh Avenue, New York, NY 10019, (212) 541-7800.

PWA Coalition, 31 West 26th Street, New York, NY 10010, (800) 828-3280.

San Francisco AIDS Foundation, 25 Van Ness Avenue, San Francisco, CA 94102, (415) 864-5855.

Sex Information and Education Council of the US (SIECUS), 130 West 42nd Street, Suite 2500, New York, NY 10036, (212) 819-9770.

US Public Health Service, Public Affairs Office, Hubert H. Humphrey Building, Room 725-H, 200 Independence Avenue, SW, Washington, DC 20201, (202) 690-6248.

AIDS RESOURCES

AIDS Alert: The Monthly Update for Health Professionals; *AIDS Guide for Health Care Workers*; and *AIDS Clinical Digest*. American Health Consultants, (800) 688-2421.

AIDS Clinical Trials Information, (800) TRIALS-A.

AIDS Educator. San Francisco AIDS Foundation, (415) 864-5855.

AIDS Hotline (national), provides many pamphlets, (800) 342-AIDS.

AIDS Patient Care: A Magazine for Health Care Professionals. Mary Ann Liebert, Inc, (212) 289-2300.

AIDS Products—Update in Development. Pharmaceutical Manufacturers Association, (202) 835-3400.

AIDS Treatment News. John S. James, (800) TREAT-1-2.

AmFAR Directory of Experimental Treatments. American Foundation for AIDS Research (AmFAR), (212) 682-7740.

ATIN (AIDS Targeted Information Newsletter). Williams and Wilkins, (800) 638-6423.

Focus: A Guide to AIDS Research and Counseling. AIDS Health Project, University of California, PO Box 0884, San Francisco, CA, 94143-0884, (415) 476-6430.

Journal of the Association of Nurses in AIDS Care. Nursecom, 1211 Locust Street, Philadelphia, PA 19107.

National AIDS Information Clearing House, (800) 458-5231.

Project Inform: Newsletter and information. Drug Hotline (800) 822-7422.

PWA Coalition Newsline and *Surviving and Thriving with AIDS*. (800) 828-3280.

RECOMMENDED FOLLOW-UP

There are several references that are "must reads" for any health care provider who wants to learn about AIDS and its treatment in depth. In addition, the Centers for Disease Control August 1987 guidelines for prevention of HIV transmission, as well as the June 1988 and July 1991 updates, are reprinted at the end of this unit for your reference.

AIDS Project Los Angeles. *AIDS: A Self-Care Manual*. Santa Monica: IBS Press; 1987.

Baker L. *You and HIV: A Day at a Time*. Philadelphia: WB Saunders; 1991.

Bartlett JG, Finkbeiner AK. *The Guide to Living with HIV Infection*. Baltimore: The Johns Hopkins Press; 1991.

Bloom DE, Carliner G. The economic impact of AIDS in the United States. *Science*. 1988;239:604–610.

Davis W. Self-care for PWAs: how to teach your patients. *AIDS Patient Care*. New York: Mary Ann Liebert, Inc; 1988.

Fischl M, Richman D, Nansen, N, et al. The safety and efficacy of zidovudine in the treatment of subjects with mildly symptomatic HIV-1 infection: a double blind placebo-controlled trial. *Ann Intern Med*. 1990;112(11):727–737.

Flaskerud JH, Ungvarski PJ. *HIV/AIDS: A Guide to Nursing Care*. 2nd ed. Philadelphia: WB Saunders; 1992.

Meisenholder J, LaCharite C, eds. *Comfort in Caring. Nursing the Person with HIV Infection*. Glenview, IL: Scott-Foreman; 1989.

O'Connor T. *Living with AIDS*. San Francisco: Crown; 1986, 1987.

Ritter M (Associated Press). Study: AIDS costs to top $5 billion. *The Durham (North Carolina) Herald-Sun*. Friday, November 29, 1991:1–2.

Sande M, Volberding P, eds. *The Medical Management of AIDS*. 3rd ed. Philadelphia: WB Saunders; 1992.

Volberding P, Jacobson M. *AIDS Clinical Review*. New York, NY: Marcel Decker; 1991.

Volberding PA, Lagakos SW, Koch MA, et al. Zidovudine in asymptomatic human immunodeficiency virus infection. *New Engl J Med.* 1990;322:941–949.

Yarchoan R, Mitsuya M, Meyers CE, Boder S. Clinical pharmacology of 3'azido2'3'deoxythymidine and related dideoxy nucleosides. *New Engl J Med.* 1989;321:726–738.

Yarchoan R, Pluta J, Frederico C. Anti-retroviral therapy of HIV-infection, current strategies and challenges for the future. *Blood.* 1991;78:859–884.

Reprinted by the
U.S. DEPARTMENT OF HEALTH AND HUMAN SERVICES
PUBLIC HEALTH SERVICE

CENTERS FOR DISEASE CONTROL   August 21, 1987 / Vol. 36 / No. 2S

Supplement

MORBIDITY AND MORTALITY WEEKLY REPORT

Recommendations for Prevention of HIV Transmission in Health-Care Settings

U. S. Department of Health and Human Services
Public Health Service
Centers for Disease Control
Atlanta, Georgia 30333

Supplements to the *MMWR* are published by the Epidemiology Program Office, Centers for Disease Control, Public Health Service, U.S. Department of Health and Human Services, Atlanta, Georgia 30333.

SUGGESTED CITATION

Centers for Disease Control. Recommendations for prevention of HIV transmission in health-care settings. *MMWR* 1987;36 (suppl no. 2S) :[inclusive page numbers].

Centers for Disease Control .... James O. Mason, M.D., Dr.P.H.
Director

The material in this report was developed (in collaboration with the Center for Prevention Services, the National Institute for Occupational Safety and Health, and the Training and Laboratory Program Office) by:

Center for Infectious Diseases ....Frederick A. Murphy, D.V.M., Ph.D.
Acting Director

Hospital Infections Program ....James M. Hughes, M.D.
Director

AIDS Program...James W. Curran, M.D.
Director

Publications and Graphics..Frances H. Porcher, M.A.
Chief

Karen L. Foster, M.A.
Consulting Editor

This report was prepared in:

Epidemiology Program Office .... Carl W. Tyler, Jr., M.D.
Director

Michael B. Gregg, M.D.
Editor, MMWR

Editorial Services .... R. Elliott Churchill, M.A.
Chief

Ruth Greenberg
Editorial Assistant

MMWR Supplement — August 21, 1987, Vol. 36, No. 2S

Recommendations for Prevention of HIV Transmission in Health-Care Settings

Introduction

Human immunodeficiency virus (HIV), the virus that causes acquired immuno-deficiency syndrome (AIDS), is transmitted through sexual contact and exposure to infected blood or blood components and perinatally from mother to neonate. HIV has been isolated from blood, semen, vaginal secretions, saliva, tears, breast milk, cerebrospinal fluid, amniotic fluid, and urine and is likely to be isolated from other body fluids, secretions, and excretions. However, epidemiologic evidence has impli-cated only blood, semen, vaginal secretions, and possibly breast milk in transmission.

The increasing prevalence of HIV increases the risk that health-care workers will be exposed to blood from patients infected with HIV, especially when blood and body-fluid precautions are not followed for all patients. Thus, this document emphasizes the need for health-care workers to consider **all** patients as potentially infected with HIV and/or other blood-borne pathogens and to adhere rigorously to infection-control precautions for minimizing the risk of exposure to blood and body fluids of all patients.

The recommendations contained in this document consolidate and update CDC recommendations published earlier for preventing HIV transmission in health-care settings: precautions for clinical and laboratory staffs (1) and precautions for health-care workers and allied professionals (2); recommendations for preventing HIV transmission in the workplace (3) and during invasive procedures (4); recom-mendations for preventing possible transmission of HIV from tears (5); and recom-mendations for providing dialysis treatment for HIV-infected patients (6). These recommendations also update portions of the "Guideline for Isolation Precautions in Hospitals" (7) and reemphasize some of the recommendations contained in "Infection Control Practices for Dentistry" (8). The recommendations contained in this docu-ment have been developed for use in health-care settings and emphasize the need to treat blood and other body fluids from **all** patients as potentially infective. These same prudent precautions also should be taken in other settings in which persons may be exposed to blood or other body fluids.

Definition of Health-Care Workers

Health-care workers are defined as persons, including students and trainees, whose activities involve contact with patients or with blood or other body fluids from patients in a health-care setting.

August 21, 1987 — Supplement

Health-Care Workers with AIDS

As of July 10, 1987, a total of 1,875 (5.8%) of 32,395 adults with AIDS, who had been reported to the CDC national surveillance system and for whom occupational information was available, reported being employed in a health-care or clinical laboratory setting. In comparison, 6.8 million persons—representing 5.6% of the U.S. labor force—were employed in health services. Of the health-care workers with AIDS, 95% have been reported to exhibit high-risk behavior; for the remaining 5%, the means of HIV acquisition was undetermined. Health-care workers with AIDS were significantly more likely than other workers to have an undetermined risk (5% versus 3%, respectively). For both health-care workers and non-health-care workers with AIDS, the proportion with an undetermined risk has not increased since 1982.

AIDS patients initially reported as not belonging to recognized risk groups are investigated by state and local health departments to determine whether possible risk factors exist. Of all health-care workers with AIDS reported to CDC who were initially characterized as not having an identified risk and for whom follow-up information was available, 66% have been reclassified because risk factors were identified or because the patient was found not to meet the surveillance case definition for AIDS. Of the 87 health-care workers currently categorized as having no identifiable risk, information is incomplete on 16 (18%) because of death or refusal to be interviewed; 38 (44%) are still being investigated. The remaining 33 (38%) health-care workers were interviewed or had other follow-up information available. The occupations of these 33 were as follows: five physicians (15%), three of whom were surgeons; one dentist (3%); three nurses (9%); nine nursing assistants (27%); seven housekeeping or maintenance workers (21%); three clinical laboratory technicians (9%); one therapist (3%); and four others who did not have contact with patients (12%). Although 15 of these 33 health-care workers reported parenteral and/or other non-needlestick exposure to blood or body fluids from patients in the 10 years preceding their diagnosis of AIDS, none of these exposures involved a patient with AIDS or known HIV infection.

Risk to Health-Care Workers of Acquiring HIV in Health-Care Settings

Health-care workers with documented percutaneous or mucous-membrane exposures to blood or body fluids of HIV-infected patients have been prospectively evaluated to determine the risk of infection after such exposures. As of June 30, 1987, 883 health-care workers have been tested for antibody to HIV in an ongoing surveillance project conducted by CDC (9). Of these, 708 (80%) had percutaneous exposures to blood, and 175 (20%) had a mucous membrane or an open wound contaminated by blood or body fluid. Of 396 health-care workers, each of whom had only a convalescent-phase serum sample obtained and tested ≥90 days post-exposure, one—for whom heterosexual transmission could not be ruled out—was seropositive for HIV antibody. For 425 additional health-care workers, both acute- and convalescent-phase serum samples were obtained and tested; none of 74 health-care workers with nonpercutaneous exposures seroconverted, and three (0.9%) of 351 with percutaneous exposures seroconverted. None of these three health-care workers had other documented risk factors for infection.

Two other prospective studies to assess the risk of nosocomial acquisition of HIV infection for health-care workers are ongoing in the United States. As of April 30, 1987, 332 health-care workers with a total of 453 needlestick or mucous-membrane exposures to the blood or other body fluids of HIV-infected patients were tested for HIV antibody at the National Institutes of Health (10). These exposed workers included 103 with needlestick injuries and 229 with mucous-membrane exposures; none had seroconverted. A similar study at the University of California of 129 health-care workers with documented needlestick injuries or mucous-membrane exposures to blood or other body fluids from patients with HIV infection has not identified any seroconversions (11). Results of a prospective study in the United Kingdom identified no evidence of transmission among 150 health-care workers with parenteral or mucous-membrane exposures to blood or other body fluids, secretions, or excretions from patients with HIV infection (12).

In addition to health-care workers enrolled in prospective studies, eight persons who provided care to infected patients and denied other risk factors have been reported to have acquired HIV infection. Three of these health-care workers had needlestick exposures to blood from infected patients (13-15). Two were persons who provided nursing care to infected persons; although neither sustained a needlestick, both had extensive contact with blood or other body fluids, and neither observed recommended barrier precautions (16,17). The other three were health-care workers with non-needlestick exposures to blood from infected patients (18). Although the exact route of transmission for these last three infections is not known, all three persons had direct contact of their skin with blood from infected patients, all had skin lesions that may have been contaminated by blood, and one also had a mucous-membrane exposure.

A total of 1,231 dentists and hygienists, many of whom practiced in areas with many AIDS cases, participated in a study to determine the prevalence of antibody to HIV; one dentist (0.1%) had HIV antibody. Although no exposure to a known HIV-infected person could be documented, epidemiologic investigation did not identify any other risk factor for infection. The infected dentist, who also had a history of sustaining needlestick injuries and trauma to his hands, did not routinely wear gloves when providing dental care (19).

Precautions To Prevent Transmission of HIV

Universal Precautions

Since medical history and examination cannot reliably identify all patients infected with HIV or other blood-borne pathogens, blood and body-fluid precautions should be consistently used for **all** patients. This approach, previously recommended by CDC (3,4), and referred to as "universal blood and body-fluid precautions" or "universal precautions," should be used in the care of **all** patients, especially including those in emergency-care settings in which the risk of blood exposure is increased and the infection status of the patient is usually unknown (20).

August 21, 1987 — Supplement

1. All health-care workers should routinely use appropriate barrier precautions to prevent skin and mucous-membrane exposure when contact with blood or other body fluids of any patient is anticipated. Gloves should be worn for touching blood and body fluids, mucous membranes, or non-intact skin of all patients, for handling items or surfaces soiled with blood or body fluids, and for performing venipuncture and other vascular access procedures. Gloves should be changed after contact with each patient. Masks and protective eyewear or face shields should be worn during procedures that are likely to generate droplets of blood or other body fluids to prevent exposure of mucous membranes of the mouth, nose, and eyes. Gowns or aprons should be worn during procedures that are likely to generate splashes of blood or other body fluids.
2. Hands and other skin surfaces should be washed immediately and thoroughly if contaminated with blood or other body fluids. Hands should be washed immediately after gloves are removed.
3. All health-care workers should take precautions to prevent injuries caused by needles, scalpels, and other sharp instruments or devices during procedures; when cleaning used instruments; during disposal of used needles; and when handling sharp instruments after procedures. To prevent needlestick injuries, needles should not be recapped, purposely bent or broken by hand, removed from disposable syringes, or otherwise manipulated by hand. After they are used, disposable syringes and needles, scalpel blades, and other sharp items should be placed in puncture-resistant containers for disposal; the puncture-resistant containers should be located as close as practical to the use area. Large-bore reusable needles should be placed in a puncture-resistant container for transport to the reprocessing area.
4. Although saliva has not been implicated in HIV transmission, to minimize the need for emergency mouth-to-mouth resuscitation, mouthpieces, resuscitation bags, or other ventilation devices should be available for use in areas in which the need for resuscitation is predictable.
5. Health-care workers who have exudative lesions or weeping dermatitis should refrain from all direct patient care and from handling patient-care equipment until the condition resolves.
6. Pregnant health-care workers are not known to be at greater risk of contracting HIV infection than health-care workers who are not pregnant; however, if a health-care worker develops HIV infection during pregnancy, the infant is at risk of infection resulting from perinatal transmission. Because of this risk, pregnant health-care workers should be especially familiar with and strictly adhere to precautions to minimize the risk of HIV transmission.

Implementation of universal blood and body-fluid precautions for **all** patients eliminates the need for use of the isolation category of "Blood and Body Fluid Precautions" previously recommended by CDC (7) for patients known or suspected to be infected with blood-borne pathogens. Isolation precautions (e.g., enteric, "AFB" [7]) should be used as necessary if associated conditions, such as infectious diarrhea or tuberculosis, are diagnosed or suspected.

Precautions for Invasive Procedures
In this document, an invasive procedure is defined as surgical entry into tissues, cavities, or organs or repair of major traumatic injuries 1) in an operating or delivery

August 21, 1987 — Supplement

room, emergency department, or outpatient setting, including both physicians' and dentists' offices; 2) cardiac catheterization and angiographic procedures; 3) a vaginal or cesarean delivery or other invasive obstetric procedure during which bleeding may occur; or 4) the manipulation, cutting, or removal of any oral or perioral tissues, including tooth structure, during which bleeding occurs or the potential for bleeding exists. The universal blood and body-fluid precautions listed above, combined with the precautions listed below, should be the minimum precautions for **all** such invasive procedures.

1. All health-care workers who participate in invasive procedures must routinely use appropriate barrier precautions to prevent skin and mucous-membrane contact with blood and other body fluids of all patients. Gloves and surgical masks must be worn for all invasive procedures. Protective eyewear or face shields should be worn for procedures that commonly result in the generation of droplets, splashing of blood or other body fluids, or the generation of bone chips. Gowns or aprons made of materials that provide an effective barrier should be worn during invasive procedures that are likely to result in the splashing of blood or other body fluids. All health-care workers who perform or assist in vaginal or cesarean deliveries should wear gloves and gowns when handling the placenta or the infant until blood and amniotic fluid have been removed from the infant's skin and should wear gloves during post-delivery care of the umbilical cord.

2. If a glove is torn or a needlestick or other injury occurs, the glove should be removed and a new glove used as promptly as patient safety permits; the needle or instrument involved in the incident should also be removed from the sterile field.

Precautions for Dentistry*

Blood, saliva, and gingival fluid from **all** dental patients should be considered infective. Special emphasis should be placed on the following precautions for preventing transmission of blood-borne pathogens in dental practice in both institutional and non-institutional settings.

1. In addition to wearing gloves for contact with oral mucous membranes of all patients, all dental workers should wear surgical masks and protective eyewear or chin-length plastic face shields during dental procedures in which splashing or spattering of blood, saliva, or gingival fluids is likely. Rubber dams, high-speed evacuation, and proper patient positioning, when appropriate, should be utilized to minimize generation of droplets and spatter.

2. Handpieces should be sterilized after use with each patient, since blood, saliva, or gingival fluid of patients may be aspirated into the handpiece or waterline. Handpieces that cannot be sterilized should at least be flushed, the outside surface cleaned and wiped with a suitable chemical germicide, and then rinsed. Handpieces should be flushed at the beginning of the day and after use with each patient. Manufacturers' recommendations should be followed for use and maintenance of waterlines and check valves and for flushing of handpieces. The same precautions should be used for ultrasonic scalers and air/water syringes.

---

*General infection-control precautions are more specifically addressed in previous recommendations for infection-control practices for dentistry (8).

3. Blood and saliva should be thoroughly and carefully cleaned from material that has been used in the mouth (e.g., impression materials, bite registration), especially before polishing and grinding intra-oral devices. Contaminated materials, impressions, and intra-oral devices should also be cleaned and disinfected before being handled in the dental laboratory and before they are placed in the patient's mouth. Because of the increasing variety of dental materials used intra-orally, dental workers should consult with manufacturers as to the stability of specific materials when using disinfection procedures.
4. Dental equipment and surfaces that are difficult to disinfect (e.g., light handles or X-ray-unit heads) and that may become contaminated should be wrapped with impervious-backed paper, aluminum foil, or clear plastic wrap. The coverings should be removed and discarded, and clean coverings should be put in place after use with each patient.

Precautions for Autopsies or Morticians' Services

In addition to the universal blood and body-fluid precautions listed above, the following precautions should be used by persons performing postmortem procedures:

1. All persons performing or assisting in postmortem procedures should wear gloves, masks, protective eyewear, gowns, and waterproof aprons.
2. Instruments and surfaces contaminated during postmortem procedures should be decontaminated with an appropriate chemical germicide.

Precautions for Dialysis

Patients with end-stage renal disease who are undergoing maintenance dialysis and who have HIV infection can be dialyzed in hospital-based or free-standing dialysis units using conventional infection-control precautions (*21*). Universal blood and body-fluid precautions should be used when dialyzing **all** patients.

Strategies for disinfecting the dialysis fluid pathways of the hemodialysis machine are targeted to control bacterial contamination and generally consist of using 500-750 parts per million (ppm) of sodium hypochlorite (household bleach) for 30-40 minutes or 1.5%-2.0% formaldehyde overnight. In addition, several chemical germicides formulated to disinfect dialysis machines are commercially available. None of these protocols or procedures need to be changed for dialyzing patients infected with HIV.

Patients infected with HIV can be dialyzed by either hemodialysis or peritoneal dialysis and do not need to be isolated from other patients. The type of dialysis treatment (i.e., hemodialysis or peritoneal dialysis) should be based on the needs of the patient. The dialyzer may be discarded after each use. Alternatively, centers that reuse dialyzers — i.e., a specific single-use dialyzer is issued to a specific patient, removed, cleaned, disinfected, and reused several times on the same patient only — may include HIV-infected patients in the dialyzer-reuse program. An individual dialyzer must never be used on more than one patient.

Precautions for Laboratories[†]

Blood and other body fluids from **all** patients should be considered infective. To supplement the universal blood and body-fluid precautions listed above, the following precautions are recommended for health-care workers in clinical laboratories.

[†]Additional precautions for research and industrial laboratories are addressed elsewhere (*22,23*).

August 21, 1987 — Supplement

1. All specimens of blood and body fluids should be put in a well-constructed container with a secure lid to prevent leaking during transport. Care should be taken when collecting each specimen to avoid contaminating the outside of the container and of the laboratory form accompanying the specimen.
2. All persons processing blood and body-fluid specimens (e.g., removing tops from vacuum tubes) should wear gloves. Masks and protective eyewear should be worn if mucous-membrane contact with blood or body fluids is anticipated. Gloves should be changed and hands washed after completion of specimen processing.
3. For routine procedures, such as histologic and pathologic studies or microbiologic culturing, a biological safety cabinet is not necessary. However, biological safety cabinets (Class I or II) should be used whenever procedures are conducted that have a high potential for generating droplets. These include activities such as blending, sonicating, and vigorous mixing.
4. Mechanical pipetting devices should be used for manipulating all liquids in the laboratory. Mouth pipetting must not be done.
5. Use of needles and syringes should be limited to situations in which there is no alternative, and the recommendations for preventing injuries with needles outlined under universal precautions should be followed.
6. Laboratory work surfaces should be decontaminated with an appropriate chemical germicide after a spill of blood or other body fluids and when work activities are completed.
7. Contaminated materials used in laboratory tests should be decontaminated before reprocessing or be placed in bags and disposed of in accordance with institutional policies for disposal of infective waste (24).
8. Scientific equipment that has been contaminated with blood or other body fluids should be decontaminated and cleaned before being repaired in the laboratory or transported to the manufacturer.
9. All persons should wash their hands after completing laboratory activities and should remove protective clothing before leaving the laboratory.

Implementation of universal blood and body-fluid precautions for **all** patients eliminates the need for warning labels on specimens since blood and other body fluids from all patients should be considered infective.

Environmental Considerations for HIV Transmission

No environmentally mediated mode of HIV transmission has been documented. Nevertheless, the precautions described below should be taken routinely in the care of **all** patients.

Sterilization and Disinfection

Standard sterilization and disinfection procedures for patient-care equipment currently recommended for use (25,26) in a variety of health-care settings — including hospitals, medical and dental clinics and offices, hemodialysis centers, emergency-care facilities, and long-term nursing-care facilities — are adequate to sterilize or disinfect instruments, devices, or other items contaminated with blood or other body fluids from persons infected with blood-borne pathogens including HIV (21,23).

Instruments or devices that enter sterile tissue or the vascular system of any patient or through which blood flows should be sterilized before reuse. Devices or items that contact intact mucous membranes should be sterilized or receive high-level disinfection, a procedure that kills vegetative organisms and viruses but not necessarily large numbers of bacterial spores. Chemical germicides that are registered with the U.S. Environmental Protection Agency (EPA) as "sterilants" may be used either for sterilization or for high-level disinfection depending on contact time.

Contact lenses used in trial fittings should be disinfected after each fitting by using a hydrogen peroxide contact lens disinfecting system or, if compatible, with heat (78 C-80 C [172.4 F-176.0 F]) for 10 minutes.

Medical devices or instruments that require sterilization or disinfection should be thoroughly cleaned before being exposed to the germicide, and the manufacturer's instructions for the use of the germicide should be followed. Further, it is important that the manufacturer's specifications for compatibility of the medical device with chemical germicides be closely followed. Information on specific label claims of commercial germicides can be obtained by writing to the Disinfectants Branch, Office of Pesticides, Environmental Protection Agency, 401 M Street, SW, Washington, D.C. 20460.

Studies have shown that HIV is inactivated rapidly after being exposed to commonly used chemical germicides at concentrations that are much lower than used in practice (27-30). Embalming fluids are similar to the types of chemical germicides that have been tested and found to completely inactivate HIV. In addition to commercially available chemical germicides, a solution of sodium hypochlorite (household bleach) prepared daily is an inexpensive and effective germicide. Concentrations ranging from approximately 500 ppm (1:100 dilution of household bleach) sodium hypochlorite to 5,000 ppm (1:10 dilution of household bleach) are effective depending on the amount of organic material (e.g., blood, mucus) present on the surface to be cleaned and disinfected. Commercially available chemical germicides may be more compatible with certain medical devices that might be corroded by repeated exposure to sodium hypochlorite, especially to the 1:10 dilution.

Survival of HIV in the Environment

The most extensive study on the survival of HIV after drying involved greatly concentrated HIV samples, i.e., 10 million tissue-culture infectious doses per milliliter (31). This concentration is at least 100,000 times greater than that typically found in the blood or serum of patients with HIV infection. HIV was detectable by tissue-culture techniques 1-3 days after drying, but the rate of inactivation was rapid. Studies performed at CDC have also shown that drying HIV causes a rapid (within several hours) 1-2 log (90%-99%) reduction in HIV concentration. In tissue-culture fluid, cell-free HIV could be detected up to 15 days at room temperature, up to 11 days at 37 C (98.6 F), and up to 1 day if the HIV was cell-associated.

When considered in the context of environmental conditions in health-care facilities, these results do not require any changes in currently recommended sterilization, disinfection, or housekeeping strategies. When medical devices are contaminated with blood or other body fluids, existing recommendations include the cleaning of these instruments, followed by disinfection or sterilization, depending on the type of medical device. These protocols assume "worst-case" conditions of

August 21, 1987 — Supplement

extreme virologic and microbiologic contamination, and whether viruses have been inactivated after drying plays no role in formulating these strategies. Consequently, no changes in published procedures for cleaning, disinfecting, or sterilizing need to be made.

Housekeeping

Environmental surfaces such as walls, floors, and other surfaces are not associated with transmission of infections to patients or health-care workers. Therefore, extraordinary attempts to disinfect or sterilize these environmental surfaces are not necessary. However, cleaning and removal of soil should be done routinely.

Cleaning schedules and methods vary according to the area of the hospital or institution, type of surface to be cleaned, and the amount and type of soil present. Horizontal surfaces (e.g., bedside tables and hard-surfaced flooring) in patient-care areas are usually cleaned on a regular basis, when soiling or spills occur, and when a patient is discharged. Cleaning of walls, blinds, and curtains is recommended only if they are visibly soiled. Disinfectant fogging is an unsatisfactory method of decontaminating air and surfaces and is not recommended.

Disinfectant-detergent formulations registered by EPA can be used for cleaning environmental surfaces, but the actual physical removal of microorganisms by scrubbing is probably at least as important as any antimicrobial effect of the cleaning agent used. Therefore, cost, safety, and acceptability by housekeepers can be the main criteria for selecting any such registered agent. The manufacturers' instructions for appropriate use should be followed.

Cleaning and Decontaminating Spills of Blood or Other Body Fluids

Chemical germicides that are approved for use as "hospital disinfectants" and are tuberculocidal when used at recommended dilutions can be used to decontaminate spills of blood and other body fluids. Strategies for decontaminating spills of blood and other body fluids in a patient-care setting are different than for spills of cultures or other materials in clinical, public health, or research laboratories. In patient-care areas, visible material should first be removed and then the area should be decontaminated. With large spills of cultured or concentrated infectious agents in the laboratory, the contaminated area should be flooded with a liquid germicide before cleaning, then decontaminated with fresh germicidal chemical. In both settings, gloves should be worn during the cleaning and decontaminating procedures.

Laundry

Although soiled linen has been identified as a source of large numbers of certain pathogenic microorganisms, the risk of actual disease transmission is negligible. Rather than rigid procedures and specifications, hygienic and common-sense storage and processing of clean and soiled linen are recommended (26). Soiled linen should be handled as little as possible and with minimum agitation to prevent gross microbial contamination of the air and of persons handling the linen. All soiled linen should be bagged at the location where it was used; it should not be sorted or rinsed in patient-care areas. Linen soiled with blood or body fluids should be placed and transported in bags that prevent leakage. If hot water is used, linen should be washed

August 21, 1987 — Supplement

with detergent in water at least 71 C (160 F) for 25 minutes. If low-temperature(≤70 C [158 F]) laundry cycles are used, chemicals suitable for low-temperature washing at proper use concentration should be used.

Infective Waste

There is no epidemiologic evidence to suggest that most hospital waste is any more infective than residential waste. Moreover, there is no epidemiologic evidence that hospital waste has caused disease in the community as a result of improper disposal. Therefore, identifying wastes for which special precautions are indicated is largely a matter of judgment about the relative risk of disease transmission. The most practical approach to the management of infective waste is to identify those wastes with the potential for causing infection during handling and disposal and for which some special precautions appear prudent. Hospital wastes for which special precautions appear prudent include microbiology laboratory waste, pathology waste, and blood specimens or blood products. While any item that has had contact with blood, exudates, or secretions may be potentially infective, it is not usually considered practical or necessary to treat all such waste as infective (*23,26*). Infective waste, in general, should either be incinerated or should be autoclaved before disposal in a sanitary landfill. Bulk blood, suctioned fluids, excretions, and secretions may be carefully poured down a drain connected to a sanitary sewer. Sanitary sewers may also be used to dispose of other infectious wastes capable of being ground and flushed into the sewer.

Implementation of Recommended Precautions

Employers of health-care workers should ensure that policies exist for:

1. Initial orientation and continuing education and training of all health-care workers—including students and trainees—on the epidemiology, modes of transmission, and prevention of HIV and other blood-borne infections and the need for routine use of universal blood and body-fluid precautions for <u>all</u> patients.
2. Provision of equipment and supplies necessary to minimize the risk of infection with HIV and other blood-borne pathogens.
3. Monitoring adherence to recommended protective measures. When monitoring reveals a failure to follow recommended precautions, counseling, education, and/or re-training should be provided, and, if necessary, appropriate disciplinary action should be considered.

Professional associations and labor organizations, through continuing education efforts, should emphasize the need for health-care workers to follow recommended precautions.

August 21, 1987 — Supplement

Serologic Testing for HIV Infection

Background
A person is identified as infected with HIV when a sequence of tests, starting with repeated enzyme immunoassays (EIA) and including a Western blot or similar, more specific assay, are repeatedly reactive. Persons infected with HIV usually develop antibody against the virus within 6-12 weeks after infection.

The sensitivity of the currently licensed EIA tests is at least 99% when they are performed under optimal laboratory conditions on serum specimens from persons infected for ≥12 weeks. Optimal laboratory conditions include the use of reliable reagents, provision of continuing education of personnel, quality control of procedures, and participation in performance-evaluation programs. Given this performance, the probability of a false-negative test is remote except during the first several weeks after infection, before detectable antibody is present. The proportion of infected persons with a false-negative test attributed to absence of antibody in the early stages of infection is dependent on both the incidence and prevalence of HIV infection in a population (Table 1).

The specificity of the currently licensed EIA tests is approximately 99% when repeatedly reactive tests are considered. Repeat testing of initially reactive specimens by EIA is required to reduce the likelihood of laboratory error. To increase further the specificity of serologic tests, laboratories must use a supplemental test, most often the Western blot, to validate repeatedly reactive EIA results. Under optimal laboratory conditions, the sensitivity of the Western blot test is comparable to or greater than that of a repeatedly reactive EIA, and the Western blot is highly specific when strict criteria are used to interpret the test results. The testing sequence of a repeatedly reactive EIA and a positive Western blot test is highly predictive of HIV infection, even in a population with a low prevalence of infection (Table 2). If the Western blot test result is indeterminant, the testing sequence is considered equivocal for HIV infection.

TABLE 1. Estimated annual number of patients infected with HIV not detected by HIV-antibody testing in a hypothetical hospital with 10,000 admissions/year*

Beginning prevalence of HIV infection	Annual incidence of HIV infection	Approximate number of HIV-infected patients	Approximate number of HIV-infected patients not detected
5.0%	1.0%	550	17-18
5.0%	0.5%	525	11-12
1.0%	0.2%	110	3-4
1.0%	0.1%	105	2-3
0.1%	0.02%	11	0-1
0.1%	0.01%	11	0-1

*The estimates are based on the following assumptions: 1) the sensitivity of the screening test is 99% (i.e., 99% of HIV-infected persons with antibody will be detected); 2) persons infected with HIV will not develop detectable antibody (seroconvert) until 6 weeks (1.5 months) after infection; 3) new infections occur at an equal rate throughout the year; 4) calculations of the number of HIV-infected persons in the patient population are based on the mid-year prevalence, which is the beginning prevalence plus half the annual incidence of infections.

When this occurs, the Western blot test should be repeated on the same serum sample, and, if still indeterminant, the testing sequence should be repeated on a sample collected 3-6 months later. Use of other supplemental tests may aid in interpreting of results on samples that are persistently indeterminant by Western blot.

Testing of Patients

Previous CDC recommendations have emphasized the value of HIV serologic testing of patients for: 1) management of parenteral or mucous-membrane exposures of health-care workers, 2) patient diagnosis and management, and 3) counseling and serologic testing to prevent and control HIV transmission in the community. In addition, more recent recommendations have stated that hospitals, in conjunction with state and local health departments, should periodically determine the prevalence of HIV infection among patients from age groups at highest risk of infection (*32*).

Adherence to universal blood and body-fluid precautions recommended for the care of all patients will minimize the risk of transmission of HIV and other blood-borne pathogens from patients to health-care workers. The utility of routine HIV serologic testing of patients as an adjunct to universal precautions is unknown. Results of such testing may not be available in emergency or outpatient settings. In addition, some recently infected patients will not have detectable antibody to HIV (Table 1).

Personnel in some hospitals have advocated serologic testing of patients in settings in which exposure of health-care workers to large amounts of patients' blood may be anticipated. Specific patients for whom serologic testing has been advocated include those undergoing major operative procedures and those undergoing treatment in critical-care units, especially if they have conditions involving uncontrolled bleeding. Decisions regarding the need to establish testing programs for patients should be made by physicians or individual institutions. In addition, when deemed appropriate, testing of individual patients may be performed on agreement between the patient and the physician providing care.

In addition to the universal precautions recommended for all patients, certain additional precautions for the care of HIV-infected patients undergoing major surgical operations have been proposed by personnel in some hospitals. For example, surgical procedures on an HIV-infected patient might be altered so that hand-to-hand passing of sharp instruments would be eliminated; stapling instruments rather than

TABLE 2. Predictive value of positive HIV-antibody tests in hypothetical populations with different prevalences of infection

	Prevalence of infection	Predictive value of positive test[*]
Repeatedly reactive enzyme immunoassay (EIA)[†]	0.2%	28.41%
	2.0%	80.16%
	20.0%	98.02%
Repeatedly reactive EIA followed by positive Western blot (WB)[§]	0.2%	99.75%
	2.0%	99.97%
	20.0%	99.99%

[*]Proportion of persons with positive test results who are actually infected with HIV.
[†]Assumes EIA sensitivity of 99.0% and specificity of 99.5%.
[§]Assumes WB sensitivity of 99.0% and specificity of 99.9%.

August 21, 1987 — Supplement

hand-suturing equipment might be used to perform tissue approximation; electro-cautery devices rather than scalpels might be used as cutting instruments; and, even though uncomfortable, gowns that totally prevent seepage of blood onto the skin of members of the operative team might be worn. While such modifications might further minimize the risk of HIV infection for members of the operative team, some of these techniques could result in prolongation of operative time and could potentially have an adverse effect on the patient.

Testing programs, if developed, should include the following principles:

- Obtaining consent for testing.

- Informing patients of test results, and providing counseling for seropositive patients by properly trained persons.

- Assuring that confidentiality safeguards are in place to limit knowledge of test results to those directly involved in the care of infected patients or as required by law.

- Assuring that identification of infected patients will not result in denial of needed care or provision of suboptimal care.

- Evaluating prospectively 1) the efficacy of the program in reducing the inci-dence of parenteral, mucous-membrane, or significant cutaneous exposures of health-care workers to the blood or other body fluids of HIV-infected patients and 2) the effect of modified procedures on patients.

Testing of Health-Care Workers

Although transmission of HIV from infected health-care workers to patients has not been reported, transmission during invasive procedures remains a possibility. Trans-mission of hepatitis B virus (HBV) — a blood-borne agent with a considerably greater potential for nosocomial spread — from health-care workers to patients has been documented. Such transmission has occurred in situations (e.g., oral and gynecologic surgery) in which health-care workers, when tested, had very high concentrations of HBV in their blood (at least 100 million infectious virus particles per milliliter, a concentration much higher than occurs with HIV infection), and the health-care workers sustained a puncture wound while performing invasive procedures or had exudative or weeping lesions or microlacerations that allowed virus to contaminate instruments or open wounds of patients (*33,34*).

The hepatitis B experience indicates that only those health-care workers who perform certain types of invasive procedures have transmitted HBV to patients. Adherence to recommendations in this document will minimize the risk of transmis-sion of HIV and other blood-borne pathogens from health-care workers to patients during invasive procedures. Since transmission of HIV from infected health-care workers performing invasive procedures to their patients has not been reported and would be expected to occur only very rarely, if at all, the utility of routine testing of such health-care workers to prevent transmission of HIV cannot be assessed. If consideration is given to developing a serologic testing program for health-care workers who perform invasive procedures, the frequency of testing, as well as the issues of consent, confidentiality, and consequences of test results — as previously outlined for testing programs for patients — must be addressed.

Management of Infected Health-Care Workers

Health-care workers with impaired immune systems resulting from HIV infection or other causes are at increased risk of acquiring or experiencing serious complications of infectious disease. Of particular concern is the risk of severe infection following exposure to patients with infectious diseases that are easily transmitted if appropriate precautions are not taken (e.g., measles, varicella). Any health-care worker with an impaired immune system should be counseled about the potential risk associated with taking care of patients with any transmissible infection and should continue to follow existing recommendations for infection control to minimize risk of exposure to other infectious agents (7,35). Recommendations of the Immunization Practices Advisory Committee (ACIP) and institutional policies concerning requirements for vaccinating health-care workers with live-virus vaccines (e.g., measles, rubella) should also be considered.

The question of whether workers infected with HIV — especially those who perform invasive procedures — can adequately and safely be allowed to perform patient-care duties or whether their work assignments should be changed must be determined on an individual basis. These decisions should be made by the health-care worker's personal physician(s) in conjunction with the medical directors and personnel health service staff of the employing institution or hospital.

Management of Exposures

If a health-care worker has a parenteral (e.g., needlestick or cut) or mucous-membrane (e.g., splash to the eye or mouth) exposure to blood or other body fluids or has a cutaneous exposure involving large amounts of blood or prolonged contact with blood — especially when the exposed skin is chapped, abraded, or afflicted with dermatitis — the source patient should be informed of the incident and tested for serologic evidence of HIV infection after consent is obtained. Policies should be developed for testing source patients in situations in which consent cannot be obtained (e.g., an unconscious patient).

If the source patient has AIDS, is positive for HIV antibody, or refuses the test, the health-care worker should be counseled regarding the risk of infection and evaluated clinically and serologically for evidence of HIV infection as soon as possible after the exposure. The health-care worker should be advised to report and seek medical evaluation for any acute febrile illness that occurs within 12 weeks after the exposure. Such an illness — particularly one characterized by fever, rash, or lymphadenopathy — may be indicative of recent HIV infection. Seronegative health-care workers should be retested 6 weeks post-exposure and on a periodic basis thereafter (e.g., 12 weeks and 6 months after exposure) to determine whether transmission has occurred. During this follow-up period — especially the first 6-12 weeks after exposure, when most infected persons are expected to seroconvert — exposed health-care workers should follow U.S. Public Health Service (PHS) recommendations for preventing transmission of HIV (36,37).

No further follow-up of a health-care worker exposed to infection as described above is necessary if the source patient is seronegative unless the source patient is at high risk of HIV infection. In the latter case, a subsequent specimen (e.g., 12 weeks following exposure) may be obtained from the health-care worker for antibody

August 21, 1987 – Supplement

testing. If the source patient cannot be identified, decisions regarding appropriate follow-up should be individualized. Serologic testing should be available to all health-care workers who are concerned that they may have been infected with HIV.

If a patient has a parenteral or mucous-membrane exposure to blood or other body fluid of a health-care worker, the patient should be informed of the incident, and the same procedure outlined above for management of exposures should be followed for both the source health-care worker and the exposed patient.

References
1. CDC. Acquired immunodeficiency syndrome (AIDS): Precautions for clinical and laboratory staffs. MMWR 1982;31:577-80.
2. CDC. Acquired immunodeficiency syndrome (AIDS): Precautions for health-care workers and allied professionals. MMWR 1983;32:450-1.
3. CDC. Recommendations for preventing transmission of infection with human T-lymphotropic virus type III/lymphadenopathy-associated virus in the workplace. MMWR 1985;34:681-6, 691-5.
4. CDC. Recommendations for preventing transmission of infection with human T-lymphotropic virus type III/lymphadenopathy-associated virus during invasive procedures. MMWR 1986;35:221-3.
5. CDC. Recommendations for preventing possible transmission of human T-lymphotropic virus type III/lymphadenopathy-associated virus from tears. MMWR 1985;34:533-4.
6. CDC. Recommendations for providing dialysis treatment to patients infected with human T-lymphotropic virus type III/lymphadenopathy-associated virus infection. MMWR 1986;35:376-8, 383.
7. Garner JS, Simmons BP. Guideline for isolation precautions in hospitals. Infect Control 1983;4 (suppl) :245-325.
8. CDC. Recommended infection control practices for dentistry. MMWR 1986;35:237-42.
9. McCray E, The Cooperative Needlestick Surveillance Group. Occupational risk of the acquired immunodeficiency syndrome among health care workers. N Engl J Med 1986;314:1127-32.
10. Henderson DK, Saah AJ, Zak BJ, et al. Risk of nosocomial infection with human T-cell lymphotropic virus type III/lymphadenopathy-associated virus in a large cohort of intensively exposed health care workers. Ann Intern Med 1986;104:644-7.
11. Gerberding JL, Bryant-LeBlanc CE, Nelson K, et al. Risk of transmitting the human immunodeficiency virus, cytomegalovirus, and hepatitis B virus to health care workers exposed to patients with AIDS and AIDS-related conditions. J Infect Dis 1987;156:1-8.
12. McEvoy M, Porter K, Mortimer P, Simmons N, Shanson D. Prospective study of clinical, laboratory, and ancillary staff with accidental exposures to blood or other body fluids from patients infected with HIV. Br Med J 1987;294:1595-7.
13. Anonymous. Needlestick transmission of HTLV-III from a patient infected in Africa. Lancet 1984;2:1376-7.
14. Oksenhendler E, Harzic M, Le Roux JM, Rabian C, Clauvel JP. HIV infection with seroconversion after a superficial needlestick injury to the finger. N Engl J Med 1986;315:582.
15. Neisson-Vernant C, Arfi S, Mathez D, Leibowitch J, Monplaisir N. Needlestick HIV seroconversion in a nurse. Lancet 1986;2:814.
16. Grint P, McEvoy M. Two associated cases of the acquired immune deficiency syndrome (AIDS). PHLS Commun Dis Rep 1985;42:4.
17. CDC. Apparent transmission of human T-lymphotropic virus type III/lymphadenopathy-associated virus from a child to a mother providing health care. MMWR 1986;35:76-9.
18. CDC. Update: Human immunodeficiency virus infections in health-care workers exposed to blood of infected patients. MMWR 1987;36:285-9.
19. Kline RS, Phelan J, Friedland GH, et al. Low occupational risk for HIV infection for dental professionals [Abstract]. In: Abstracts from the III International Conference on AIDS, 1-5 June 1985. Washington, DC: 155.
20. Baker JL, Kelen GD, Sivertson KT, Quinn TC. Unsuspected human immunodeficiency virus in critically ill emergency patients. JAMA 1987;257:2609-11.
21. Favero MS. Dialysis-associated diseases and their control. In: Bennett JV, Brachman PS, eds. Hospital infections. Boston: Little, Brown and Company, 1985:267-84.

22. Richardson JH, Barkley WE, eds. Biosafety in microbiological and biomedical laboratories, 1984. Washington, DC : US Department of Health and Human Services, Public Health Service. HHS publication no. (CDC) 84-8395.
23. CDC. Human T-lymphotropic virus type III/lymphadenopathy-associated virus: Agent summary statement. MMWR 1986;35:540-2, 547-9.
24. Environmental Protection Agency. EPA guide for infectious waste management. Washington, DC :U.S. Environmental Protection Agency, May 1986 (Publication no. EPA/530-SW-86-014).
25. Favero MS. Sterilization, disinfection, and antisepsis in the hospital. In: Manual of clinical microbiology. 4th ed. Washington, DC: American Society for Microbiology, 1985;129-37.
26. Garner JS, Favero MS. Guideline for handwashing and hospital environmental control, 1985. Atlanta: Public Health Service, Centers for Disease Control, 1985. HHS publication no. 99-1117.
27. Spire B, Montagnier L, Barré-Sinoussi F, Chermann JC. Inactivation of lymphadenopathy associated virus by chemical disinfectants. Lancet 1984;2:899-901.
28. Martin LS, McDougal JS, Loskoski SL. Disinfection and inactivation of the human T lymphotropic virus type III/lymphadenopathy-associated virus. J Infect Dis 1985; 152:400-3.
29. McDougal JS, Martin LS, Cort SP, et al. Thermal inactivation of the acquired immunodeficiency syndrome virus-III/lymphadenopathy-associated virus, with special reference to antihemophilic factor. J Clin Invest 1985;76:875-7.
30. Spire B, Barré-Sinoussi F, Dormont D, Montagnier L, Chermann JC. Inactivation of lymphadenopathy-associated virus by heat, gamma rays, and ultraviolet light. Lancet 1985;1:188-9.
31. Resnik L, Veren K, Salahuddin SZ, Tondreau S, Markham PD. Stability and inactivation of HTLV-III/LAV under clinical and laboratory environments. JAMA 1986;255:1887-91.
32. CDC. Public Health Service (PHS) guidelines for counseling and antibody testing to prevent HIV infection and AIDS. MMWR 1987;3:509-15..
33. Kane MA, Lettau LA. Transmission of HBV from dental personnel to patients. J Am Dent Assoc 1985;110:634-6.
34. Lettau LA, Smith JD, Williams D, et. al. Transmission of hepatitis B with resultant restriction of surgical practice. JAMA 1986;255:934-7.
35. Williams WW. Guideline for infection control in hospital personnel. Infect Control 1983;4 (suppl) :326-49.
36. CDC. Prevention of acquired immune deficiency syndrome (AIDS): Report of inter-agency recommendations. MMWR 1983;32:101-3.
37. CDC. Provisional Public Health Service inter-agency recommendations for screening donated blood and plasma for antibody to the virus causing acquired immunodeficiency syndrome. MMWR 1985;34:1-5.

Reprinted by the
U.S. DEPARTMENT OF HEALTH AND HUMAN SERVICES
Public Health Service
Centers for Disease Control

from MMWR, June 24, 1988, Vol. 37, No. 24, pp. 377-382,387-388

Perspectives in Disease Prevention and Health Promotion

Update: Universal Precautions for Prevention of Transmission of Human Immunodeficiency Virus, Hepatitis B Virus, and Other Bloodborne Pathogens in Health-Care Settings

Introduction

The purpose of this report is to clarify and supplement the CDC publication entitled "Recommendations for Prevention of HIV Transmission in Health-Care Settings" (*1*).*

In 1983, CDC published a document entitled "Guideline for Isolation Precautions in Hospitals" (*2*) that contained a section entitled "Blood and Body Fluid Precautions." The recommendations in this section called for blood and body fluid precautions when a patient was known or suspected to be infected with bloodborne pathogens. In August 1987, CDC published a document entitled "Recommendations for Prevention of HIV Transmission in Health-Care Settings" (*1*). In contrast to the 1983 document, the 1987 document recommended that blood and body fluid precautions be consistently used for all patients regardless of their bloodborne infection status. This extension of blood and body fluid precautions to **all** patients is referred to as "Universal Blood and Body Fluid Precautions" or "Universal Precautions." Under universal precautions, blood and certain body fluids of all patients are considered potentially infectious for human immunodeficiency virus (HIV), hepatitis B virus (HBV), and other bloodborne pathogens.

---

*The August 1987 publication should be consulted for general information and specific recommendations not addressed in this update.

Copies of this report and of the *MMWR* supplement entitled *Recommendations for Prevention of HIV Transmission in Health-Care Settings* published in August 1987 are available through the National AIDS Information Clearinghouse, P.O. Box 6003, Rockville, MD 20850.

Universal precautions are intended to prevent parenteral, mucous membrane, and nonintact skin exposures of health-care workers to bloodborne pathogens. In addition, immunization with HBV vaccine is recommended as an important adjunct to universal precautions for health-care workers who have exposures to blood (*3,4*).

Since the recommendations for universal precautions were published in August 1987, CDC and the Food and Drug Administration (FDA) have received requests for clarification of the following issues: 1) body fluids to which universal precautions apply, 2) use of protective barriers, 3) use of gloves for phlebotomy, 4) selection of gloves for use while observing universal precautions, and 5) need for making changes in waste management programs as a result of adopting universal precautions.

Body Fluids to Which Universal Precautions Apply

Universal precautions apply to blood and to other body fluids containing visible blood. Occupational transmission of HIV and HBV to health-care workers by blood is documented (*4,5*). **Blood is the single most important source of HIV, HBV, and other bloodborne pathogens in the occupational setting. Infection control efforts for HIV, HBV, and other bloodborne pathogens must focus on preventing exposures to blood as well as on delivery of HBV immunization.**

Universal precautions also apply to semen and vaginal secretions. Although both of these fluids have been implicated in the sexual transmission of HIV and HBV, they have not been implicated in occupational transmission from patient to health-care worker. This observation is not unexpected, since exposure to semen in the usual health-care setting is limited, and the routine practice of wearing gloves for performing vaginal examinations protects health-care workers from exposure to potentially infectious vaginal secretions.

Universal precautions also apply to tissues and to the following fluids: cerebrospinal fluid (CSF), synovial fluid, pleural fluid, peritoneal fluid, pericardial fluid, and amniotic fluid. The risk of transmission of HIV and HBV from these fluids is unknown; epidemiologic studies in the health-care and community setting are currently inadequate to assess the potential risk to health-care workers from occupational exposures to them. However, HIV has been isolated from CSF, synovial, and amniotic fluid (*6–8*), and HBsAg has been detected in synovial fluid, amniotic fluid, and peritoneal fluid (*9–11*). One case of HIV transmission was reported after a percutaneous exposure to bloody pleural fluid obtained by needle aspiration (*12*). Whereas aseptic procedures used to obtain these fluids for diagnostic or therapeutic purposes protect health-care workers from skin exposures, they cannot prevent penetrating injuries due to contaminated needles or other sharp instruments.

Body Fluids to Which Universal Precautions Do Not Apply

Universal precautions do not apply to feces, nasal secretions, sputum, sweat, tears, urine, and vomitus unless they contain visible blood. The risk of transmission of HIV and HBV from these fluids and materials is extremely low or nonexistent. HIV has been isolated and HBsAg has been demonstrated in some of these fluids; however, epidemiologic studies in the health-care and community setting have not implicated these fluids or materials in the transmission of HIV and HBV infections (*13,14*). Some of the above fluids and excretions represent a potential source for nosocomial and community-acquired infections with other pathogens, and recommendations for preventing the transmission of nonbloodborne pathogens have been published (*2*).

Precautions for Other Body Fluids in Special Settings

Human breast milk has been implicated in perinatal transmission of HIV, and HBsAg has been found in the milk of mothers infected with HBV (*10,13*). However, occupational exposure to human breast milk has not been implicated in the transmission of HIV nor HBV infection to health-care workers. Moreover, the health-care worker will not have the same type of intensive exposure to breast milk as the nursing neonate. Whereas universal precautions do not apply to human breast milk, gloves may be worn by health-care workers in situations where exposures to breast milk might be frequent, for example, in breast milk banking.

Saliva of some persons infected with HBV has been shown to contain HBV-DNA at concentrations 1/1,000 to 1/10,000 of that found in the infected person's serum (*15*). HBsAg-positive saliva has been shown to be infectious when injected into experimental animals and in human bite exposures (*16–18*). However, HBsAg-positive saliva has not been shown to be infectious when applied to oral mucous membranes in experimental primate studies (*18*) or through contamination of musical instruments or cardiopulmonary resuscitation dummies used by HBV carriers (*19,20*). Epidemiologic studies of nonsexual household contacts of HIV-infected patients, including several small series in which HIV transmission failed to occur after bites or after percutaneous inoculation or contamination of cuts and open wounds with saliva from HIV-infected patients, suggest that the potential for salivary transmission of HIV is remote (*5,13,14,21,22*). One case report from Germany has suggested the possibility of transmission of HIV in a household setting from an infected child to a sibling through a human bite (*23*). The bite did not break the skin or result in bleeding. Since the date of seroconversion to HIV was not known for either child in this case, evidence for the role of saliva in the transmission of virus is unclear (*23*). Another case report suggested the possibility of transmission of HIV from husband to wife by contact with saliva during kissing (*24*). However, follow-up studies did not confirm HIV infection in the wife (*21*).

Universal precautions do not apply to saliva. General infection control practices already in existence — including the use of gloves for digital examination of mucous membranes and endotracheal suctioning, and handwashing after exposure to saliva — should further minimize the minute risk, if any, for salivary transmission of HIV and HBV (*1,25*). Gloves need not be worn when feeding patients and when wiping saliva from skin.

Special precautions, however, are recommended for dentistry (*1*). Occupationally acquired infection with HBV in dental workers has been documented (*4*), and two possible cases of occupationally acquired HIV infection involving dentists have been reported (*5,26*). During dental procedures, contamination of saliva with blood is predictable, trauma to health-care workers' hands is common, and blood spattering may occur. Infection control precautions for dentistry minimize the potential for nonintact skin and mucous membrane contact of dental health-care workers to blood-contaminated saliva of patients. In addition, the use of gloves for oral examinations and treatment in the dental setting may also protect the patient's oral mucous membranes from exposures to blood, which may occur from breaks in the skin of dental workers' hands.

Use of Protective Barriers

Protective barriers reduce the risk of exposure of the health-care worker's skin or mucous membranes to potentially infective materials. For universal precautions, protective barriers reduce the risk of exposure to blood, body fluids containing visible blood, and other fluids to which universal precautions apply. Examples of protective barriers include gloves, gowns, masks, and protective eyewear. Gloves should reduce the incidence of contamination of hands, but they cannot prevent penetrating injuries due to needles or other sharp instruments. Masks and protective eyewear or face shields should reduce the incidence of contamination of mucous membranes of the mouth, nose, and eyes.

Universal precautions are intended to supplement rather than replace recommendations for routine infection control, such as handwashing and using gloves to prevent gross microbial contamination of hands (*27*). Because specifying the types of barriers needed for every possible clinical situation is impractical, some judgment must be exercised.

The risk of nosocomial transmission of HIV, HBV, and other bloodborne pathogens can be minimized if health-care workers use the following general guidelines:[†]

1. Take care to prevent injuries when using needles, scalpels, and other sharp instruments or devices; when handling sharp instruments after procedures; when cleaning used instruments; and when disposing of used needles. Do not recap used needles by hand; do not remove used needles from disposable syringes by hand; and do not bend, break, or otherwise manipulate used needles by hand. Place used disposable syringes and needles, scalpel blades, and other sharp items in puncture-resistant containers for disposal. Locate the puncture-resistant containers as close to the use area as is practical.

2. Use protective barriers to prevent exposure to blood, body fluids containing visible blood, and other fluids to which universal precautions apply. The type of protective barrier(s) should be appropriate for the procedure being performed and the type of exposure anticipated.

3. Immediately and thoroughly wash hands and other skin surfaces that are contaminated with blood, body fluids containing visible blood, or other body fluids to which universal precautions apply.

Glove Use for Phlebotomy

Gloves should reduce the incidence of blood contamination of hands during phlebotomy (drawing blood samples), but they cannot prevent penetrating injuries caused by needles or other sharp instruments. The likelihood of hand contamination with blood containing HIV, HBV, or other bloodborne pathogens during phlebotomy depends on several factors: 1) the skill and technique of the health-care worker, 2) the frequency with which the health-care worker performs the procedure (other factors being equal, the cumulative risk of blood exposure is higher for a health-care worker who performs more procedures), 3) whether the procedure occurs in a routine or emergency situation (where blood contact may be more likely), and 4) the prevalence of infection with bloodborne pathogens in the patient population. The likelihood of infection after skin exposure to blood containing HIV or HBV will depend on the concentration of virus (viral concentration is much higher for hepatitis B than for HIV), the duration of contact, the presence of skin lesions on the hands of the health-care worker, and — for HBV — the immune status of the health-care worker. Although not accurately quantified, the risk of HIV infection following intact skin contact with infective blood is certainly much less than the 0.5% risk following percutaneous

[†]The August 1987 publication should be consulted for general information and specific recommendations not addressed in this update.

needlestick exposures (5). In universal precautions, all blood is assumed to be potentially infective for bloodborne pathogens, but in certain settings (e.g., volunteer blood-donation centers) the prevalence of infection with some bloodborne pathogens (e.g., HIV, HBV) is known to be very low. Some institutions have relaxed recommendations for using gloves for phlebotomy procedures by skilled phlebotomists in settings where the prevalence of bloodborne pathogens is known to be very low.

Institutions that judge that routine gloving for all phlebotomies is not necessary should periodically reevaluate their policy. Gloves should always be available to health-care workers who wish to use them for phlebotomy. In addition, the following general guidelines apply:

1. Use gloves for performing phlebotomy when the health-care worker has cuts, scratches, or other breaks in his/her skin.
2. Use gloves in situations where the health-care worker judges that hand contamination with blood may occur, for example, when performing phlebotomy on an uncooperative patient.
3. Use gloves for performing finger and/or heel sticks on infants and children.
4. Use gloves when persons are receiving training in phlebotomy.

Selection of Gloves

The Center for Devices and Radiological Health, FDA, has responsibility for regulating the medical glove industry. Medical gloves include those marketed as sterile surgical or nonsterile examination gloves made of vinyl or latex. General purpose utility ("rubber") gloves are also used in the health-care setting, but they are not regulated by FDA since they are not promoted for medical use. There are no reported differences in barrier effectiveness between intact latex and intact vinyl used to manufacture gloves. Thus, the type of gloves selected should be appropriate for the task being performed.

The following general guidelines are recommended:

1. Use sterile gloves for procedures involving contact with normally sterile areas of the body.
2. Use examination gloves for procedures involving contact with mucous membranes, unless otherwise indicated, and for other patient care or diagnostic procedures that do not require the use of sterile gloves.
3. Change gloves between patient contacts.
4. Do not wash or disinfect surgical or examination gloves for reuse. Washing with surfactants may cause "wicking," i.e., the enhanced penetration of liquids through undetected holes in the glove. Disinfecting agents may cause deterioration.
5. Use general-purpose utility gloves (e.g., rubber household gloves) for housekeeping chores involving potential blood contact and for instrument cleaning and decontamination procedures. Utility gloves may be decontaminated and reused but should be discarded if they are peeling, cracked, or discolored, or if they have punctures, tears, or other evidence of deterioration.

Waste Management

Universal precautions are not intended to change waste management programs previously recommended by CDC for health-care settings (1). Policies for defining, collecting, storing, decontaminating, and disposing of infective waste are generally determined by institutions in accordance with state and local regulations. Information regarding waste management regulations in health-care settings may be obtained from state or local health departments or agencies responsible for waste management.

Reported by: Center for Devices and Radiological Health, Food and Drug Administration. Hospital Infections Program, AIDS Program, and Hepatitis Br, Div of Viral Diseases, Center for Infectious Diseases, National Institute for Occupational Safety and Health, CDC.

Editorial Note: Implementation of universal precautions does not eliminate the need for other category- or disease-specific isolation precautions, such as enteric precautions for infectious diarrhea or isolation for pulmonary tuberculosis (*1,2*). In addition to universal precautions, detailed precautions have been developed for the following procedures and/or settings in which prolonged or intensive exposures to blood occur: invasive procedures, dentistry, autopsies or morticians' services, dialysis, and the clinical laboratory. These detailed precautions are found in the August 21, 1987, "Recommendations for Prevention of HIV Transmission in Health-Care Settings" (*1*). In addition, specific precautions have been developed for research laboratories (*28*).

References
1. Centers for Disease Control. Recommendations for prevention of HIV transmission in health-care settings. MMWR 1987;36(suppl no. 2S).
2. Garner JS, Simmons BP. Guideline for isolation precautions in hospitals. Infect Control 1983:4;245–325.
3. Immunization Practices Advisory Committee. Recommendations for protection against viral hepatitis. MMWR 1985;34:313-24,329–35.
4. Department of Labor, Department of Health and Human Services. Joint advisory notice: protection against occupational exposure to hepatitis B virus (HBV) and human immunodeficiency virus (HIV). Washington, DC:US Department of Labor, US Department of Health and Human Services, 1987.
5. Centers for Disease Control. Update: Acquired immunodeficiency syndrome and human immunodeficiency virus infection among health-care workers. MMWR 1988;37:229–34,239.
6. Hollander H, Levy JA. Neurologic abnormalities and recovery of human immunodeficiency virus from cerebrospinal fluid. Ann Intern Med 1987;106:692–5.
7. Wirthrington RH, Cornes P, Harris JRW, et al. Isolation of human immunodeficiency virus from synovial fluid of a patient with reactive arthritis. Br Med J 1987;294:484.
8. Mundy DC, Schinazi RF, Gerber AR, Nahmias AJ, Randall HW. Human immunodeficiency virus isolated from amniotic fluid. Lancet 1987;2:459–60.
9. Onion DK, Crumpacker CS, Gilliland BC. Arthritis of hepatitis associated with Australia antigen. Ann Intern Med 1971;75:29–33.
10. Lee AKY, Ip HMH, Wong VCW. Mechanisms of maternal-fetal transmission of hepatitis B virus. J Infect Dis 1978;138:668–71.
11. Bond WW, Petersen NJ, Gravelle CR, Favero MS. Hepatitis B virus in peritoneal dialysis fluid: A potential hazard. Dialysis and Transplantation 1982;11:592–600.
12. Oskenhendler E, Harzic M, Le Roux J-M, Rabian C, Clauvel JP. HIV infection with seroconversion after a superficial needlestick injury to the finger [Letter]. N Engl J Med 1986;315:582.
13. Lifson AR. Do alternate modes for transmission of human immunodeficiency virus exist? A review. JAMA 1988;259:1353–6.
14. Friedland GH, Saltzman BR, Rogers MF, et al. Lack of transmission of HTLV-III/LAV infection to household contacts of patients with AIDS or AIDS-related complex with oral candidiasis. N Engl J Med 1986;314:344–9.
15. Jenison SA, Lemon SM, Baker LN, Newbold JE. Quantitative analysis of hepatitis B virus DNA in saliva and semen of chronically infected homosexual men. J Infect Dis 1987;156:299–306.
16. Cancio-Bello TP, de Medina M, Shorey J, Valledor MD, Schiff ER. An institutional outbreak of hepatitis B related to a human biting carrier. J Infect Dis 1982;146:652–6.
17. MacQuarrie MB, Forghani B, Wolochow DA. Hepatitis B transmitted by a human bite. JAMA 1974;230:723–4.

18. Scott RM, Snitbhan R, Bancroft WH, Alter HJ, Tingpalapong M. Experimental transmission of hepatitis B virus by semen and saliva. J Infect Dis 1980;142:67–71.
19. Glaser JB, Nadler JP. Hepatitis B virus in a cardiopulmonary resuscitation training course: Risk of transmission from a surface antigen-positive participant. Arch Intern Med 1985;145:1653–5.
20. Osterholm MT, Bravo ER, Crosson JT, et al. Lack of transmission of viral hepatitis type B after oral exposure to HBsAg-positive saliva. Br Med J 1979;2:1263–4.
21. Curran JW, Jaffe HW, Hardy AM, et al. Epidemiology of HIV infection and AIDS in the United States. Science 1988;239:610–6.
22. Jason JM, McDougal JS, Dixon G, et al. HTLV-III/LAV antibody and immune status of household contacts and sexual partners of persons with hemophilia. JAMA 1986;255:212–5.
23. Wahn V, Kramer HH, Voit T, Brüster HT, Scrampical B, Scheid A. Horizontal transmission of HIV infection between two siblings [Letter]. Lancet 1986;2:694.
24. Salahuddin SZ, Groopman JE, Markham PD, et al. HTLV-III in symptom-free seronegative persons. Lancet 1984;2:1418–20.
25. Simmons BP, Wong ES. Guideline for prevention of nosocomial pneumonia. Atlanta: US Department of Health and Human Services, Public Health Service, Centers for Disease Control, 1982.
26. Klein RS, Phelan JA, Freeman K, et al. Low occupational risk of human immunodeficiency virus infection among dental professionals. N Engl J Med 1988;318:86–90.
27. Garner JS, Favero MS. Guideline for handwashing and hospital environmental control, 1985. Atlanta: US Department of Health and Human Services, Public Health Service, Centers for Disease Control, 1985; HHS publication no. 99-1117.
28. Centers for Disease Control. 1988 Agent summary statement for human immunodeficiency virus and report on laboratory-acquired infection with human immunodeficiency virus. MMWR 1988;37(suppl no. S4:1S-22S).

CENTERS FOR DISEASE CONTROL

July 12, 1991 / Vol. 40 / No. RR-8

MORBIDITY AND MORTALITY WEEKLY REPORT

*Recommendations
and
Reports*

Recommendations for Preventing Transmission of Human Immunodeficiency Virus and Hepatitis B Virus to Patients During Exposure-Prone Invasive Procedures

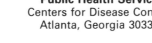
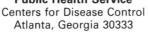

U.S. DEPARTMENT OF HEALTH AND HUMAN SERVICES
Public Health Service
Centers for Disease Control
Atlanta, Georgia 30333

CDC
CENTERS FOR DISEASE CONTROL

The *MMWR* series of publications is published by the Epidemiology Program Office, Centers for Disease Control, Public Health Service, U.S. Department of Health and Human Services, Atlanta, Georgia 30333.

SUGGESTED CITATION

Centers for Disease Control. Recommendations for preventing transmission of human immunodeficiency virus and hepatitis B virus to patients during exposure-prone invasive procedures. *MMWR* 1991;40(No. RR-8):[inclusive page numbers].

Centers for Disease Control ....William L. Roper, M.D., M.P.H.
Director
Walter R. Dowdle, Ph.D.
Deputy Director
Gary R. Noble, M.D., M.P.H.
Deputy Director (HIV)

This report was prepared for publication by:

National Center for Infectious Diseases ....Frederick A. Murphy, D.V.M., Ph.D.
Director

Hospital Infections Program...................................William J. Martone, M.D., M.Sc.
Director

Division of HIV/AIDS...James W. Curran, M.D., M.P.H.
Director

Division of Viral and Rickettsial Diseases...............Brian W. J. Mahy, Ph.D., Sc.D.
Director

in collaboration with:

National Center for Prevention Services ....Alan R. Hinman, M.D., M.P.H.
Director

National Institute for Occupational
Safety and Health..J. Donald Millar, M.D., M.P.H.
Director

The production of this report as an *MMWR* serial publication was coordinated in:

Epidemiology Program Office.................................Stephen B. Thacker, M.D., M.Sc.
Director
Richard A. Goodman, M.D., M.P.H.
Editor MMWR *Series*

Scientific Communications Program.................................R. Elliott Churchill, M.A.
Director
Suzanne Hewitt
Production Coordinator
Morie Miller
Editorial Assistant

Recommendations for Preventing Transmission of Human Immunodeficiency Virus and Hepatitis B Virus to Patients During Exposure-Prone Invasive Procedures

The CDC staff members listed below served as authors of this document.

Coordinators
Jacquelyn A. Polder, B.S.N., M.P.H.
David M. Bell, M.D.

James Curran, M.D., M.P.H.
Lawrence Furman, D.D.S., M.P.H.
Barbara Gooch, D.M.D., M.P.H.
James Hughes, M.D.
Harold Jaffe, M.D.
Harold Margolis, M.D.
Donald Marianos, D.D.S., M.P.H.
William Martone, M.D., M.Sc.
Linda Martin, Ph.D.
Craig Shapiro, M.D.

Single copies of this document are available from the National AIDS Clearinghouse, P.O. Box 6003, Rockville, MD 20850; telephone 800-458-5231.

Vol. 40 / No. RR-8   MMWR   **1**

Recommendations for Preventing Transmission of Human Immunodeficiency Virus and Hepatitis B Virus to Patients During Exposure-Prone Invasive Procedures

This document has been developed by the Centers for Disease Control (CDC) to update recommendations for prevention of transmission of human immunodeficiency virus (HIV) and hepatitis B virus (HBV) in the health-care setting. Current data suggest that the risk for such transmission from a health-care worker (HCW) to a patient during an invasive procedure is small; a precise assessment of the risk is not yet available. This document contains recommendations to provide guidance for prevention of HIV and HBV transmission during those invasive procedures that are considered exposure-prone.

INTRODUCTION

Recommendations have been made by the Centers for Disease Control (CDC) for the prevention of transmission of the human immunodeficiency virus (HIV) and the hepatitis B virus (HBV) in health-care settings (*1-6*). These recommendations emphasize adherence to universal precautions that require that blood and other specified body fluids of **all** patients be handled as if they contain blood-borne pathogens (*1,2*).

Previous guidelines contained precautions to be used during invasive procedures (defined in Appendix) and recommendations for the management of HIV- and HBV-infected health-care workers (HCWs) (*1*). These guidelines did not include specific recommendations on testing HCWs for HIV or HBV infection, and they did not provide guidance on which invasive procedures may represent increased risk to the patient.

The recommendations outlined in this document are based on the following considerations:

- Infected HCWs who adhere to universal precautions and who do not perform invasive procedures pose no risk for transmitting HIV or HBV to patients.
- Infected HCWs who adhere to universal precautions and who perform certain exposure-prone procedures (see page 4) pose a small risk for transmitting HBV to patients.
- HIV is transmitted much less readily than HBV.

In the interim, until further data are available, additional precautions are prudent to prevent HIV and HBV transmission during procedures that have been linked to HCW-to-patient HBV transmission or that are considered exposure-prone.

2   MMWR   July 12, 1991

BACKGROUND

Infection-Control Practices

Previous recommendations have specified that infection-control programs should incorporate principles of universal precautions (i.e., appropriate use of hand washing, protective barriers, and care in the use and disposal of needles and other sharp instruments) and should maintain these precautions rigorously in all health-care settings (1,2,5). Proper application of these principles will assist in minimizing the risk of transmission of HIV or HBV from patient to HCW, HCW to patient, or patient to patient.

As part of standard infection-control practice, instruments and other reusable equipment used in performing invasive procedures should be appropriately disinfected and sterilized as follows (7):

- Equipment and devices that enter the patient's vascular system or other normally sterile areas of the body should be sterilized before being used for each patient.
- Equipment and devices that touch intact mucous membranes but do not penetrate the patient's body surfaces should be sterilized when possible or undergo high-level disinfection if they cannot be sterilized before being used for each patient.
- Equipment and devices that do not touch the patient or that only touch intact skin of the patient need only be cleaned with a detergent or as indicated by the manufacturer.

Compliance with universal precautions and recommendations for disinfection and sterilization of medical devices should be scrupulously monitored in all health-care settings (1, 7, 8). Training of HCWs in proper infection-control technique should begin in professional and vocational schools and continue as an ongoing process. Institutions should provide all HCWs with appropriate inservice education regarding infection control and safety and should establish procedures for monitoring compliance with infection-control policies.

All HCWs who might be exposed to blood in an occupational setting should receive hepatitis B vaccine, preferably during their period of professional training and before any occupational exposures could occur (8, 9).

Transmission of HBV During Invasive Procedures

Since the introduction of serologic testing for HBV infection in the early 1970s, there have been published reports of 20 clusters in which a total of over 300 patients were infected with HBV in association with treatment by an HBV-infected HCW. In 12 of these clusters, the implicated HCW did not routinely wear gloves; several HCWs also had skin lesions that may have facilitated HBV transmission (10-22). These 12 clusters included nine linked to dentists or oral surgeons and one cluster each linked to a general practitioner, an inhalation therapist, and a cardiopulmonary-bypass-pump technician. The clusters associated with the inhalation therapist and the cardiopulmonary-bypass-pump technician — and some of the other 10 clusters — could possibly have been prevented if current recommendations on universal precautions, including glove use, had been in effect. In the remaining eight clusters, transmission occurred despite glove use by the HCWs; five clusters were linked to obstetricians or gynecologists, and three were linked to cardiovascular surgeons (6, 22-28). In

Vol. 40 / No. RR-8   MMWR   3

addition, recent unpublished reports strongly suggest HBV transmission from three surgeons to patients in 1989 and 1990 during colorectal (CDC, unpublished data), abdominal, and cardiothoracic surgery (*29*).

Seven of the HCWs who were linked to published clusters in the United States were allowed to perform invasive procedures following modification of invasive techniques (e.g., double gloving and restriction of certain high-risk procedures) (*6,11-13,15,16, 24*). For five HCWs, no further transmission to patients was observed. In two instances involving an obstetrician/gynecologist and an oral surgeon, HBV was transmitted to patients after techniques were modified (*6, 12*).

Review of the 20 published studies indicates that a combination of risk factors accounted for transmission of HBV from HCWs to patients. Of the HCWs whose hepatitis B e antigen (HBeAg) status was determined (17 of 20), all were HBeAg positive. The presence of HBeAg in serum is associated with higher levels of circulating virus and therefore with greater infectivity of hepatitis-B-surface-antigen (HBsAg)-positive individuals; the risk of HBV transmission to an HCW after a percutaneous exposure to HBeAg-positive blood is approximately 30% (*30-32*). In addition, each report indicated that the potential existed for contamination of surgical wounds or traumatized tissue, either from a major break in standard infection-control practices (e.g., not wearing gloves during invasive procedures) or from unintentional injury to the infected HCW during invasive procedures (e.g., needle sticks incurred while manipulating needles without being able to see them during suturing).

Most reported clusters in the United States occurred before awareness increased of the risks of transmission of blood-borne pathogens in health-care settings and before emphasis was placed on the use of universal precautions and hepatitis B vaccine among HCWs. The limited number of reports of HBV transmission from HCWs to patients in recent years may reflect the adoption of universal precautions and increased use of HBV vaccine. However, the limited number of recent reports does not preclude the occurrence of undetected or unreported small clusters or individual instances of transmission; routine use of gloves does not prevent most injuries caused by sharp instruments and does not eliminate the potential for exposure of a patient to an HCW's blood and transmission of HBV (*6, 22-29*).

Transmission of HIV During Invasive Procedures

The risk of HIV transmission to an HCW after percutaneous exposure to HIV-infected blood is considerably lower than the risk of HBV transmission after percutaneous exposure to HBeAg-positive blood (0.3% versus approximately 30%) (*33-35*). Thus, the risk of transmission of HIV from an infected HCW to a patient during an invasive procedure is likely to be proportionately lower than the risk of HBV transmission from an HBeAg-positive HCW to a patient during the same procedure. As with HBV, the relative infectivity of HIV probably varies among individuals and over time for a single individual. Unlike HBV infection, however, there is currently no readily available laboratory test for increased HIV infectivity.

Investigation of a cluster of HIV infections among patients in the practice of one dentist with acquired immunodeficiency syndrome (AIDS) strongly suggested that HIV was transmitted to five of the approximately 850 patients evaluated through June 1991 (*36-38*). The investigation indicates that HIV transmission occurred during dental care, although the precise mechanisms of transmission have not been determined. In two other studies, when patients cared for by a general surgeon and a surgical resident who had AIDS were tested, all patients tested, 75 and 62, respectively, were negative for HIV infection (*39, 40*). In a fourth study, 143 patients who had been treated by a dental student with HIV infection and were later tested were all negative for HIV infection (*41*). In another investigation, HIV antibody testing was offered to all patients whose surgical procedures had been performed by a general surgeon within 7 years before the surgeon's diagnosis of AIDS; the date at which the surgeon became infected with HIV is unknown (*42*). Of 1,340 surgical patients contacted, 616 (46%) were tested for HIV. One patient, a known intravenous drug user, was HIV positive when tested but may already have been infected at the time of surgery. HIV test results for the 615 other surgical patients were negative (95% confidence interval for risk of transmission per operation = 0.0%-0.5%).

The limited number of participants and the differences in procedures associated with these five investigations limit the ability to generalize from them and to define precisely the risk of HIV transmission from HIV-infected HCWs to patients. A precise estimate of the risk of HIV transmission from infected HCWs to patients can be determined only after careful evaluation of a substantially larger number of patients whose exposure-prone procedures have been performed by HIV-infected HCWs.

Exposure-Prone Procedures

Despite adherence to the principles of universal precautions, certain invasive surgical and dental procedures have been implicated in the transmission of HBV from infected HCWs to patients, and should be considered exposure-prone. Reported examples include certain oral, cardiothoracic, colorectal (CDC, unpublished data), and obstetric/gynecologic procedures (*6, 12, 22-29*).

Certain other invasive procedures should also be considered exposure-prone. In a prospective study CDC conducted in four hospitals, one or more percutaneous injuries occurred among surgical personnel during 96 (6.9%) of 1,382 operative procedures on the general surgery, gynecology, orthopedic, cardiac, and trauma services (*43*). Percutaneous exposure of the patient to the HCW's blood may have occurred when the sharp object causing the injury recontacted the patient's open wound in 28 (32%) of the 88 observed injuries to surgeons (range among surgical specialties = 8%-57%; range among hospitals = 24%-42%).

> **Characteristics of exposure-prone procedures include digital palpation of a needle tip in a body cavity or the simultaneous presence of the HCW's fingers and a needle or other sharp instrument or object in a poorly visualized or highly confined anatomic site. Performance of exposure-prone procedures presents a recognized risk of percutaneous injury to the HCW, and—if such an injury occurs—the HCW's blood is likely to contact the patient's body cavity, subcutaneous tissues, and/or mucous membranes.**

Experience with HBV indicates that invasive procedures that do not have the above characteristics would be expected to pose substantially lower risk, if any, of transmission of HIV and other blood-borne pathogens from an infected HCW to patients.

Vol. 40 / No. RR-8   MMWR   5

RECOMMENDATIONS

Investigations of HIV and HBV transmission from HCWs to patients indicate that, when HCWs adhere to recommended infection-control procedures, the risk of transmitting HBV from an infected HCW to a patient is small, and the risk of transmitting HIV is likely to be even smaller. However, the likelihood of exposure of the patient to an HCW's blood is greater for certain procedures designated as exposure-prone. To minimize the risk of HIV or HBV transmission, the following measures are recommended:

- **All HCWs should adhere to universal precautions, including the appropriate use of hand washing, protective barriers, and care in the use and disposal of needles and other sharp instruments. HCWs who have exudative lesions or weeping dermatitis should refrain from all direct patient care and from handling patient-care equipment and devices used in performing invasive procedures until the condition resolves. HCWs should also comply with current guidelines for disinfection and sterilization of reusable devices used in invasive procedures.**

- **Currently available data provide no basis for recommendations to restrict the practice of HCWs infected with HIV or HBV who perform invasive procedures not identified as exposure-prone, provided the infected HCWs practice recommended surgical or dental technique and comply with universal precautions and current recommendations for sterilization/disinfection.**

- **Exposure-prone procedures should be identified by medical/surgical/dental organizations and institutions at which the procedures are performed.**

- **HCWs who perform exposure-prone procedures should know their HIV antibody status. HCWs who perform exposure-prone procedures and who do not have serologic evidence of immunity to HBV from vaccination or from previous infection should know their HBsAg status and, if that is positive, should also know their HBeAg status.**

- **HCWs who are infected with HIV or HBV (and are HBeAg positive) should not perform exposure-prone procedures unless they have sought counsel from an expert review panel and been advised under what circumstances, if any, they may continue to perform these procedures.* Such circumstances would include notifying prospective patients of the HCW's seropositivity before they undergo exposure-prone invasive procedures.**

---

*The review panel should include experts who represent a balanced perspective. Such experts might include all of the following: a) the HCW's personal physician(s), b) an infectious disease specialist with expertise in the epidemiology of HIV and HBV transmission, c) a health professional with expertise in the procedures performed by the HCW, and d) state or local public health official(s). If the HCW's practice is institutionally based, the expert review panel might also include a member of the infection-control committee, preferably a hospital epidemiologist. HCWs who perform exposure-prone procedures outside the hospital/institutional setting should seek advice from appropriate state and local public health officials regarding the review process. Panels must recognize the importance of confidentiality and the privacy rights of infected HCWs.

6 MMWR July 12, 1991

- Mandatory testing of HCWs for HIV antibody, HBsAg, or HBeAg is not recommended. The current assessment of the risk that infected HCWs will transmit HIV or HBV to patients during exposure-prone procedures does not support the diversion of resources that would be required to implement mandatory testing programs. Compliance by HCWs with recommendations can be increased through education, training, and appropriate confidentiality safeguards.

HCWS WHOSE PRACTICES ARE MODIFIED BECAUSE OF HIV OR HBV STATUS

HCWs whose practices are modified because of their HIV or HBV infection status should, whenever possible, be provided opportunities to continue appropriate patient-care activities. Career counseling and job retraining should be encouraged to promote the continued use of the HCW's talents, knowledge, and skills. HCWs whose practices are modified because of HBV infection should be reevaluated periodically to determine whether their HBeAg status changes due to resolution of infection or as a result of treatment (44).

NOTIFICATION OF PATIENTS AND FOLLOW-UP STUDIES

The public health benefit of notification of patients who have had exposure-prone procedures performed by HCWs infected with HIV or positive for HBeAg should be considered on a case-by-case basis, taking into consideration an assessment of specific risks, confidentiality issues, and available resources. Carefully designed and implemented follow-up studies are necessary to determine more precisely the risk of transmission during such procedures. Decisions regarding notification and follow-up studies should be made in consultation with state and local public health officials.

ADDITIONAL NEEDS

- Clearer definition of the nature, frequency, and circumstances of blood contact between patients and HCWs during invasive procedures.
- Development and evaluation of new devices, protective barriers, and techniques that may prevent such blood contact without adversely affecting the quality of patient care.
- More information on the potential for HIV and HBV transmission through contaminated instruments.
- Improvements in sterilization and disinfection techniques for certain reusable equipment and devices.
- Identification of factors that may influence the likelihood of HIV or HBV transmission after exposure to HIV- or HBV-infected blood.

Vol. 40 / No. RR-8   MMWR   7

References
 1. CDC. Recommendations for prevention of HIV transmission in health-care settings. MMWR
    1987;36(suppl. no. 2S):1-18S.
 2. CDC. Update: Universal precautions for prevention of transmission of human immunode-
    ficiency virus, hepatitis B virus, and other bloodborne pathogens in health-care settings.
    MMWR 1988;37:377-82,387-8.
 3. CDC. Hepatitis Surveillance Report No. 48. Atlanta: U.S. Department of Health and Human
    Services, Public Health Service, 1982:2-3.
 4. CDC. CDC Guideline for Infection Control in Hospital Personnel, Atlanta, Georgia: Public
    Health Service, 1983. 24 pages. (GPO# 6AR031488305).
 5. CDC. Guidelines for prevention of transmission of human immunodeficiency virus and
    hepatitis B virus to health-care and public-safety workers. MMWR 1989;38;(suppl. no.
    S-6):1-37.
 6. Lettau LA, Smith JD, Williams D, et al. Transmission of hepatitis B with resultant restriction
    of surgical practice. JAMA 1986;255:934-7.
 7. CDC. Guidelines for the prevention and control of nosocomial infections: guideline for
    handwashing and hospital environmental control. Atlanta, Georgia: Public Health Service,
    1985. 20 pages. (GPO# 544-436/24441).
 8. Department of Labor, Occupational Safety and Health Administration. Occupational expo-
    sure to bloodborne pathogens: proposed rule and notice of hearing. Federal Register
    1989;54:23042-139.
 9. CDC. Protection against viral hepatitis: recommendations of the immunization practices
    advisory committee (ACIP). MMWR 1990;39:(no. RR-2).
10. Levin ML, Maddrey WC, Wands JR, Mendeloff AI. Hepatitis B transmission by dentists.
    JAMA 1974; 228:1139-40.
11. Rimland D, Parkin WE, Miller GB, Schrack WD. Hepatitis B outbreak traced to an oral
    surgeon. N Engl J Med 1977;296:953-8.
12. Goodwin D, Fannin SL, McCracken BB. An oral-surgeon related hepatitis-B outbreak.
    California Morbidity 1976;14.
13. Hadler SC, Sorley DL, Acree KH, et al. An outbreak of hepatitis B in a dental practice. Ann
    Intern Med 1981;95:133-8.
14. Reingold AL, Kane MA, Murphy BL, Checko P, Francis DP, Maynard JE. Transmission of
    hepatitis B by an oral surgeon. J Infect Dis 1982;145:262-8.
15. Goodman RA, Ahtone JL, Finton RJ. Hepatitis B transmission from dental personnel to
    patients: unfinished business [Editorial]. Ann Intern Med 1982;96:119.
16. Ahtone J, Goodman RA. Hepatitis B and dental personnel: transmission to patients and
    prevention issues. J Am Dent Assoc 1983;106:219-22.
17. Shaw FE, Jr, Barrett CL, Hamm R, et al. Lethal outbreak of hepatitis B in a dental practice.
    JAMA 1986;255:3260-4.
18. CDC. Outbreak of hepatitis B associated with an oral surgeon, New Hampshire. MMWR
    1987;36:132-3.
19. Grob PJ, Moeschlin P. Risk to contacts of a medical practitioner carrying HBsAg. [Letter]. N
    Engl J Med 1975;293:197.
20. Grob PJ, Bischof B, Naeff F. Cluster of hepatitis B transmitted by a physician. Lancet
    1981;2:1218-20.
21. Snydman DR, Hindman SH, Wineland MD, Bryan JA, Maynard JE. Nosocomial viral hepatitis
    B. A cluster among staff with subsequent transmission to patients. Ann Intern Med
    1976;85:573-7.
22. Coutinho RA, Albrecht-van Lent P, Stoutjesdijk L, et al. Hepatitis B from doctors [Letter].
    Lancet 1982;1:345-6.
23. Anonymous. Acute hepatitis B associated with gynaecological surgery. Lancet 1980;1:1-6.
24. Carl M, Blakey DL, Francis DP, Maynard JE. Interruption of hepatitis B transmission by
    modification of a gynaecologist's surgical technique. Lancet 1982;1:731-3.
25. Anonymous. Acute hepatitis B following gynaecological surgery. J Hosp Infect 1987;9:34-8.
26. Welch J, Webster M, Tilzey AJ, Noah ND, Banatvala JE. Hepatitis B infections after
    gynaecological surgery. Lancet 1989;1:205-7.
27. Haeram JW, Siebke JC, Ulstrup J, Geiram D, Helle I. HBsAg transmission from a cardiac
    surgeon incubating hepatitis B resulting in chronic antigenemia in four patients. Acta Med
    Scand 1981;210:389-92.

28. Flower AJE, Prentice M, Morgan G, et al. Hepatitis B infection following cardiothoracic surgery [Abstract]. 1990 International Symposium on Viral Hepatitis and Liver Diseases, Houston. 1990;94.
29. Heptonstall J. Outbreaks of hepatitis B virus infection associated with infected surgical staff in the United Kingdom. Communicable Disease Reports 1991 (in press).
30. Alter HJ, Seef LB, Kaplan PM, et al. Type B hepatitis: the infectivity of blood positive for e antigen and DNA polymerase after accidental needlestick exposure. N Engl J Med 1976; 295:909-13.
31. Seeff LB, Wright EC, Zimmerman HJ, et al. Type B hepatitis after needlestick exposure: prevention with hepatitis B immunoglobulin: final report of the Veterans Administration Cooperative Study. Ann Intern Med 1978;88:285-93.
32. Grady GF, Lee VA, Prince AM, et al. Hepatitis B immune globulin for accidental exposures among medical personnel: final report of a multicenter controlled trial. J Infect Dis 1978;138:625-38.
33. Henderson DK, Fahey BJ, Willy M, et al. Risk for occupational transmission of human immunodeficiency virus type 1 (HIV-1) associated with clinical exposures: a prospective evaluation. Ann Intern Med 1990;113:740-6.
34. Marcus R, CDC Cooperative Needlestick Study Group. Surveillance of health-care workers exposed to blood from patients infected with the human immunodeficiency virus. N Engl J Med 1988;319:1118-23.
35. Gerberding JL, Bryant-LeBlanc CE, Nelson K, et al. Risk of transmitting the human immunodeficiency virus, cytomegalovirus, and hepatitis B virus to health-care workers exposed to patients with AIDS and AIDS-related conditions. J Infect Dis 1987;156:1-8.
36. CDC. Possible transmission of human immunodeficiency virus to a patient during an invasive dental procedure. MMWR 1990;39:489-93.
37. CDC. Update: transmission of HIV infection during an invasive dental procedure - Florida. MMWR 1991;40:21-27,33.
38. CDC. Update: transmission of HIV infection during invasive dental procedures - Florida. MMWR 1991;40:377-81.
39. Porter JD, Cruikshank JG, Gentle PH, Robinson RG, Gill ON. Management of patients treated by a surgeon with HIV infection. [Letter] Lancet 1990;335:113-4.
40. Armstrong FP, Miner JC, Wolfe WH. Investigation of a health-care worker with symptomatic human immunodeficiency virus infection: an epidemiologic approach. Milit Med 1987; 152:414-8.
41. Comer RW, Myers DR, Steadman CD, Carter MJ, Rissing JP, Tedesco FJ. Management considerations for an HIV positive dental student. J Dent Educ 1991;55:187-91.
42. Mishu B, Schaffner W, Horan JM, Wood LH, Hutcheson R, McNabb P. A surgeon with AIDS: lack of evidence of transmission to patients. JAMA 1990;264:467-70.
43. Tokars J, Bell D, Marcus R, et al. Percutaneous injuries during surgical procedures [Abstract]. VII International Conference on AIDS. Vol 2. Florence, Italy, June 16-21, 1991:83.
44. Perrillo RP, Schiff ER, Davis GL, et al. A randomized, controlled trial of interferon alfa-2b alone and after prednisone withdrawal for the treatment of chronic hepatitis B. N Engl J Med 1990;323:295-301.

Vol. 40 / No. RR-8   MMWR   9

APPENDIX

Definition of Invasive Procedure

An invasive procedure is defined as "surgical entry into tissues, cavities, or organs or repair of major traumatic injuries" associated with any of the following: "1) an operating or delivery room, emergency department, or outpatient setting, including both physicians' and dentists' offices; 2) cardiac catheterization and angiographic procedures; 3) a vaginal or cesarean delivery or other invasive obstetric procedure during which bleeding may occur; or 4) the manipulation, cutting, or removal of any oral or perioral tissues, including tooth structure, during which bleeding occurs or the potential for bleeding exists."

Reprinted from: Centers for Disease Control. Recommendation for prevention of HIV transmission in health-care settings. *MMWR* 1987;36 (suppl. no. 2S):6S-7S.

CARE AND MANAGEMENT OF PATIENTS WITH HIV INFECTION

Chapter 2: Basic Concepts of the Immune Response and the Immunology of HIV Infection

Kent J. Weinhold, PhD
Associate Professor of Experimental Surgery
Duke University Medical Center

CONTENTS

Introduction 67
Objectives 67
   I.   General Overview of the Immune System 69
      A. Nonspecific Responses 69
      B. Specific Responses 69
  II.   Organization and Distribution of the Immune System 72
      A. External Secretory System 72
      B. Internal Secretory System 72
Review Questions (I & II) 74
  III. The Cells of the Immune System 75
      A. Myeloid Cell Line 75
      B. Lymphoid Cell Line 75
  IV. Function of the Cells of the Immune System 76
      A. Macrophages 76
      B. Neutrophils 77
      C. Eosinophils 77
      D. Basophils and Mast Cells 77
      E. Lymphocytes 78
Review Questions (III & IV) 81
   V. Characteristics and Properties of Antigens (Immunogens) 83
      A. Natural Antigens 83
      B. Factors Influencing Antigenicity (Immunogenicity) 83
      C. Histocompatibility (Self) Antigens 84
  VI. Structure and Function of Antibodies (Immunoglobulins) 85
      A. Molecular Structure 85
      B. Function 85
      C. Polyclonal and Monoclonal Antibodies 86
Review Questions (V & VI) 87
  VII. Complement 88
 VIII. Immune Responses to Bacteria and Viruses 90
      A. Bacterial Infection 90
      B. Viral Infection 91
Review Questions (VII & VIII) 92
  IX. Immune Dysfunction in Acquired Immunodeficiency
         Syndrome (AIDS) 93
Review Questions (IX) 97
Summary 98
Answers to Review Questions 99
References 100
Recommended Follow-up 102

INTRODUCTION

Current knowledge of the immune system is increasing at a phenomenal rate due to recent advances in the molecular sciences and biotechnology. These new developments are already having a significant impact on diagnosis and treatment in many areas of medical practice including allergy, autoimmune diseases, cancer, toxicology, and immunodeficiency diseases such as AIDS. Health professionals in all disciplines are finding themselves more involved in caring for patients with diseases that have some underlying immunological component and in using new classes of immunopharmacologic agents that were nonexistent only a few years ago. For the health professional to answer questions adequately about immunologic diseases or agents, it is important to be familiar with concepts of immunology.

This chapter reviews current knowledge about the body's immune system and the immune dysfunction that is a direct result of HIV infection. It is intended to be a comprehensive review of present-day knowledge about immune defense mechanisms and immune dysfunction. Due to the complexity of this chapter, you may find it helpful to read the chapter quickly to gain familiarity, and then reread it for detail. Although some material may not be directly applicable to your clinical practice now, you may find it helpful to review the material again as your involvement in the care of HIV-infected patients increases.

OBJECTIVES

Objectives presented here are intended to focus the reader's attention on expected learning outcomes.

On completion of the chapter, the reader should be able to:

1. Identify the basic functions of the immune system.

2. Distinguish between nonspecific and specific immune responses.

3. Distinguish between humoral and cell-mediated responses and identify the blood cells associated with each.

4. Describe the relationship between the external and internal secretory systems.

5. State the functions of each of the following cells in immune defense of the body:

    •   monocytes and macrophages
    •   neutrophils
    •   basophils and mast cells
    •   eosinophils
    •   B cells
    •   T helper/inducer cells
    •   T cytotoxic/suppressor cells
    •   natural killer cells

6. Describe factors that affect the immunogenicity of foreign antigens.

7. Describe the function of antibodies in the immune response.

8. Distinguish between monoclonal and polyclonal antibodies.

9. Describe the body's response to bacterial and viral infections.

10. Describe the replicative cycle of the human immunodeficiency virus (HIV).

11. Describe the immunologic consequences of HIV infection.

I. GENERAL OVERVIEW OF THE IMMUNE SYSTEM

Our body has an immune system to perform at least three basic functions:

- to protect the body against invasion by foreign substances, including pathogenic bacteria, viruses, fungi, and other parasites, and also against nonviable substances such as environmental pollutants (the tissues and cells of the immune system act as efficient "filters" to remove these foreign substances so that they do not cause damage to the body);

- to maintain homeostasis by removing worn out, damaged, or dead cells; and

- to act as a surveillance system to destroy mutant and cancer cells.

These immune system functions may involve both nonspecific and specific elements.

A. NONSPECIFIC RESPONSES

Several nonspecific mechanical, chemical, and biochemical factors protect the body against microorganism invasion and subsequent infection. The epithelial layer of the skin is a barrier to infection. Desquamation of dead skin cells with their adherent microorganisms helps to prevent their invasion. The trapping activity of mucus and mucus-coated hairs, the explosive effects of a simple sneeze or cough, and the lavaging action of tears, urine, and saliva all prevent infection. Tears and saliva also contain enzymes and secretory antibodies that inhibit some bacteria. The acidity of gastric and vaginal secretions and the lactic acid of sweat also inhibit most bacteria. Neutrophils and macrophages play a central role in the nonspecific immune response as phagocytic cells. Activated macrophages and natural killer cells are part of our nonspecific defense against cancer cells and viruses. The activities of these cells are further enhanced by antibodies and/or various lymphokines produced during the specific immune response.

B. SPECIFIC RESPONSES

There are two specific responses that protect against infection and cancer: humoral and cell-mediated immune responses. Both responses require specific recognition of foreign antigens for activation. Although the two responses are distinct, they are not entirely independent, and cooperation between them is important. The cells associated with these immune responses are the plasma cells (activated B lymphocytes) and the T lymphocytes. These cells belong to a group of blood cells known as leukocytes or white blood cells (see Table 2.1).

TABLE 2.1. Major Types of Leukocytes (White Blood Cells)

A. Granulocytes

    1. Neutrophils
    2. Eosinophils
    3. Basophils

B. Agranulocytes

    1. Monocytes (in the blood)

    2. Macrophages (in the tissues)

    3. Lymphocytes

        a. small

            1) B lymphocytes
            2) T lymphocytes

        b. medium

        c. large

        d. plasma cells

Both T and B lymphocytes can recognize specific molecules associated with foreign substances. The molecules may be soluble cellular synthetic products, cell surface determinants, or degradation products of the foreign substance. These substances that can induce an immune response are called immunogens. Lymphocytes respond to immunogens by synthesizing specific proteins called antibodies (immunoglobulins) and lymphokines. These proteins in turn work directly to neutralize or kill foreign substances or cells, or indirectly to promote the functions of other leukocytes such as neutrophils and macrophages.

1. Humoral Response. The humoral immune response is primarily mediated by B lymphocytes; its product is antibody. Antibodies are effective against bacterial infections and viral reinfections, and help in the process of removing nonviable foreign substances. Humoral immune responses are aided by a group of blood proteins synthesized by the liver that are collectively known as complement.

When antibodies combine with antigens, "immune complexes" are formed. These complexes initiate the activation of complement that then binds to the complex. Various by-products of this reaction serve as attractants to phagocytic cells and serve as receptors to phagocytic cells to initiate the process of ingestion of the complex (phagocytosis). Because these complexes attract white blood cells, they produce inflammation.

2. Cell-mediated Response. The cell-mediated immune response is primarily mediated by T lymphocytes, which become activated and secrete lymphokines that in turn:

- combat fungi and viruses,
- protect the body against mutant and cancer cells, and
- destroy foreign tissues such as those encountered in transplanted organs.

The cell that suffers the greatest damage in AIDS is the T lymphocyte. Since these cells are an integral part of the cell-mediated and humoral responses, the immune deficit produced in AIDS is profound and ultimately lethal.

II. ORGANIZATION AND DISTRIBUTION OF THE IMMUNE SYSTEM

The lymphoreticular (lymphoid or lymphatic) system contains the anatomical structures associated with the immune system (see Figure 2.1). Lymph circulates through the system through lymphatic vessels, which are present in all parts of the body. Lymph is the primary fluid that bathes the major tissues of the body. Although the immune system is one integrated system, it can be subdivided into an external and an internal secretory system. Both systems contain cells that are capable of participating in humoral and cell-mediated immune responses.

A. EXTERNAL SECRETORY SYSTEM

The external secretory system may be viewed as the body's first line of defense. Lymphatic tissue is distributed adjacent to mucosal surfaces in the respiratory, gastrointestinal, and genitourinary tracts and mammary glands. Aggregates of lymphoid tissue are found in the tonsils, adenoids, salivary glands, appendix, and Peyer's patch. Specific immune responses may be made by the production and excretion of antibodies in mucus or milk, such as secretory IgA, which recognizes and neutralizes various bacteria and viruses as they come in contact with these body surfaces.

B. INTERNAL SECRETORY SYSTEM

The internal secretory system comprises the majority of what will be dealt with in subsequent sections. It is connected to the external system by lymphatic vessels that drain into regional lymph nodes. Foreign materials or microorganisms that have evaded or overwhelmed the external system are met by the humoral arm (antibody and complement) and cellular arm (neutrophils, lymphocytes, etc.) of the internal system. Regional lymph nodes and the spleen serve as major sites for antigen recognition and antibody synthesis. Other organs found in the internal system include the thymus, the liver, and the bone marrow. The major classes of antibodies produced by the internal secretory system by the lymph nodes and spleen and that circulate in the blood and lymph are IgM, IgG, and IgA. Complement proteins are produced by the liver and are not products of immune cells.

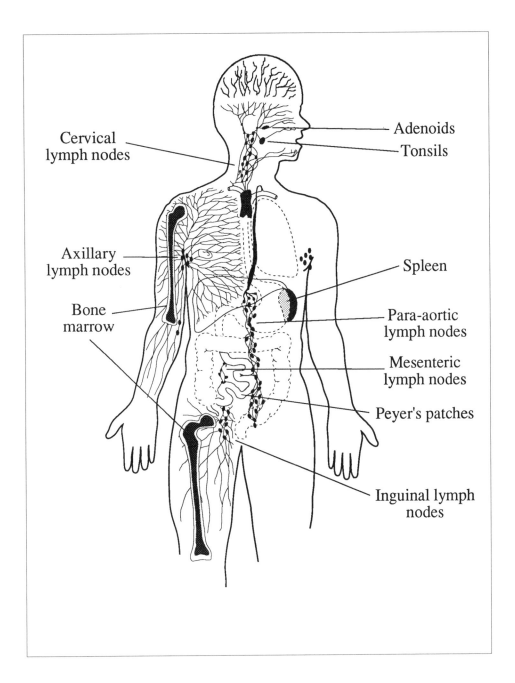

FIGURE 2.1. A Diagram of the Human Lymphoid System

REVIEW QUESTIONS (I & II)

DIRECTIONS. Circle the letter corresponding to the correct response in each of the following.

1. The major product of the humoral immune response is

   a. antibodies.
   b. enzymes.
   c. hormones.
   d. mucus.

2. Antibodies are produced by activated B lymphocytes called

   a. macrophages.
   b. neutrophils.
   c. plasma cells.
   d. platelets.

3. In order for the immune system to work normally, there must be a complex interaction between T and B lymphocytes.

   a. true
   b. false

4. The cell that suffers the most damage in AIDS is the

   a. B lymphocyte.
   b. macrophage.
   c. plasma cell.
   d. T lymphocyte.

5. The only defenses available on mucosal surfaces of the body are mucus and enzymes.

   a. true
   b. false

Check your responses on page 99.

III. THE CELLS OF THE IMMUNE SYSTEM

The cells of the immune system consist of the circulating and tissue leukocytes (see Table 2.1). Leukocytes are produced from precursor cells in bone marrow and then released into the bloodstream. Some cells are terminally differentiated whereas others are capable of further differentiation.

A. MYELOID CELL LINE

Myeloid stem cells give rise to monocytes and granulocytes, so called because they contain granules in their cytoplasm. Monocytes are found in the blood, but are predestined to enter tissues where they further differentiate into macrophages. Macrophages are found not only in lymphatic tissues but also in many other areas of the body, such as the lung and liver. There are three types of granulocytes, classified partly on the staining characteristics of the granules to hematoxylin and eosin dyes. These include the neutrophils (neutral staining), basophils (basic staining), and eosinophils (acidic staining). These granulocytes have a short life span and are constantly being replenished.

B. LYMPHOID CELL LINE

Lymphoid stem cells in the bone marrow give rise to B and T lymphocytes. B cells mature in the bone marrow in response to differentiation factors. After maturation, the B cells colonize in the lymphoid organs. Immature T cells are released into the bloodstream and travel to the thymus, where further maturation takes place over three days. Mature T cells tend to circulate in the blood and lymph. During maturation, B cells and T cells acquire specific surface markers (antigens) that identify the two types of lymphocytes.

The T-cell lineage divides into two parallel lines, and these two subpopulations each acquire antigens that specifically characterize them. One population, the helper/inducer T cells, acquires the CD4 differentiation antigen. The other population, the suppressor/cytotoxic T cells, acquires the CD8 differentiation antigen. CD4 cells represent 65% of the peripheral blood T lymphocytes, CD8 cells represent the other 35%. The normal ratio of CD4 to CD8 cells is 1.8:2.2; this ratio is lower or inverted in patients with AIDS, due both to the destruction of CD4 cells during the course of this illness as well as the concomitant activation and expansion of CD8 cell populations.

There are also subpopulations of CD4 and CD8 cells, but a discussion of subpopulations is beyond the scope of this chapter. Other lymphocytes found in blood and other tissues include null cells, killer cells, and natural killer cells.

IV. FUNCTION OF THE CELLS OF THE IMMUNE SYSTEM

Each of the cells of the immune system has functions that are crucial to the integration of immune responses. The effects of the AIDS virus on various cells in the system have greatly enhanced our knowledge of many of these functions.

A. MACROPHAGES

Macrophages play a number of roles in protecting the body, as summarized below.

1. Phagocytosis. Monocytes and macrophages are important phagocytic cells in the body; however, macrophages enhance phagocytic activity more than monocytes. Macrophages respond to chemotactic factors released at a site of invasion of a microorganism. They have a variety of surface receptors, the most important being Fc receptors for IgG antibody and receptors for specific components of complement. Phagocytosis of antibody- or complement-coated foreign particles is more efficient because of these specific interactions. This facilitated phagocytosis is called opsonization, and IgG and specific components of complement are referred to as opsonins. Opsonization of organisms that do not activate complement is performed by antibodies which act as a bridge to the Fc receptor on the phagocyte. Organisms that fix complement proteins may be phagocytosed after complement activation and the subsequent exposure of C3b, to which cell surface receptors or macrophages and monocytes may attach.

The particles ingested by macrophages are destroyed by interaction with enzymes present in lysosomal granules in the cytoplasm and through the respiratory burst metabolic pathway, which generates reactive oxygen compounds such as hydrogen peroxide, hydroxyl radical, singlet oxygen, and hypochlorite ions.

2. Antigen Processing/Presentation. In order to optimally stimulate the immune system, most antigens must first be broken down or processed into smaller components. Although a number of different cell lineages are capable of performing this task, the macrophage/monocyte is the major contributor. Complex antigens are taken up by the macrophage, processed into smaller fragments, and presented at the surface membrane in conjunction with major histocompatibility complex (MHC) antigens. This complex enables T lymphocytes to recognize the antigen, and the cascade of immunologic activation is initiated.

3. Thermoregulation. When stimulated by bacteria and bacterial products or during tissue damage, macrophages also secrete a protein called interleukin-1 (IL-

1). IL-1 acts on the thermoregulatory center in the anterior hypothalamus to raise body temperature and induce fever.

4. Inflammation. Macrophages participate in the inflammatory process by secreting:

- complement components,
- hormonal mediators such as cyclic AMP,
- clotting factors, and
- compounds such as leukotrienes and prostaglandins.

When activated by gamma interferon, these macrophages become directly cytotoxic to tumor cells and can secrete a variety of tumoricidal substances, including protease enzymes, tumor necrosis factor (TNF), and IL-1.

5. Healing. Macrophages also promote healing by secreting elastases, collagenases, hyaluronidase, and IL-1.

B. NEUTROPHILS

Like macrophages, neutrophils are important phagocytic cells. They are the first cells to accumulate at the site of bacterial infections in response to chemotactic factors. In order for a neutrophil to ingest a foreign particle, it must bind firmly to it. For efficient phagocytosis, this is accomplished by interaction with an opsonized (antibody- or complement-coated) particle. The ingested particles are destroyed by lysosomal enzymes and activated oxygen species. Whereas macrophages are capable of sustained phagocytosis, neutrophils have a limited phagocytic capacity and are rapidly exhausted. Because of this and because they usually destroy all ingested foreign material, neutrophils do not function as antigen-presenting cells. Dead neutrophils are actually chemotactic for macrophages, attracting these cells to the invasion site. All of these processes cause inflammation within the involved tissues.

C. EOSINOPHILS

Eosinophils comprise 2% to 5% of the leukocytes. Eosinophil function includes ingesting immune complexes and developing immunity to parasites. They are not as phagocytic as neutrophils.

D. BASOPHILS AND MAST CELLS

Basophils constitute about 0.5% of the blood leukocytes and normally are not found in tissues except when they respond to factors released by T lymphocytes.

In tissues, basophils release histamine, leukotrienes, prostaglandins, and other inflammatory mediators. Mast cells, which are associated with mucosal and connective tissues, are functionally related to basophils. They are more abundant and thus are more active inflammatory cells than basophils. Basophils and mast cells are the primary inflammatory cells involved in allergy, asthma, and anaphylaxis. Like macrophages, they produce a variety of inflammatory substances, including histamines and leukotrienes.

E. LYMPHOCYTES

Two major types of lymphocytes are found in the immune system: B lymphocytes and T lymphocytes. These cells are morphologically indistinguishable and are differentiated from each other by characteristic cell surface antigens. Prior to activation and differentiation, B lymphocytes have surface immunoglobulins which serve as the specific receptor for only one antigen.

1. B lymphocytes. B lymphocytes are the primary cells involved in humoral immune responses. When exposed to an immunogen, they proliferate and differentiate into plasma cells, the major antibody-producing cells of the body. This process is specific: each clone or cell population of B cells can interact with only one specific antigenic (immunogenic) determinant on a foreign particle. B lymphocytes tend not to circulate in the lymphatic or blood systems, and reside primarily in lymphatic tissues. Plasma cells are found primarily in the spleen, medulla of lymph nodes, and bone marrow, but can be found distributed throughout the body. Whereas B lymphocytes have a long life span, the life span of plasma cells is short. One subpopulation lives about three days and another subpopulation has a life span of three to four weeks.

Not all B cells responding to immunogens become plasma cells. Another population of B cells develops into memory B cells, which resemble the other lymphocytes morphologically. On subsequent exposure to the same immunogen, these sensitized memory B cells respond with less lag time than unprimed B lymphocytes.

2. T lymphocytes. T lymphocytes are found scattered throughout the body and, in contrast to B lymphocytes, tend to be circulatory cells. T lymphocytes comprise about 70% of the lymphocytes in blood and over 90% in thoracic duct lymph. They are also found in lymphatic tissues where they are particularly involved in antibody production. As stated previously, T lymphocytes can be divided into two subpopulations based on the presence of cell surface differentiation antigens.

a. T helper/inducer cells. CD4 T lymphocytes (formerly called T4 cells) exhibit T helper/inducer functions. T helper/inducer cells stimulate the growth and differentiation of B lymphocytes and antigen-presenting cells in humoral immune responses (antibody production) to thymus-dependent antigens. They also secrete a number of lymphokine mediators, some of which are listed in Table 2.2. It is apparent that lymphokines have a wide variety of specific effects on both humoral and cell-mediated immune responses against bacteria, viruses, and tumor cells, and in regulation of leukocyte growth and differentiation. Some lymphokines are being developed as drugs.

TABLE 2.2.   Biological Activity of Lymphokines Secreted from Activated T Lymphocytes (Compiled from Foon KA. Biological response modifiers: the new immunotherapy. *Cancer Res.* 1989;49:1621–1639; and Tizzard I. *Immunology: An Introduction.* 2nd ed. Philadelphia: Saunders College Publishing; 1988.)

Lymphokine	Activity
Interleukin-2 (IL-2)	Induces T cells to proliferate Enhances activity of natural killer (NK) cells and cytotoxic T cells
Interleukin-3 (IL-3)	Regulates growth and differentiation of leukocytes in the bone marrow
Interleukin-4 (IL-4)	Enhances antibody production through B-cell activation
Interleukin-5 (IL-5)	Promotes growth and differentiation of B lymphocytes into IgA-secreting cells
Interleukin-6 (IL-6)	Promotes the differentiation of B lymphocytes to plasma cells
Interleukin-7 (IL-7)	Induces growth of immature T and B cells
Granulocyte macrophage colony stimulating factor (GM-CSF)	Enhances production of neutrophils in the bone marrow
Lymphotoxins	Directly cytotoxic to target cells
Tumor necrosis factor (TNF)	Cytotoxic to tumor cells
Macrophage inhibition factor/Macrophage activating factor (MIF/MAF)	Inhibits macrophage migration Activates macrophages to become more bacteriostatic and antiviral

b. Cytotoxic/suppressor T cells. CD8 or cytotoxic/suppressor T cells are the other major class of T lymphocytes. These cells are further characterized according to their specific activities. When activated, they are capable of binding to and directly killing tumor cells and some virus-infected cells. These cells are responsible for rejection of a primary graft, such as a skin graft or organ transplant. In this role, the CD8 cell is referred to as a cytotoxic T lymphocyte, sometimes abbreviated CTL. These cells have proven to be important effectors in controlling a number of viral infections in man. For example, in influenza virus infection, the presence of virus-specific CTL greatly limits the degree of virus replication, thereby reducing symptoms and expediting recovery. CD8 cells are also responsible for regulating and terminating humoral and cell-mediated immune responses. They probably play an important role in preventing autoimmune disease and are the cells largely responsible for the immunosuppression observed in cancer patients. When a CD8 cell is exercising these activities, it is referred to as a T suppressor cell. In a number of different neoplastic diseases, CD8 cells can be found infiltrating solid tumors. The cells, referred to as tumor-infiltrating lymphocytes or TIL can be isolated, expanded *ex vivo,* and reintroduced into patients as part of an overall treatment strategy. In this context, the CD8 cells are believed to exhibit CTL activities.

3. Natural Killer Cells. Natural killer (NK) cells represent an important class of cytotoxic lymphocytes that are neither T nor B lymphocytes and are characterized by specific antigenic markers. Natural killer cells are a hetero-geneous group of large granular lymphocytes that comprise about 10% to 15% of the blood and splenic lymphocytes. They do not recirculate like T cells and are not found in the thoracic duct lymph. These cells are the primary cells involved in immune surveillance against tumors, and have activity against some parasites and viruses. NK cells also express a receptor for the Fc portion of IgG. Specific antibody bound to these effectors can direct the lysis of tumor cells as well as HIV-1-infected targets by a process termed antibody-dependent cellular cyto-toxicity or ADCC. NK cells have recently been shown to have cytotoxic activity against HIV-infected cells. They bind to and kill certain tumor cells, primarily in solid tumors, without prior activation. They become even more cytocidal when activated by gamma interferon or IL-2. When cultured for three days in the presence of the lymphokine IL-2, these large granular lymphocytes alter their morphology, become even more tumoricidal, and begin nonspecifically to attack all killer types. These lymphokine-activated killer cells, also known as LAK cells, are currently being used in several experimental treatment trials in cancer patients.[1]

REVIEW QUESTIONS (III & IV)

DIRECTIONS. Circle the letter corresponding to the correct response in each of the following.

1. The cell of the immune system most capable of sustained phagocytosis is the

    a. eosinophil.
    b. lymphocyte.
    c. macrophage.
    d. neutrophil.

2. The cell most responsible for mediating allergic reactions, such as asthma and anaphylaxis, is the

    a. basophil.
    b. eosinophil.
    c. monocyte.
    d. neutrophil.

3. T lymphocytes are the most plentiful circulating lymphocytes. The subtype that interacts with B lymphocytes and antigen-presenting cells in humoral immune responses and secretes lymphokines with a wide variety of specific effects on both humoral and cell-mediated immune responses is the

    a. helper cell (CD4).
    b. natural killer cell.
    c. plasma cell.
    d. suppressor cell (CD8).

4. Lymphokines are substances produced by lymphoid cells that enhance the effectiveness of other cells of the immune system.

    a. true
    b. false

5. Large granular lymphocytes that may have cytotoxic activity against tumor cells and cells infected with HIV are known as

    a. helper cells (CD4).
    b. macrophages.
    c. natural killer cells.
    d. suppressor cells (CD8).

Check your responses on page 99.

V. CHARACTERISTICS AND PROPERTIES OF ANTIGENS (IMMUNOGENS)

Antigens are substances that can induce an immune response. Recently the term *immunogen* was coined to refer to foreign antigens that stimulate a specific immune response.

A. NATURAL ANTIGENS

Natural antigens contain many different antigenic determinants or areas on their surface that stimulate a specific immune response. Thus, antigens are multi-specific and multideterminant. A synonym often used for *antigenic determinant* is *epitope*. In a humoral immune response, the epitope is that part of the antigen that is recognized specifically by the B lymphocyte. In order for an immune response to occur to most epitopes, however, a T helper/inducer lymphocyte must recognize some carrier portion of the molecule. Most natural antigens contain both the epitope and the carrier; therefore, they are fully capable of stimulating an immune response, hence acting as an immunogen. Natural antigens can stimulate both humoral and cell-mediated immune responses, depending on the antigen. Some small molecules, such as in certain drugs like methyldopa and penicillin, are incomplete antigens and represent only the epitope portion. They are known as haptens and are not immunogenic until combined with a carrier molecule, usually a body protein.

B. FACTORS INFLUENCING ANTIGENICITY (IMMUNOGENICITY)

Several factors influence antigenicity (immunogenicity), including size, complexity, structural stability, degradability, and foreignness.

   1. Size. Generally, the larger the molecule, the better its immunogenicity. Good immunogens generally have a molecular size of 10,000 or larger.

   2. Complexity. The more complex the antigen, the better its immunogenicity. Polysaccharides, which are repetitive polymers of simple sugars such as dextran, are poor antigens. In contrast, proteins, glycoproteins, and lipoproteins, whose structures tend to be complex, are good antigens and capable of stimulating both humoral and cell-mediated immune responses.

C. HISTOCOMPATIBILITY (SELF) ANTIGENS

Antigens found on the surface of most nucleated cells in the body are called histocompatibility antigens. They have a fundamental role in recognition of self (one's own proteins) and in regulation of immune responses. They were first recognized for their role in eliciting graft rejection.

Each individual's histocompatibility antigens are unique and genetically determined. There is a region on the sixth chromosome that contains the genes that code for these antigens. This region is called the major histocompatibility complex (MHC). There are four genes within this MHC region on chromosome six, and the proteins that they code for are called human leukocyte antigens (HLA). The position of each of these genes on the chromosome in the MHC is called a locus. The HLA loci are designated HLA-A, HLA-B, HLA-C, and HLA-D.

The HLA are further divided into Class I or Class II antigens.

- Class I antigens are coded for by the HLA-A, HLA-B, and HLA-C loci and are found on most nucleated cells. They regulate cytotoxic T-cell activity involved in destruction of virus-infected cells.

- Class II antigens are coded for by the HLA-D locus and are found on B lymphocytes, activated T lymphocytes, and some macrophages. They regulate immune response by controlling the interactions between B lymphocytes, T lymphocytes, and antigen-presenting macrophages and by regulating infectious and immunological disease susceptibility. During an immune response against foreign or infected cells, CD4 lymphocytes must recognize both Class II antigens and the foreign antigen on antigen-presenting cells to initiate an immune response.

VI. STRUCTURE AND FUNCTION OF ANTIBODIES (IMMUNOGLOBULINS)

Antibodies are the synthetic products of plasma cells. They belong to a group of glycoproteins known as immunoglobulins.

A. MOLECULAR STRUCTURE

There are five classes of immunoglobulins: IgA, IgD, IgE, IgG, and IgM. The basic structural unit of these proteins is composed of two heavy chains and two light chains. IgD, IgE, and IgG contain one structural unit, but IgA contains two units and IgM contains five. Another protein, called a secretory component, is added to the IgA dimer; in this form IgA is known as secretory IgA (sIgA). The secretory component enables IgA to be released into mucus secretions and protects the antibody from degradation. Within the structural unit, the light chains are attached to the heavy chains by disulfide linkages, and each heavy chain is held together by additional disulfide bonds. The number and placement of these disulfide bonds vary from one antibody to another, and this, in part, gives rise to the differences between the antibody classes.

One section (fragment) of antibodies binds specifically to antigens and is known as Fab. The other major section is known as Fc and has receptors for white blood cells and complement. Complement is bound and activated through these factors, resulting in chemotaxis, opsonization, and phagocytosis of antigen-antibody complexes.

B. FUNCTION

Following the complex interactions outlined in previous sections involving the recognition and synthesis of antibodies to foreign substances, immunoglobulins are secreted into plasma and circulate through the body. For many antigens, IgM is the initial antibody produced, followed by IgG several days to weeks later. These antibodies bind to various antigens, and, through the action of complement (see below), result in lysis and/or phagocytosis of invading organisms. If the host survives the first infection with a particular organism, this initial reaction results in immunity from subsequent infection with the same organism. Antibodies to certain toxins (usually proteins) may also be produced, and thus prevent diseases produced by such toxins, including diphtheria, tetanus, toxic shock syndrome, and scarlet fever. The principal biologic functions of human immunoglobulins are summarized in Table 2.3.

TABLE 2.3. Biologic Functions of Human Immunoglobulins

Function	IgG	IgA	IgM	IgD*	IgE*
Fix complement	+	–	+	–	–
Opsonin for bacteria	+	–	–	–	–
Neutralize bacterial toxins	+	–	–	–	–
Neutralize viral toxins	–	–	+	–	–
Antiviral activity	+	+	+	–	–
Antifungal activity	–	–	+	–	–
Defense at mucosal surfaces	–	+	–	–	–

*Function is not known.

C. POLYCLONAL AND MONOCLONAL ANTIBODIES

Since most antigens in nature contain multiple epitopes, they will stimulate many different populations or clones of B lymphocytes to differentiate into plasma cells. A multideterminant antigen stimulates production of many different antibodies and activation of several different clones of B lymphocytes. Thus, the immune response to a multideterminant antigen is polyclonal, and the antibodies produced are referred to as polyclonal antibodies. New technologies have now been developed to isolate a specific lymphocyte population that produces antibody to only one epitope. The antibodies produced from these specific clones are called monoclonal antibodies. These antibodies are being evaluated in many different aspects of medicine, including diagnosis of diseases such as cancer, targeting of cytotoxic drugs to tumor cells, treatment of drug overdoses, inhibition of graft rejection, and specific immunoassay of drugs.[1,2]

REVIEW QUESTIONS (V & VI)

DIRECTIONS. Circle the letter corresponding to the correct response in each of the following.

1. Simple substances with small molecular weights generally make the best antigens.

    a. true
    b. false

2. The major importance of histocompatibility antigens such as HLA is in the rejection of organ transplants.

    a. true
    b. false

3. Antibodies are produced by B lymphocytes known as plasma cells and serve to enhance recognition of microorganisms and toxins, thus making their destruction and removal more efficient.

    a. true
    b. false

4. Different classes of antibodies tend to serve specialized functions within the immune system.

    a. true
    b. false

5. Monoclonal antibodies respond to a broad group of antigens and are hence protective in many kinds of infections.

    a. true
    b. false

Check your responses on page 99.

VII. COMPLEMENT

Complement is the collective name for a group of about 12 different proteins, which consist, for the most part, of enzymes. They are present in the blood in an inactive form, but the presence of an antigen-antibody complex triggers them to produce a sequential "cascade" of reactions that results in cell lysis, chemotaxis, inflammation, and increased phagocytosis. The various complement proteins are designated by specific numbers (e.g., C3, C5). Complement proteins are produced in the liver, blood monocytes, tissue macrophages, fibroblasts, epithelial cells of the gastrointestinal and genitourinary tracts, adipocytes, and glial cells.

The complement cascade can be activated by either of two pathways: the classical and the alternate. The classical pathway is activated by IgG or IgM bound to cell surfaces. The alternate pathway can be activated by many substances, including bacterial endotoxins, snake venom, IgA, IgD, and IgE.

In the classical pathway (see Figure 2.2), IgG or IgM antibody binds the first component of complement, C1, which is formed by the interaction of its three q, r, and s subunits. Components C3, C4, and C5 then become activated by limited proteolytic cleavage, and two subunits designated "a" and "b" are formed. C2a, C3b, C4b, and C5b become attached to the cell membrane and are required for further addition of the complement sequence. They also act as opsonins. Full activation of complement leads to cell lysis, which plays an important role in killing certain bacteria and viruses. In the alternate pathway, proteins other than C1, C4, and C2 are used for activation, but the rest of the components are the same as in the classical pathway.

The cleaved proteins that do not bind to the cell membrane surface are also biologically active. C3a and C5a are chemotactic factors. These components have been referred to as biological amplifiers in that they enhance the speed and intensity of the immune response. C3a, C4a, and C5a stimulate the release of histamine from mast cells, increase vascular permeability, and contract smooth muscle independent of histamine.

The complement system is not affected in any major way by HIV infection.

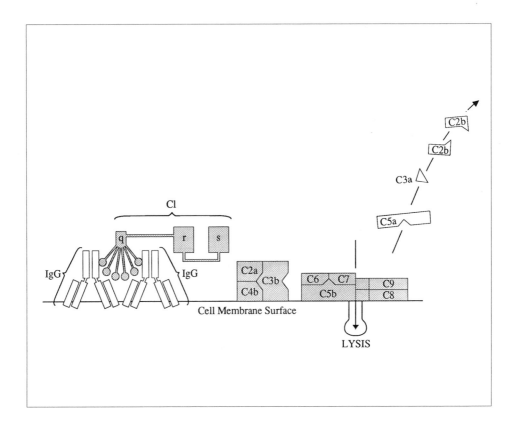

FIGURE 2.2.   Overview of the Complement Cascade (Reprinted with permission from Frank MM. *Complement*. Kalamazoo, MI: The Upjohn Company; 1975:16–17 or 1985:15.)

VIII. IMMUNE RESPONSES TO BACTERIA AND VIRUSES

One important aspect of the immune system is its ability to "learn" from previous exposure to an organism. Second exposure produces a quicker and longer-lasting response.

Initial exposure to an infectious agent stimulates a primary immune response. The primary humoral immune response is characterized by a lag period of several days in which the antigens from the infectious agent are processed by macrophages and presented to the B lymphocytes. IgM is produced, followed by a weak IgG antibody response. After the primary response has ended only memory cells will remain.

Upon second exposure to the same infectious agent, memory B and T helper/inducer cells become activated in a shorter time than in the primary response. The amount of IgM produced is similar to the amount produced during the primary response, but the IgG response is enhanced and long-lived. Memory cells are also formed during the second exposure to the infectious agent. Cell-mediated immune responses are stimulated in a similar fashion except that either cytotoxic T lymphocytes are activated or lymphokines are produced.

A. BACTERIAL INFECTION

The immunogenic components of bacteria are associated primarily with the cell walls and exotoxins produced by the organisms, and also with the capsules, flagella, and pili of the organisms, if present. Response differs depending on whether bacteria are extracellular (such as pneumococci, *Haemophilus*, and *Escherichia coli*) or intracellular (such as *Salmonella*, *Listeria*, and mycobacteria).

1. Extracellular Bacteria. Upon initial exposure to extracellular bacteria, which remain outside host cells, the primary humoral immune responses (antibody production) are most important in recovering from infection and preventing reinfection. Cell-mediated immunity is relatively unimportant. IgG antibodies act as opsonins and neutralize exotoxins; IgM antibodies cause agglutination and are very efficient at activating complement; and IgA antibodies help to protect the respiratory, gastrointestinal, and genitourinary tracts by blocking bacterial infection. Second exposure stimulates the secondary humoral immune response and augments antibody production.

2. Intracellular Bacteria. Immune responses to intracellular bacteria, organisms that invade and spend time inside host cells, involve greater participation of cell-mediated than humoral immunity during both primary and secondary immune responses. Although antibodies may be produced during both responses, they generally are of little consequence in terminating an infection. Lymphokines, working directly or through activation of macrophages and cytotoxic T lymphocytes, are the important mediators of the primary and secondary cell-mediated immune responses.

B. VIRAL INFECTION

The immunogenic constituents of viruses depend on whether the viruses are enveloped or not. The immunologic component of a nonenveloped virus is the protein coat surrounding the DNA or RNA. Immunologic constituents in enveloped viruses include hemagglutinin, hemolysin, and neuraminidase. Antibodies against these proteins protect against infection.

Upon initial exposure to an extracellular virus (such as influenza, measles, or mumps), cell-mediated immunity is stimulated and is important in killing and limiting the initial infection. Interferon, released early during viral infections, may help to limit spread of the virus to other cells. In many viral diseases, humoral immunity is also stimulated, but antibodies may not be produced soon enough to stop dissemination or to terminate the initial infection. Again, lymphokines, working directly or through activation of macrophages and cytotoxic T lymphocytes, are the important mediators of the primary response.

The humoral immune response plays a more important role in the secondary response. Circulating antibodies protect against reinfection. IgG and IgM antibodies neutralize virus infectivity, IgM antibodies cause agglutination of virus-infected cells, and full activation of complement can induce lysis of some large viruses. Secretory IgA is very important for protecting against respiratory and intestinal viruses.

The immune responses to intracellular viruses, such as herpes simplex and zoster, cytomegalovirus, and retroviruses, are less well understood. These viruses tend to remain in the body as latent infections. The immune response to these viruses involves a significant cell-mediated immune component. Antibodies are generally only protective when the virus is active, but may help in blocking reactivation of a latent virus infection.

REVIEW QUESTIONS (VII & VIII)

DIRECTIONS. Circle the letter corresponding to the correct response in each of the following.

1. Complement proteins are produced by lymphocytes in response to specific bacteria and viruses.

    a. true
    b. false

2. The complement system acts as a biologic amplifier that enhances the efficiency and intensity of phagocytosis and inflammation.

    a. true
    b. false

3. Immunologic memory plays an important role in both humoral and cell-mediated immunity.

    a. true
    b. false

4. Since infection with the AIDS virus primarily affects the CD4 T helper lymphocyte, would you predict that patients with AIDS will have more infections with extracellular or intracellular bacteria?

    a. extracellular bacteria
    b. intracellular bacteria

5. To which of the following viral diseases would an HIV-infected patient be likely to have the best resistance?

    a. cytomegalovirus
    b. herpes simplex
    c. mumps
    d. shingles

Check your responses on page 99.

IX. IMMUNE DYSFUNCTION IN ACQUIRED IMMUNODEFICIENCY SYNDROME (AIDS)

The acquired immunodeficiency syndrome (AIDS) was first described as a disease characterized by either an opportunistic infection, frequently *Pneumocystis carinii* pneumonia, or Kaposi's sarcoma, a rare cancer associated with certain immuno-suppressed states. Immune dysfunction, dysregulation, and deficiency are the hallmarks of AIDS. This is generally reflected in depression of cell-mediated immune responses in the AIDS patient.

In 1983–84, it was found that a human retrovirus (RNA virus), termed lymphadenopathy-associated virus (LAV) or human T lymphotropic virus type III (HTLV-III), was the etiologic agent of AIDS. This AIDS virus is now known as the human immunodeficiency virus type 1 (HIV-1). Persons infected with the virus can be identified by the presence of HIV-1 antibody in the blood, using a screening test with the ELISA technique for diagnosis of HIV infection. Positive tests are always confirmed with a Western Blot Test that measures antibodies to specific proteins of HIV. Currently available studies suggest that ultimately all HIV-infected persons will progress to full-blown AIDS.

The major target cell for HIV-1 is the CD4 T helper/inducer lymphocyte, although other immune cells such as monocytes and macrophages may also be infected. The virus binds to the CD4 cell by virtue of a high-affinity interaction between the major envelope glycoprotein of the virus (gp120) and the CD4 molecule expressed on the surface of these cells.[3] After binding to susceptible cells, the virus enters the cytoplasm and uncoats. Using its enzyme reverse transcriptase, a DNA copy of the viral RNA genome is made and duplicated. This process of reverse transcription is the target of many currently used antiretroviral agents such as zidovudine, didanosine, and zalcitabine. The new double-stranded DNA now can become integrated into the DNA of the host cell. In this integrated state, the virus can remain latent or "silent," or it can direct the production of new progeny virions. It is in this productive state that the virus buds from the cell surface and causes overt cytopathology and cell death.

The immunologic/virologic cascade of events that leads to the development of AIDS is far more complex than the simple destruction of CD4 cells. The immunologic consequences that follow HIV-1 infection include: 1) progressive immunosuppression;[4] 2) generation of antiviral immune reactivities;[5-7] 3) immuno-pathogenesis with possible autoimmune components;[8] and 4) chronic immune activation.[9] These phenomena can best be put into perspective if discussed within the context of the natural history of HIV-1 infection. An overview of the immunologic and virologic hallmarks associated with HIV-1 infection are presented in Figure 2.3.

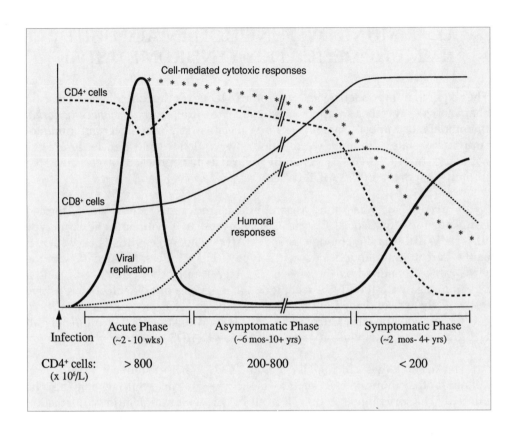

FIGURE 2.3. Course of Immunologic/Virologic Events During HIV-1 Infection

The course of disease following HIV-1 infection can be divided into three phases: 1) an acute phase occurring shortly after infection; 2) an asymptomatic phase of highly variable duration; and 3) a symptomatic phase characterized by infection with opportunistic pathogens. Acute or primary HIV-1 infection is characterized clinically by acute onset of symptoms which can include fever, lethargy, myalgias, headaches, photophobia, sore throat, lymphadenopathy, and maculopapular rash.[10] Active viral replication occurs during the acute phase. Levels of serum p24 as well as plasma viremia may be higher in the acute phase than in any other stage, including the terminal phases of AIDS. These extremely high levels of antigenemia are rapidly resolved during acute infection. This has been interpreted by many investigators as indicative of an immunologic response capable of suppressing viral replication. Other investigators suggest that this is simply a redistribution of replicating virus from the peripheral circulating lymphocytes into secondary lymphoid organs such as the spleen and lymph nodes. Few humoral antiviral responses have been readily detected during the acute phase of infection. Thus, standard ELISA and Western Blot assays may not be capable of identifying acutely infected individuals. This "window period" reinforces the need for careful history-taking in the screening of potential blood donors to decline the donations of those with a history of risk behavior or clinical illness compatible with acute HIV infection. Additional testing for p24 anti-genemia or polymerase chain reaction (PCR) testing for HIV nucleic acids could overcome the shortcomings of serologic testing in acute-phase patients.

As individuals pass from acute infection and enter the asymptomatic phase, viral replication has diminished to levels just barely above the threshold of detection. Serologically, antiviral antibodies rise in titer and are readily demon-strable by ELISA and Western Blot analyses. Antibodies capable of neutralizing HIV-1 infectivity *in vitro* also become apparent. In addition, high titers of antibodies are present which direct the lysis of virus-infected cells by a mechanism termed antibody-dependent cellular cytotoxicity or ADCC.[11] Anti-HIV-1 cytotoxic T lymphocyte (CTL) activities against a number of HIV-1 struc-tural determinants (i.e., envelope, capsid, reverse transcriptase, etc.) are also present throughout the asymptomatic period. Collectively, these antiviral immune reactivities are taken as evidence of a "protective" or beneficial immune response which is responsible for keeping overall virus replication at a low level. If true, these same immunologic reactivities would be sought in the context of preventive vaccine strategies.

Despite the presence of the various potentially beneficial anti-HIV-1 immune responses, the initial signs of immunologic impairment are manifest during the early portions of this phase.[12] The very first element of immunologic respon-siveness that is lost is the ability to respond to "recall" antigens such as tetanus toxoid, PPD, *Candida albicans*, etc. Although such responses are dependent on many elements of the immune system, it is the functional integrity of the memory subset of CD4 that is first compromised following HIV-1 infection. The basis for this relatively early immunologic impairment is poorly understood. It is important to note that this occurs *prior to* any dramatic decline in CD4 cell numbers. Thus begins a progressive cascade of functional impairments which continues throughout eventual disease progression, ultimately leading to the loss of mitogen responsiveness in late-stage disease.

It is important to keep in mind that virus replication continues throughout the asymptomatic phase, albeit at a relatively low level. It is, however, during this time when the generation of viral variants takes place. The initial infecting virus now becomes a viral swarm with a variety of different biological properties including altered tropisms, pathogenicities, and antigenic expression.[13] During viral replication, the step of reverse transcription is believed to be a mistake-prone process that is responsible for the generation of HIV-1 variants. The antiviral immune response present during this time probably adds selective pressures which favor the generation of escape mutants. Ultimately, the failure of the immune response to contain these constantly evolving variants leads to a renewal of virus replication by viruses with enhanced pathogenic properties such as the ability to form syncytia following infection of CD4 cells.

During these later stages of disease, most antiviral responsiveness begins to wane. This late decline is thought to be linked both to the accelerated rate of CD4 cell loss and the increase in suppressor cell activity. The hallmark of late-stage disease is heightened viral replication and chronic immunologic activation. CD8 lymphocytes bearing multiple activation markers rapidly become the dominant T-cell population.[14] The following are products of this activation and can be used as surrogate markers for disease progression:

- IFN-α
- TNF-α
- TGF-β
- soluble CD8
- beta$_2$-microglobulin
- neoptrin
- expression of lymphocyte activation markers

Despite the enormous progress made in sorting out the many immunologic and virologic events that occur as a result of HIV-1 infection, we have yet to define the elements responsible for the destruction of CD4 lymphocytes. Viral infection alone may not be sufficient since the percentage of peripheral blood mononuclear cells harboring virus at any stage of disease seldom, if ever, exceeds 1% to 2%.[15] Cross-reactivity between virion components and normally expressed cellular antigens could mean that antiviral immune responses could also be autoimmune,[16] resulting in the destruction of noninfected cells. Alternatively, it has been proposed that the interaction of certain viral components and cellular receptors triggers a process termed apoptosis, or programmed cell death, whereby cells could be eliminated in the absence of virus infection.[17] Clearly, a better understanding of the processes that drive this progressive elimination of crucial immunologic elements will greatly assist in the development of future interventive therapeutic strategies.

REVIEW QUESTIONS (IX)

DIRECTIONS. Circle the letter corresponding to the correct response in each of the following.

1. The causative agent of AIDS is

    a. cytomegalovirus.
    b. herpes simplex.
    c. HIV-1.
    d. *Pneumocystis carinii.*

2. A positive test for HIV-1 by ELISA means that a person has AIDS or will ultimately develop AIDS.

    a. true
    b. false

3. Mechanisms that are known to damage or destroy CD4 cells are direct HIV infection and cytotoxic antibodies.

    a. true
    b. false

4. CD4 lymphocytes are the only cells infected by the AIDS virus.

    a. true
    b. false

5. Once an individual has developed AIDS, antibody synthesis should still be intact and normal responses to bacterial and viral antigens should be expected.

    a. true
    b. false

Check your responses on page 99.

SUMMARY

Infection with HIV-1 has many phases. It progresses from the initial hyperactivity of the immune system with B-cell proliferation, to the more quiescent phases where the virus remains latent in many infected cells, to the gradual decline in cell-mediated function that is generally measured by profound diminution of CD4 cells. Since the CD4 cell is at the heart of the regulation of many immune responses, including those of B cells, macrophages, and other phagocytic cells, the immune deficit, involving all arms of the immune system, is profound once the first infection develops in an AIDS patient.

ANSWERS TO REVIEW QUESTIONS

I & II

1. a
2. c
3. a
4. d
5. b

III & IV

1. c
2. a
3. a
4. a
5. c

V & VI

1. b
2. b
3. a
4. a
5. b

VII & VIII

1. b
2. a
3. a
4. b
5. c

IX

1. c
2. a
3. a
4. b
5. b

REFERENCES

1.   Foon KA. Biological response modifiers: the new immunotherapy. *Cancer Res.* April 1, 1989;49:1621–1639.

2.   Smith TW, Haber E, Yeatman L, Butler VP Jr. Reversal of advanced digoxin intoxication with Fab fragments of digoxin-specific antibodies. *N Engl J Med.* April 8, 1976;294(15):797–800.

3.   Klatzmann D, Champagne E, Chamaret S, et al. T-lymphocyte T4 molecule behaves as the receptor for human retrovirus LAV. *Nature.* December 1984;312:767–768.

4.   Lane HC, Fanci AS. Immunologic abnormalities in the acquired immuno-deficiency syndrome. *Ann Rev Immunol.* 1985;3:477–500.

5.   Walker BD, Plata F. Cytotoxic T lymphocytes against HIV [editorial]. *AIDS.* 1990;4(3):177–184.

6.   Ho DD, Rota TR, Hirsch MS. Antibody to lymphadenopathy-associated virus in AIDS. *N Engl J Med.* March 7, 1985;312(10):649–650.

7.   Walker CM, Moody DJ, Stites DP, Levy JA. CD8+ lymphocytes can control HIV infection in vitro by suppressing virus replication. *Science.* December 19, 1986;234:1563–1566.

8.   Via CS, Morse HC III, Shearer GM. Altered immunoregulation and autoimmune aspects of HIV infection: relevant murine models. In: Gallagher RB, ed. *HIV and the Immune System.* Elsevier Trends Books; 1991:107–116.

9.   Giorgi JV, Detels R. T-cell subset alterations in HIV-infected homosexual men: NIAID multicenter AIDS cohort study. *Clin Immunol and Immunopathol.* 1989;52:10–18.

10. Tindall B, Cooper DA. Primary HIV infection: host responses and intervention strategies. *AIDS.* 1991;5(1):1–14.

11. Tyler DS, Lyerly HK, Weinhold KJ. Minireview: anti-HIV-1 ADCC. *AIDS Res Hum Retrovir.* 1989;5(6):557–561.

12. Shearer GM, Clerici M. Early T-helper cell defects in HIV infection. *AIDS.* 1991;5(3):245–253.

13. Schuitemaker H, Koot M, Kootstra NA, et al. Biological phenotype of human immunodeficiency virus type 1 clones at different stages of infection: progression of disease is associated with a shift from monocytotropic to T-cell-tropic virus populations. *J Virol.* March 1992; 66(3):1354–1360.

14. Schnittman SM, Lane HC, Greenhouse J, et al. Preferential infection of CD4+ memory T cells by human immunodeficiency virus type 1: evidence for a role in the selective T-cell functional defects observed in infected individuals. *Proc Natl Acad Sci USA.* August 1990;87:6058–6062.

15. Fahey JL, Taylor JMG, Detels R, et al. The prognostic value of cellular and serologic markers in infection with human immunodeficiency virus type 1. *N Engl J Med.* January 18,1990;322(3):166–172.

16. Golding H, Shearer GM, Hillman K, et al. Common epitope in human immunodeficiency virus (HIV) I-gp41 and HLA class II elicits immuno-suppressive autoantibodies capable of contributing to immune dysfunction in HIV I–infected individuals. *J Clin Invest.* April 1989;83:1430–1435.

17. Meyaard L, Otto SA, Jonker RR, et al. Programmed death of T cells in HIV-1 infection. *Science.* July 10, 1992;257:217–219.

RECOMMENDED FOLLOW-UP

In addition to the reference list, the reader may wish to consult the following sources:

Tizzard I. *Immunology: An Introduction*. 2nd ed. Philadelphia: Saunders College Publishing; 1988.

Amman AJ. Immunodeficiency diseases. In: Stites DP, Stobs JD, Wells JV, eds. *Basic and Clinical Immunology*, 6th ed. Norwalk/Los Altos: Appleton & Lange; 1987:317–355.

Gallagher RB. *HIV and the Immune System*. Cambridge: Elsevier Trends Books; 1991.

CARE AND MANAGEMENT OF PATIENTS WITH HIV INFECTION

Chapter 3: Diagnosis and Treatment of the Patient with HIV Infection

John A. Bartlett, MD
Assistant Professor of Medicine
Principal Investigator, AIDS Clinical Trials Unit
Duke University Medical Center

Harry A. Gallis, MD
Associate Professor of Medicine
Duke University Medical Center

Kenneth W. Shipp, BS Pharm
Clinical Pharmacist
AIDS Treatment Evaluation Unit
Duke University Medical Center

Karen L. Nabors, PharmD
Pharmacy Resident, Department of Pharmacy
Duke University Medical Center

CONTENTS

Introduction 107
Objectives 107
   I.　　Disease Classification 108
Review Questions (I) 110
  II.　　Primary Therapy of HIV Infection 111
 III.　　Experimental Therapies for HIV Infection 114
       A.　Antiviral Agents 114
       B.　Immune-based Therapies 115
  IV.　　AIDS Dementia Complex 117
Review Questions (II, III, & IV) 118
   V.　　Therapy of Opportunistic Infections 119
       A.　Candidiasis 119
       B.　Pneumocystis Infection 120
       C.　Cytomegalovirus Infection 121
       D.　Cryptococcus Infections 122
       E.　Toxoplasmosis 123
       F.　Mycobacterium Infections 123
       G.　Syphilis 124
       H.　Other Infections 124
  VI.　　Kaposi's Sarcoma and Other Malignancies 125
Review Questions (V & VI) 126
Summary 129
Answers to Review Questions 130
References 131

INTRODUCTION

This chapter provides an overview of the diagnosis and treatment of HIV infection and its consequent opportunistic infections and malignancies. The chapter is not intended as a comprehensive review of the subject matter. Health professionals should refer to the chapter specific to their profession for more detailed coverage of certain topics. You should also be aware that treatment of HIV infection is a rapidly changing field. You are encouraged to refer to professional journals to supplement and update this chapter.

OBJECTIVES

Objectives presented here are intended to focus the reader's attention on expected learning outcomes.

On completion of the chapter, the reader should be able to:

1. State the proposed criteria used by the Centers for Disease Control (CDC) for classifying the stages of HIV infection.

2. Describe tests used to diagnose and follow the course of HIV infection.

3. Describe the indications, dose, and expected side effects of the primary therapy for HIV infection.

4. Recognize the two broad areas of drug development for HIV treatment and list some of the agents that are currently under investigation.

5. Describe the presenting symptoms, clinical course, and standard therapy for the following opportunistic infections:

    *   candidiasis
    *   *Pneumocystis carinii* pneumonia
    *   cytomegalovirus infection
    *   cryptococcosis
    *   toxoplasmosis
    *   mycobacteriosis
    *   syphilis

6. Describe the presenting symptoms, clinical course, and standard therapy for Kaposi's sarcoma.

I. DISEASE CLASSIFICATION

The accurate staging of patients infected with HIV is essential in guiding therapeutic decisions and providing important prognostic information to patients. The physician must stage the disease from both a physical and immunological standpoint. The Centers for Disease Control (CDC) has developed a proposed classification system for HIV infection (see Table 3.1).[1]

TABLE 3.1.   1992 Revised Classification System for HIV Infection and Expanded AIDS Surveillance Case Definition for Adolescents and Adults

	CLINICAL CATEGORIES		
CD4+ T-CELL CATEGORIES	(A) Asymptomatic, acute (primary) HIV, or PGL	(B) Symptomatic, not (A) or (C) conditions	(C) AIDS-indicator conditions
(1) ≥ 500/μL	A1	B1	C1
(2) 200–499/μL	A2	B2	C2
(3) < 200/μL AIDS-indicator T-cell count	A3	B3	C3

In staging the patient immunologically, lymphocyte subset analysis has been found to be of the greatest prognostic significance. The most commonly used test is the absolute CD4 cell count, since cells that express the CD4 receptor (primarily T helper cells) are the primary target for the human immunodeficiency virus.

Studies have shown that patients can be stratified in their risk of developing AIDS based on their absolute CD4 count and its percentage of the total T-cell count. For example, if the CD4 cell count is greater than $400/mm^3$, the four-year cumulative risk for developing AIDS is 18%, whereas if the CD4 cell count is less than $200/mm^3$ the four-year incidence is 84%.[2] The percentage of lymphocytes that bear CD4 molecules on their surface is also a predictor of progression to AIDS,[3] but has been less widely used as a guide to therapeutic decisions.

Other laboratory data have also been found to be prognostic indicators. A complete blood count should be done at the initial visit. Patients who are anemic, lymphopenic, or thrombocytopenic also have a poorer prognosis. Other nonspecific immunologic markers of prognostic significance include beta$_2$-microglobulin and neoptrin levels. The detection of viral p24 antigen in the bloodstream is also a viral marker of poor prognosis.

Other screening tests that are useful include liver enzymes and serologic tests for syphilis, toxoplasmosis, and cytomegalovirus (CMV). AIDS patients with positive serologies for syphilis should be treated very aggressively to avoid relapse and the potential for later complications. Serologic evidence of exposure to CMV and toxoplasma may be useful in assessing future infectious complications. A PPD should be placed. If this is positive, isoniazid prophylaxis should be instituted once the patient has been fully evaluated for signs of active tuberculosis. Positive skin test reactivity to other common pathogens is useful in assessing the status of cell-mediated immunity. A baseline chest x-ray is useful to rule out active pulmonary infection and as a comparison for future situations.

REVIEW QUESTIONS (I)

DIRECTIONS. Circle the letter corresponding to the correct response in each of the following.

1. The proposed CDC staging system will utilize a comprehensive approach to patients which includes

    a. clinical symptoms.
    b. AIDS-indicator conditions.
    c. a laboratory assessment of immunologic integrity.
    d. all of the above.

2. The most useful laboratory marker of immunologic staging is

    a. the hematocrit.
    b. result of skin tests.
    c. absolute CD4 lymphocyte count.
    d. sedimentation rate.

3. Other laboratory markers of prognostic significance include

    a. erythrocyte sedimentation rate.
    b. viral p24 antigen.
    c. carcinoembryonic antigen.
    d. eosinophil count.

Check your responses on page 130.

II. PRIMARY THERAPY OF HIV INFECTION

Currently there are three approved antiviral therapies for HIV infection: zidovudine (AZT), didanosine (ddI), and zalcitabine (ddC). All act as reverse transcriptase inhibitors, blocking viral replication. Originally, the FDA approved zidovudine only in cases of documented *Pneumocystis carinii* pneumonia and for individuals with CD4 counts of less than 200 cells/mm^3. In March 1990, based on the results of two randomized, double-blind, placebo-controlled studies, the FDA approved a change in the indications to include all HIV-infected patients with CD4 counts of 500 cells/mm^3 or less.[4,5] More recently the FDA approved didanosine as a single agent for patients intolerant of zidovudine or those who deteriorate clinically or immunologically on zidovudine. Zalcitabine is approved for use in combination with zidovudine in patients who are clinically or immunologically deteriorating on zidovudine monotherapy.

Treatment with zidovudine prolongs survival in patients with AIDS, as well as improves clinical well-being and performance.[6] Zidovudine therapy also slows progression of HIV infection when given to patients with early symptomatic HIV infection[4] and when given to patients with asymptomatic HIV infection who have CD4 counts of 500 cells/mm^3 or less.[5] The recommended dose of zidovudine for all adults with HIV infection is 100 mg five times daily. Clinical studies are ongoing to evaluate less frequent dosing schedules. Higher doses of zidovudine (200 mg five times daily) may be necessary in treating patients with HIV-associated dementia. Doses must be reduced for hematologic toxicities, especially severe anemia and granulocytopenia and for significant renal or hepatic dysfunction. See the manufacturer's prescribing information for guidelines.

Zidovudine is well tolerated in the majority of patients at the currently recommended dose levels. In the clinical trial involving asymptomatic patients, nausea was the only statistically significant toxicity, which occurred more often in patients receiving 500 mg per day than in patients receiving placebo.[5] In the study involving mildly asymptomatic patients, serious anemia and granulocytopenia were the major side effects, which occurred in 5% and 4% of zidovudine patients, respectively.[4] Patients experienced more frequent and more severe side effects, primarily anemia and granulocytopenia, in an earlier study that used higher doses in patients with more advanced disease (AIDS or advanced ARC).[6]

The anemia associated with zidovudine is macrocytic and the MCV may reach 130. Folate and B12 levels may be checked, but, if normal, the elevated MCV of zidovudine-associated anemia will not respond to the exogenous administration of either folate or B12. In patients with serum erythropoietin levels less than 500, the use of recombinant erythropoietin may improve zidovudine-associated anemia.[7] Granulocytopenia may occur in patients on zidovudine; fortunately it is well tolerated by these patients.[8] Many clinicians will continue zidovudine if the absolute granulocyte count remains above 500/mm^3. For patients with severe granulocytopenia, GCSF may raise the granulocyte count.[9]

Long-term zidovudine therapy may also result in a drug-related myopathy due to inhibition of DNA polymerase in the mitochondria of striated muscle.[10] The myopathy is usually proximally located and painful, and may be difficult to distinguish from the myopathy associated with the underlying HIV infection. Discontinuation of zidovudine therapy should result in clinical improvement within one month, and neither didanosine nor zalcitabine has been associated with striated muscle myopathies.

Zidovudine-resistant virus has now been isolated from HIV-infected patients on prolonged zidovudine therapy.[11] The emergence of these isolates appears to be related to the preexisting burden of HIV in a given patient and thus to the stage of their disease.[12,13] Patients with early-stage HIV infection and a relatively low viral burden experience the emergence of resistant isolates relatively slowly. In contrast, patients with advanced disease on zidovudine are virtually certain to develop resistant isolates within one year. The most common mechanism of zidovudine resistance is a series of four nucleotide mutations in the gene encoding reverse transcriptase.[14] Fortunately, most isolates that are zidovudine resistant maintain their sensitivity to didanosine or zalcitabine. It is currently recommended that concern about zidovudine resistance should not delay decisions regarding the initiation of zidovudine therapy, but should reaffirm the need for developing strategies of salvage therapy. Switching to another anti-retroviral agent (e.g., didanosine) or combining agents (e.g., zidovudine and zalcitabine) represent potentially successful salvage strategies.

Didanosine has demonstrated evidence of clinical activity through anti-retroviral and immunologic effects similar to those seen with zidovudine.[15-17] It is currently indicated for patients with progressive HIV infection who are intolerant of zidovudine or are deteriorating either clinically or immunologically on zidovudine. Direct comparative trials of zidovudine and didanosine remain in progress, and their comparative efficacy is not yet known. A recently completed study which evaluated patients with CD4 counts less than 300/mm^3 who had taken zidovudine for at least four months demonstrated fewer opportunistic infections and less CD4 lymphocyte decline among patients who switched from zidovudine to didanosine.[18] This study may have provided an important clinical correlate to the observations of frequent zidovudine resistance in this population and the lack of cross-resistant isolates.

Didanosine is administered twice daily and the dosage must be adjusted to the patient's weight. It is best absorbed in a basic environment and is thus produced in a formulation containing an antacid. It is necessary to take two didanosine pills simultaneously to obtain the proper mixture of drug and antacid, and they should be administered either one-half hour before meals or at least two hours after meals. The pills must be chewed, crushed, or dissolved in tap water prior to swallowing.

The toxicities of didanosine include peripheral neuropathy, pancreatitis, hepatitis, hyperuricemia, and hypertriglyceridemia.[19] Peripheral neuropathies may occur in 7% to 34% of patients.[16,18] Clearly, patients with preexisting neuropathies or those taking other neuropathic drugs are most predisposed to this complication. The neuropathy usually does not occur in the first two months of therapy, and begins with sensory symptoms in the lower extremities. Discontinuation of didanosine as rapidly as possible results in early resolution, and didanosine may then be resumed at a lower dosage. Pancreatitis occurs in 1% to 9% of patients,[16,18] and once again those patients with a history of pancreatitis or taking drugs with pancreatic toxicity are most predisposed. Alcohol should be consumed very cautiously. Most clinicians monitor the serum amylase monthly and will discontinue didanosine if amylase elevations exceed two times normal.

Zalcitabine has shown preliminary evidence of clinical activity in combination with zidovudine.[20,21] Although these studies are uncontrolled, they suggest that the clinical benefits, antiretroviral effects, and immunologic effects of combination therapy are more prolonged than expected with single-agent therapy. Controlled studies are currently in progress. Zalcitabine is now approved for the combination treatment of progressive HIV infection in patients with clinical or immunologic deterioration. As a single agent, zalcitabine is inferior to zidovudine and is recommended only in combination treatment.

The toxicities of zalcitabine are similar to those of didanosine with regard to peripheral neuropathies and pancreatitis.[22] The neuropathic toxicity of zalcitabine is probably greater than that of didanosine and the pancreatic toxicity is probably less. Zalcitabine frequently results in a transient erythematous maculopapular rash in many patients within the first two weeks of treatment.[23] The rash may be accompanied by systemic symptoms, but is self-limited and should not interrupt therapy. Zalcitabine has also been associated with aphthous oral and esophageal ulcers.[24]

Thus clinicians may now offer salvage therapy to patients who progress on zidovudine. They may choose between switching to didanosine or adding zalcitabine. The relative efficacy of each approach is uncertain at the present time and is the subject of ongoing trials. In addition, preliminary studies utilizing concurrent zidovudine and didanosine have suggested important clinical, virologic, and immunologic effects.

III. EXPERIMENTAL THERAPIES FOR HIV INFECTION

Two broad areas of drug development are being pursued for the improved treatment of HIV infection: antiviral therapies and immune-based therapies. Antiviral therapies exert a direct effect on the replicative cycle of HIV, while immune-based therapies attempt to therapeutically manipulate selective components of the host immune response against HIV. Ultimately, the optimal treatment of HIV infection will probably involve multiple agents, perhaps different antiviral drugs whose mechanisms of action attack the virus at different points in its life cycle, and perhaps immunomodulators.

A. ANTIVIRAL AGENTS

1. Reverse Transcriptase Inhibitors. The conversion of viral RNA to DNA by the enzyme reverse transcriptase is a biologic process unique to retroviruses. The HIV reverse transcriptase has been intensively studied and its three-dimensional structure elucidated by x-ray crystallography. It is thus an ideal target for drug development, and all of the presently available agents for prescription inhibit this enzyme. Reverse transcriptase inhibitors fall into two categories: nucleoside analogues and non-nucleoside analogues. The nucleoside analogues include zidovudine, didanosine, zalcitabine, and other agents in development such as d4T, FLT, and 3TC. The non-nucleoside analogues include drugs such as foscarnet, nevirapine, the L compounds, and the TIBO compounds. Foscarnet is now FDA approved for the treatment of CMV disease and it has activity against HIV. However, its use as an antiretroviral agent will probably be limited by the need for intravenous administration and its toxicities. Nevirapine, the L compounds, and the TIBO compounds have demonstrated antiviral activity in clinical trials, but all have been complicated by the rapid development of viral resistance.

Any new inhibitor of reverse transcriptase must offer advantages over presently available agents. These advantages could include more potent antiviral activity as a single agent, additive or synergistic effects with presently available agents, decreased or non-overlapping toxicities compared to presently available agents, activity against resistant isolates, and lower cost. The results of clinical trials should be scrutinized as clinicians critically evaluate the usefulness of this rapidly expanding group of agents.

2. Alpha Interferon. Alpha interferon is a naturally occurring human protein that is produced in response to viral infections. It has many biologic effects including these antiviral effects: inhibition of transcription/translation, inhibition of viral messenger RNA, inhibition of protein synthesis, and inhibition of assembly of the final viral particle. Alpha interferon is also effective in the treatment of Kaposi's sarcoma and has been approved for the treatment of Kaposi's sarcoma in AIDS patients with greater than 200 CD4 cells. The usefulness of alpha interferon as an antiviral agent continues to be explored. Its antiretroviral effects have been well demonstrated both alone and in combination with zidovudine. However, it has not yet demonstrated efficacy in improving natural history endpoints. The toxicities of alpha interferon may be troubling and include flu-like symptoms and neutropenia. The ultimate role of alpha interferon in the treatment of HIV infection remains to be determined.

3. **Protease Inhibitors.** In the process of producing new viral particles, HIV-infected cells produce large proteins that are then divided into smaller functional proteins, such as p24 and reverse transcriptase, by the protease enzyme. Inhibitors of this enzyme definitively interrupt the HIV life cycle. Investigators have defined the three-dimensional structure of HIV protease and are now designing drugs that may be able to inhibit HIV protease without significantly interfering with the structurally similar human aspartic proteases. Several pharmaceutical companies are developing protease inhibitors and have begun initial clinical testing.

4. **TAT Inhibitors.** The transactivating (TAT) protein of HIV is a key element in promoting its explosive ability to replicate. The TAT protein binds to long terminal repeat (LTR) sequences of the HIV genome and thus up-regulates viral transcription and translation. At least one compound has been identified that inhibits TAT, and it has demonstrated significant antiviral activity *in vitro*. Clinical trials are now beginning to evaluate this compound.

5. **TNF Inhibitors.** Tumor necrosis factor (TNF), also known as cachectin, is a cytokine produced in response to many disease states including sepsis, tuberculosis, malignancy, and HIV infection. It appears to be important in the pathogenesis of cachexia from many causes, including progressive HIV infection, and perhaps also in the pathogenesis of HIV-associated neurologic disease. In addition, the exposure of HIV-infected macrophages to TNF increases viral replication, which can be blocked by TNF inhibitors. Thus, TNF inhibitors could potentially be useful in HIV-infected patients to reverse cachexia, to treat HIV-associated neurologic disease, and to inhibit viral replication. Pentoxifylline (Trental®) is an agent that is FDA approved for the treatment of intermittent claudication, but also inhibits TNF production. A recently completed phase I study of pentoxifylline suggested clinical improvements in cachexia and antiviral effects.[25] Further study is planned, including more potent inhibitors of TNF.

B. IMMUNE-BASED THERAPIES

During the prolonged asymptomatic period of HIV infection, vigorous host immune responses against HIV can be measured, including neutralizing antibodies, helper cell responses, and cytotoxic T lymphocytes. It has been hypothesized that these responses are important in the suppression of HIV replication following acute HIV infection, and that they are responsible for the relatively low levels of detectable virus during the asymptomatic period. In progressive HIV infection, the amount of detectable virus increases concurrent with decreases in the measurable host immune response. Therefore, the strategy of immune-based therapies has been developed to augment these potentially beneficial responses.

Immune-based therapies fall into three broad categories: active immunotherapy, including vaccines and stimulating cytokines; passive immunotherapy, including purified HIV-specific immune globulin; and adoptive immunotherapy.

1. Active Immunotherapy. The premise of active immunotherapy is to use a stimulus to generate a new immune response or augment a preexisting response against HIV. In general, the use of active immunotherapy requires an intact immunologic response in the patient and thus may not be utilized in patients in the later stages of HIV infection. HIV vaccines are being evaluated in HIV-infected persons both to assess safety and immunogenicity and also to observe for potential therapeutic effects. Uncontrolled studies have suggested stabilization of CD4 lymphocyte counts among the recipients of HIV vaccines.[26] These observations must be confirmed in controlled studies before considering the widespread use of therapeutic vaccines.

Cytokine therapy has also been employed to augment specific aspects of the HIV-infected patient's immune response. Interleukin-2 has undergone the most thorough evaluation. In preliminary studies, it has stimulated cell-mediated responses against HIV and resulted in transient rises in absolute CD4 lymphocyte counts.[27,28] Further controlled studies are necessary to assess any therapeutic value of these preliminary observations and to better design optimal schedules of drug administration.

2. Passive Immunotherapy. Passive immunotherapy proposes to use important immunologic elements of the host immune response and to exogenously administer them to persons deficient in that response. Purified p24 antibody has been evaluated in preliminary clinical trials and was not associated with immunologic, antiviral, or clinical benefits.[29] HIV-specific immune globulin is now being evaluated for prevention of maternal-fetal transmission, and HIV monoclonal antibodies are also being proposed for evaluation in this setting.

3. Adoptive Immunotherapy. In adoptive immunotherapy, elements of the patient's immune system are temporarily removed from the body, improved in function and/or number, and then returned in an attempt to heighten immunologic responsiveness. Currently the *ex vivo* expansion of CD8 lymphocytes, especially cytotoxic T lymphocytes, is a subject of active research. Preliminary trials suggest that such an approach is safe and perhaps of immediate therapeutic use in patients with Kaposi's sarcoma.[30]

IV. AIDS DEMENTIA COMPLEX

HIV is clearly neurotropic as well as lymphotropic, making it perhaps the most challenging CNS infection. Manifestations range from myelopathy and peripheral neuropathy to the so-called AIDS dementia complex. Initial HIV infection may result in aseptic meningitis. The most serious presentation is subacute encephalitis, leading to the AIDS dementia complex. Early in the course of the disease, patients complain of forgetfulness, loss of concentration, and slowness of thought. There can be motor deficits, with loss of balance and leg weakness, as well as apathy, social withdrawal, and depression. The course, once detected, is usually progressive over months. Late manifestations are psychosis, psychomotor retardation, incontinence, ataxia, and motor weakness. Some researchers suggest that patients who are asymptomatic HIV carriers may also have evidence of central nervous system disorders.

Pathologic examination reveals rarefaction and demyelination, particularly in the white matter and basal ganglia. Clinical signs are usually general, not focal. The CSF may be normal or show modest elevations in protein and slight to moderate mononuclear pleocytosis. A CT scan may show cortical atrophy while magnetic resonance imaging reveals increased signal in the white matter.

Dementia coupled with progressive disease, as is seen with HIV, is problematic. Therapy must be directed at the virus itself. One controlled study has shown benefits with zidovudine therapy.[31] Patients improved in cognitive function but not in affective disorders. At the same time, patients reported less distress from HIV symptoms than those who received placebo. The usefulness of zidovudine for HIV-associated dementia may be dose related, and 200 mg five times daily is recommended in tolerant patients. Uncontrolled studies have also suggested therapeutic benefits to didanosine treatment in patients with neuro-cognitive deficits.

REVIEW QUESTIONS (II, III, & IV)

DIRECTIONS. Circle the letter corresponding to the correct response in each of the following.

1. Zidovudine has been shown effective in patients with

    a. asymptomatic HIV infection with CD4 counts less than 500 cells per mm^3.
    b. early symptomatic HIV infection.
    c. *Pneumocystis carinii* pneumonia.
    d. all of the above.

2. Potential therapeutic strategies for patients progressing on zidovudine include

    a. switching to didanosine.
    b. increasing the zidovudine dose.
    c. adding zalcitabine.
    d. options a and c.

3. The predominant toxicities of didanosine and zalcitabine include

    a. hematologic suppression.
    b. peripheral neuropathies and pancreatitis.
    c. myopathies.
    d. nephrotoxicity.

4. Early symptoms of AIDS dementia complex include all of the following *except*

    a. depression.
    b. forgetfulness.
    c. incontinence.
    d. leg weakness.

5. Treatment of AIDS dementia complex with zidovudine has produced only subjective feelings of improvement.

    a. true
    b. false

Check your responses on page 130.

V. THERAPY OF OPPORTUNISTIC INFECTIONS

The hallmark of progressive immunosuppression (AIDS) is the development of opportunistic infections. Six basic principles are important in diagnosing and treating AIDS-related infections.[32]

1. These infections are rarely curable and usually require long-term suppressive therapy, if not life-long therapy.

2. Many infections represent reactivation of endogenous infections (CMV, herpes, *Mycobacterium tuberculosis*, *Toxoplasma gondii*, histoplasma, coccidioides).

3. Infections may be multiple and concurrent. This must be kept in mind when judging response to therapy.

4. Endogenous infections usually represent the geographic locality of acquisition (histoplasmosis, coccidioidomycosis). Travel and exposure history thus becomes important when attempting to diagnose an illness.

5. Several bacterial infections (pneumococcal, *Haemophilus*, and *Salmonella* infections) are also being recognized as HIV-associated diseases.

6. Infections are usually more severe and may be widely disseminated at the time of diagnosis (cryptococcosis, mycobacteriosis, pneumocystosis).

A. CANDIDIASIS

Although not indicative of AIDS, mucocutaneous candidiasis is the most commonly seen fungal infection. It may become clinically manifest as oral thrush, esophagitis, or vaginitis. Systemic candidal infections are uncommon.

Nystatin and clotrimazole are topical therapies which can be employed. For clinically refractory cases, either ketoconazole or fluconazole may be used. Recently an AIDS-associated gastropathy has been reported that can significantly decrease ketoconazole absorption. The same phenomenon has been found with concomitant therapy with H_2-blockers such as ranitidine and cimetidine. Adding hydrochloric acid, in the form of acidulin, can increase ketoconazole absorption.[33] Fluconazole does not require gastric acidity and represents another therapeutic option. Intermittent amphotericin B may be required in particularly refractory cases.

B. PNEUMOCYSTIS INFECTION

Historically, the most common opportunistic infection seen in AIDS was *Pneumocystis carinii* pneumonia (PCP), occurring in more than 80% of cases. This number may be decreasing with the use of preventive strategies. This organism, ubiquitous in the environment, rarely causes disease in non-immunocompromised hosts. In patients with AIDS, it may present with nonspecific symptoms of malaise, mild cough, and easy fatigability over several weeks. Alternatively, high fevers, dyspnea, tachypnea, prostration, and rapid progression with severe hypoxemia may be present. The chest x-ray may be normal initially, but will progress to show diffuse interstitial infiltrates. Patients receiving aerosolized pentamidine as prophylaxis may present with unusual radiographic appearances such as disease restricted to the upper lobes, lobar infiltrates, cavitations, or nodular disease.[34] The diagnosis may be obscure. A high index of suspicion is needed in patients with dyspnea, and arterial blood gases should be analyzed. Gallium scans may assist with diagnosis, but a significant percentage of false positives occur.

Diagnosis is based on identification of organisms, commonly with the aid of fiberoptic bronchoscopy. Bronchoalveolar lavage is nearly always diagnostic in patients not on prophylaxis, but in patients on prophylaxis even transbronchial biopsy is associated with a lower diagnostic yield.[34] Saline-induced sputum induction with rapid staining may be successful in diagnosing patients not on prophylaxis.

Pneumocystis carinii may occur concomitantly with other pathogens in up to 40% of AIDS patients. If the patient does not appear to respond to therapy, other pathogens should be sought before therapy is altered. Likewise, organisms may still be present after an apparent clinical cure. It is therefore difficult to judge whether treatment is effective based on sampling for the organism. However, once a clinical "remission" is obtained, patients are then placed on post-PCP suppressive therapy.

Seventy-five percent of patients with first episodes of PCP are expected to survive with proper therapy. The potential options for oral treatment include the approved drugs trimethoprim/sulfamethoxazole (TMP/SMX) and atovaquone, and two combinations of drugs which are not FDA indicated for PCP but have achieved therapeutic success in preliminary studies—dapsone and trimethoprim, and clindamycin and primaquine. Also available for mild episodes of PCP, but not FDA indicated, is aerosolized pentamidine. Intravenous treatment can be offered with TMP/SMX or pentamidine. No one treatment has established therapeutic superiority, but each has unique toxicities. The initial dose of TMP/SMX is 15 to 20 mg/kg per day (based on TMP) divided into four equal doses. Most clinicians choose TMP/SMX as their agent of first choice given its extensive evaluation in treating PCP, oral formulation, low cost, and widespread availability. Unfortunately, it causes significant toxicities in many patients, including rash, fever, nausea, leukopenia, anemia, and hepatotoxicity. Atovaquone, 750 mg three times daily, is effective in the treatment of PCP and is well tolerated, although it has a lower rate of therapeutic success than TMP/SMX. It must be given with food and is absorbed through the enterohepatic circulation. The combination of trimethoprim (15 to 20 mg/kg per day divided into four equal doses) and dapsone (100 mg daily as a single dose) has similar efficacy for mild to moderate episodes and is orally administered. However, its toxicities are also similar to those of TMP/SMX. Clindamycin (300 to 600 mg four times daily) and primaquine (30 mg daily) have also been evaluated in preliminary studies with promising results. This combination can also be orally administered. Its potential toxicities include gastrointestinal distress (clindamycin), *Clostridium difficile*–associated diarrhea (clindamycin), and a very common, self-limited erythematous rash (primaquine). Pentamidine may be given intravenously to treat PCP, or in aerosolized form to treat mild episodes. Intravenous pentamidine is given as a single daily dose (4 mg/kg per day) and causes frequent toxicity including nausea, metallic taste, hypoglycemia, pancreatitis, nephrotoxicity, and hypotension. Aerosolized pentamidine should be given as two 300-mg doses daily, but is plagued by a high failure rate.

All patients with PCP should receive therapy for at least three weeks. In addition, all should receive prophylaxis immediately given the extremely high relapse rate (60% in the first year post-PCP).

In patients with moderate impairment of oxygenation due to PCP ($PO_2 < 70$ on room air), corticosteroid therapy may be beneficial in preventing progression to respiratory failure. Several studies have shown therapeutic benefit to a prednisone taper of 40 mg twice daily for days 1 through 5, 40 mg once daily for days 6 through 10, and 20 mg once daily for days 11 through 16.[35]

Any patient with a history of PCP, an absolute CD4 lymphocyte count of less than 200/mm³ or CD4 percentage less than 20%, or another AIDS-defining illness is at high risk for PCP and should receive prophylaxis. The potential options for prophylaxis include TMP/SMX double strength (DS) three times weekly, dapsone 50 mg daily, or aerosolized pentamidine 300 mg monthly. TMP/SMX is superior to aerosolized pentamidine in preventing relapse of PCP, probably reflecting the advantage of systemic prophylaxis.[36] Most clinicians choose TMP/SMX DS three times weekly initially, and will then try dapsone if the patient is intolerant of TMP/SMX. Aerosolized pentamidine is expensive and awkward to deliver, but may be used in patients intolerant of TMP/SMX or dapsone.

C. CYTOMEGALOVIRUS INFECTION

Cytomegalovirus (CMV) infection presents a diagnostic and therapeutic challenge. Active CMV usually represents reactivation of latent disease. Its manifestations are variable, but it most commonly presents as retinitis (15% to 46% of AIDS cases). Pneumonitis, esophagitis, colitis, fever, hepatitis, and adrenal necrosis are other features.[37,38]

In CMV retinitis, early infection is usually asymptomatic. Later it can present as scotoma or seeing floaters. Pain, photophobia, and erythema are not usually present. The disease is progressive and eventually results in blindness. Ganciclovir and foscarnet are approved drugs used to treat CMV retinitis. They inhibit the CMV DNA polymerase. Both drugs are virustatic and not virucidal, so relapse will occur if maintenance therapy is not continued. Approximately 85% of patients will respond to a two-week course of ganciclovir 5 mg/kg intravenously every 12 hours. Areas of involvement may clear, but these areas remain visually nonfunctional. Maintenance therapy should then be given with ganciclovir 5 mg/kg intravenously five days per week.

Foscarnet is also effective in treating CMV retinitis. Acute therapy is given for two weeks at a dose of 60 mg/kg every eight hours, and maintenance therapy at 90 mg/kg once daily. Foscarnet must be administered intravenously, preferably through a central venous catheter, and frequently with normal saline following the foscarnet infusion. Foscarnet has numerous potential toxicities including proteinuria, renal insufficiency, abnormalities of calcium and phosphorus metabolism, seizures, neutropenia, and anemia.[39]

One clinical trial directly compared the efficacy of ganciclovir to that of foscarnet in treating CMV retinitis.[40] The drugs demonstrated equal efficacy in treating the retinitis, but foscarnet recipients had a significant prolongation of survival. This prolongation may reflect the antiretroviral activity of foscarnet. Many clinicians have continued to prescribe ganciclovir as initial therapy given the relatively high cost and multiple toxicities of foscarnet.

D. CRYPTOCOCCUS INFECTIONS

Cryptococcus is the major cause of meningitis in AIDS patients. It may be indolent, presenting as fever alone without any evidence of CNS involvement. The more common symptoms of fever and headache are present in 80% to 90% of cases. In patients with suspected CNS disease, computerized tomography should be done first, followed by lumbar puncture. In patients with AIDS, the CSF indices of cell count, protein, and glucose may be normal or only mildly abnormal. The cryptococcal antigen titer is helpful but not always positive, even in culture-proven cryptococcosis. In these situations, culture from extraneural sites (e.g., blood, skin, lung, liver, bone marrow) may be helpful.

Fluconazole is effective both as primary therapy and as maintenance therapy in cryptococcal meningitis. Given orally, fluconazole can achieve 60% to 80% of serum levels in CSF. A clinical trial directly comparing fluconazole with amphotericin B suggested equivalent efficacy, although amphotericin B sterilized the CSF more quickly.[41] Many clinicians now prescribe fluconazole 400 mg daily to treat less severely ill patients with cryptococcal meningitis. After 12 weeks of high-dose therapy, the dose can be reduced to 200 mg daily as maintenance therapy. Fluconazole is superior to amphotericin B in preventing relapse of cryptococcal meningitis,[42] and offers the relative advantages of much less toxicity and oral administration when compared to amphotericin B.

Amphotericin B is the drug of choice in treating severe cryptococcosis. 5-Flucytosine is synergistic with amphotericin B, but bone marrow toxicity limits its usefulness in AIDS. The dose of amphotericin B should be 0.3 to 0.8 mg/kg per day. A minimum total dose of 1 g should be used. If flucytosine is used, the dose should not exceed 50 to 100 mg/kg per day. Serum levels should be monitored to maintain serum concentration of 25 to 100 mcg/mL.

E. TOXOPLASMOSIS

Central nervous system toxoplasmosis is another common life-threatening opportunistic infection. It usually presents with fever and CNS symptoms, including seizures, confusion, and focal neurological findings such as hemiparesis and cranial nerve palsies. Diagnosis is usually based on the clinical picture—CT scan results commonly showing multiple ring enhancing lesions and response to empiric therapy. Lymphoma and other infections should also be considered. Definitive diagnosis can be made with a tissue biopsy stained by immunoperoxidase technique.

Pyrimethamine (50 mg per day) and sulfadiazine (100 mg/kg per day up to a maximum of 8 g per day) are the drugs of choice for the treatment of toxoplasmosis. Patients who are intolerant of sulfadiazine may be treated with clindamycin 300 to 600 mg four times daily and pyrimethamine. Other agents under evaluation include azithromycin and atovaquone. The therapeutic response is usually rapid (1 to 2 weeks), but therapy should be continued indefinitely to avoid relapse. Folinic acid, at doses as high as 50 mg per day, appears to be useful in limiting the hematologic toxicity of pyrimethamine. A recent study of TMP/SMX DS three times weekly to prevent PCP suggested that this regimen also prevented CNS toxoplasmosis.[43] This encouraging preliminary observation needs to be confirmed in further studies.

F. MYCOBACTERIUM INFECTIONS

The mycobacterium species *Mycobacterium avium-intracellulare* (MAI) and *Mycobacterium tuberculosis* are also common causes of infection. MAI usually presents as a wasting syndrome characterized by fever, malaise, night sweats, weight loss, and diarrhea. This organism can be readily recovered from blood, bone marrow, lymph nodes, and stool. Therapy for disseminated MAI infection has considerably improved utilizing multiple agents, some FDA indicated for this condition and others used outside of label indications. Multidrug regimens including clarithromycin, ciprofloxacin, rifampin, clofazimine, ethambutol, or amikacin are resulting in decreased mycobacteremia and improvements in clinical symptoms.[44,45] Two recent studies have demonstrated delay in MAI infections among patients with CD4 lymphocyte counts less than 200/mm^3 receiving rifabutin 300 mg daily.[46,47] Rifabutin is now available commercially for this indication.

Tuberculosis is increasing rapidly among persons with HIV infection. The yearly rate of progression to clinical tuberculosis in HIV-infected persons with positive PPD skin tests is 8% per year. Pulmonary tuberculosis is a manifestation of moderate immunodeficiency and often precedes the diagnosis of AIDS. PPD skin tests are unreliable in AIDS; they may be positive only in early HIV disease. Granuloma formation is rare because an intact immune response is necessary for that process. Thus, a high index of suspicion must be maintained among persons at risk. In identified cases, therapy with isoniazid, rifampin, ethambutol, or pyrazinamide is recommended pending the results of sensitivity testing. Standard duration of therapy results in a high rate of clinical cure without relapse.

G. SYPHILIS

Syphilis in conjunction with AIDS presents another diagnostic challenge, since some patients may be seronegative in the presence of disease documented by biopsy. Since the organism frequently disseminates to the CNS at an early stage in the infection, some authorities recommend treatment with a regimen appropriate for neurosyphilis in all stages. In some patients presenting with biopsy-confirmed secondary syphilis, both the treponemal and nontreponemal tests for syphilis are negative. Therapy for HIV-positive patients who have documented neurosyphilis should consist of high-dose intravenous penicillin for 10 days.

H. OTHER INFECTIONS

Many other infectious complications accompany HIV but are beyond the scope of this book. CNS infections with papovavirus (progressive multifocal leukoencephalopathy), herpes simplex encephalitis, varicella-zoster encephalitis, and viral myelitis have been noted. Bacteremias are becoming more common, particularly *Salmonella, Shigella,* and *Streptococcus pneumoniae.* Disseminated coccidioidomycosis and histoplasmosis are found in their respective endemic areas, as is strongyloidiasis. Gastrointestinal disorders are seen with cryptosporidiosis and isosporiasis.

VI. KAPOSI'S SARCOMA AND OTHER MALIGNANCIES

Before the advent of AIDS, Kaposi's sarcoma (KS) was a relatively rare malignancy in the United States. At present the epidemic form is predominantly a disease of homosexual men.

KS can be relatively asymptomatic except for cosmetic effects of cutaneous lesions. In most patients, KS never progresses beyond cutaneous involvement. However, early visceral involvement may occur, especially of the lymph nodes and gastrointestinal tract. KS may also involve the lungs and pleura, and in these locations it is very difficult to diagnose without open biopsy. Survival tends to be longer in patients with KS with no associated opportunistic infections than in patients who present with opportunistic infections.

Radiation therapy is highly effective and palliative in KS. It is probably most beneficial for controlling local painful lesions or for relieving lymphatic obstruction. Cytotoxic therapy has also been used, but its limitations are obvious in patients who are already immunocompromised. Intravenous or intralesional vinblastine may be useful in patients with cutaneous disease. Doxorubicin HCl, bleomycin, and vinblastine may be successful in palliating patients with pulmonary KS. Alpha interferon (IFN-α) has been studied extensively as a therapeutic modality. Its effectiveness depends on the pretreatment status of the patient's immune system. Patients with CD4 counts greater than $400/mm^3$ showed significant reduction in tumor load, whereas patients with CD4 counts less than $150/mm^3$ had no response.

Another important malignancy in AIDS patients is non-Hodgkins lymphoma (NHL). NHL is clearly increasing in incidence, perhaps a reflection of prolonged survival times among persons with AIDS and as a late manifestation of their immunosuppression. NHL can be found in extra-CNS or CNS locations. Extra-CNS disease responds well to conventional chemotherapy. However, CNS lymphoma is relatively refractory and associated with a very poor prognosis.

REVIEW QUESTIONS (V & VI)

DIRECTIONS. Circle the letter corresponding to the correct response in each of the following.

1. Opportunistic infections in persons with AIDS

    a. usually occur with progressive immunosuppression (CD4 ≤200/mm³).
    b. are usually not due to reactivation of chronic endogenous infections.
    c. can usually be treated with short courses of antibiotics.
    d. show little variation from one area to another.

2. Treatment of mucocutaneous candidiasis with ketoconazole may be significantly impaired by simultaneous use of H_2-blockers.

    a. true
    b. false

3. Early signs and symptoms of *Pneumocystis carinii* pneumonia can include all of the following *except*

    a. dyspnea and tachypnea.
    b. malaise and mild cough.
    c. normal chest x-ray.
    d. thick, green, tenacious mucus.

4. In the initial treatment of PCP, TMP/SMX is usually employed because of a history of therapeutic successes, oral administration, easy availability, and low cost.

    a. true
    b. false

5. Prophylaxis for PCP should probably be provided for all of the following patients with

    a. a previous history of PCP.
    b. CD4 counts < 200/mm³.
    c. Kaposi's sarcoma.
    d. all of the above.

6. Which of the following is *not* a common feature of early CMV retinitis?

    a. no symptoms at all
    b. loss of peripheral vision
    c. pain
    d. scotoma

7. The drug of choice for treatment of CMV is

    a. acyclovir.
    b. ganciclovir.
    c. TMP/SMX.
    d. zidovudine.

8. All of the following drugs are effective in treating cryptococcal meningitis *except*

    a. amphotericin B.
    b. fluconazole.
    c. 5-flucytosine.
    d. ketoconazole.

9. Patients with HIV infection and a history of a positive PPD should receive isoniazid prophylaxis.

    a. true
    b. false

10. Which of the following statements about syphilis in patients with HIV infection is *not* true?

    a. CNS infiltration occurs rarely in the early stages of infection.
    b. Serology may be negative in biopsy-documented disease.
    c. Therapy for syphilis is no more aggressive for the AIDS patient than for the non-AIDS patient.
    d. Therapy usually involves penicillin G or procaine penicillin given with oral probenecid.

11.   Patients with Kaposi's sarcoma and no associated opportunistic infections

    a.   are usually IV drug users.
    b.   survive longer than patients whose first AIDS symptom is an opportunistic infection.
    c.   should always receive aggressive chemotherapy.
    d.   usually survive only 10 to 12 months.

Check your responses on page 130.

SUMMARY

Future successful treatment of the human immunodeficiency virus will likely consist of antiviral therapy coupled with immunologic reconstitution. A number of antiviral drugs are currently under evaluation that hold promise for the immediate future in controlling viral replication. The goal of immunologic reconstitution remains elusive. New therapies are being studied for many of the opportunistic infections that have heretofore shortened the life expectancy of many patients. Many of these agents are orally administered and less toxic than standard therapy. Health care professionals, when well-versed in the intricacies of providing care for AIDS patients, can make a substantial impact on quality of life.

ANSWERS TO REVIEW QUESTIONS

I		V & VI	
1.	d	1.	b
2.	c	2.	a
3.	b	3.	d
		4.	a
II, III, & IV		5.	d
		6.	c
1.	d	7.	b
2.	d	8.	d
3.	b	9.	a
4.	c	10.	a
5.	b	11.	b

REFERENCES

1. Revised Adult and Adolescent HIV Classification System and Expanded Surveillance Case Definition for Severe HIV Disease (AIDS). Atlanta, GA: Centers for Disease Control; July 1992.

2. Kaplan JE, Spira TJ, Fishbein DB, et al. A six-year follow-up of HIV-infected homosexual men with lymphadenopathy: evidence for an increased risk for developing AIDS after the third year of lymphadenopathy. *JAMA*. November 11, 1988;260(18):2694–2697.

3. Burcham J, Marmor M, Dubin N, et al. CD4% is the best predictor of development of AIDS in a cohort of HIV-infected homosexual men. *AIDS*. 1991;5:365–372.

4. Fischl MA, Richman DD, Hansen N, et al. The safety and efficacy of zidovudine (AZT) in the treatment of subjects with mildly symptomatic human immunodeficiency virus type I (HIV) infection: a double-blind, placebo-controlled trial. *Ann Intern Med*. May 15, 1990;112(10):727–737.

5. Volberding PA, Lagakos SW, Koch MA, et al. Zidovudine in asymptomatic human immunodeficiency virus infection: a controlled trial in persons with fewer than 500 CD4-positive cells per cubic millimeter. *N Engl J Med*. April 5, 1990;322(14):941–949.

6. Fischl MA, Richman DD, Grieco MH, et al. The efficacy of azidothymidine (AZT) in the treatment of patients with AIDS and AIDS-related complex: a double-blind, placebo-controlled trial. *N Engl J Med*. July 23, 1987;317(4):185–191.

7. Fischl M, Galpin JE, Levine JD, et al. Recombinant human erythropoietin for patients with AIDS treated with zidovudine. *N Engl J Med*. May 24, 1990;322(21):1488–1493.

8. Shaunak S, Bartlett JA. Zidovudine-induced neutropenia: are we too cautious? *Lancet*. July 8, 1989;2:91–93.

9. Groopman JE, Mitsuyasu RT, DeLeo MJ, et al. Effect of recombinant human granulocyte-macrophage colony-stimulating factor on myelopoiesis in the acquired immunodeficiency syndrome. *N Engl J Med*. September 3, 1987;317(10):593–598.

10. Dalakas MC, Illa I, Pezeshkpour GH, et al. Mitochondrial myopathy caused by long-term zidovudine therapy. *N Engl J Med*. April 19, 1990; 322(16):1098–1105.

11.   Larder BA, Darby G, Richman DD. HIV with reduced sensitivity to zidovudine (AZT) isolated during prolonged therapy. *Science.* March 31, 1989;243:1731–1734.

12.   Richman DD, Grimes JM, Lagakos SW. Effect of stage of disease and drug dose on zidovudine susceptibilities of isolates of human immuno-deficiency virus. *J AIDS.* 1990;3(8):743–746.

13.   Boucher CAB, Tersmette M, Lange JMA, et al. Zidovudine sensitivity of human immunodeficiency viruses from high-risk, symptom-free indivi-duals during therapy. *Lancet.* September 8, 1990;336:585–590.

14.   Larder BA, Kemp SD. Multiple mutations in HIV-1 reverse transcriptase confer high-level resistance to zidovudine (AZT). *Science.* December 1, 1989;246:1155-1158.

15.   Yarchoan R, Mitsuya H, Thomas RV, et al. In vivo activity against HIV and favorable toxicity profile of 2′,3′-dideoxyinosine. *Science.* July 28, 1989;245:412–415.

16.   Lambert JS, Seidlin M, Reichman RC, et al. 2′,3′-dideoxyinosine (ddI) in patients with the acquired immunodeficiency syndrome or AIDS-related complex. *N Engl J Med.* May 10, 1990;322(19):1333–1340.

17.   Cooley TP, Kunches LM, Saunders CA, et al. Once-daily administration of 2′,3′-dideoxyinosine (ddI) in patients with the acquired immuno-deficiency syndrome or AIDS-related complex. *N Engl J Med.* May 10, 1990;322(19):1340–1345.

18.   Kahn JO, Lagakos SW, Richman DD, et al. A controlled trial comparing continued zidovudine with didanosine in human immunodeficiency virus infection. *N Engl J Med.* August 27, 1992;327(9):581–587.

19.   Yarchoan R, Pluda JM, Thomas RV, et al. Long-term toxicity/activity profile of 2′,3′-dideoxyinosine in AIDS or AIDS-related complex. *Lancet.* September 1, 1990;336:526–529.

20.   Yarchoan R, Perno CF, Thomas RV, et al. Phase I studies of 2′,3′-dideoxycytidine in severe human immunodeficiency virus infection as a single agent and alternating with zidovudine (AZT). *Lancet.* January 16, 1988;1:76–80.

21.   Meng TC, Fischl MA, Boota AM, et al. Combination therapy with zidovudine and dideoxycytidine in patients with advanced human immunodeficiency virus infection: a phase I/II study. *Ann Intern Med.* January 1, 1992;116(1):13–20.

22. Merigan TC, Skowron G, Bozzette SA, et al. Circulating p24 antigen levels and responses to dideoxycytidine in human immunodeficiency virus (HIV) infections. *Ann Intern Med.* February 1, 1989;110(3):189–194.

23. McNeely MC, Yarchoan R, Broder S, et al. Dermatologic complications associated with administration of 2′,3′-dideoxycytidine in patients with human immunodeficiency virus infection. *Journal of American Academy of Dermatology.* 1989;21:1213–1217.

24. Indorf AS, Pegram PS. Esophageal ulceration related to zalcitabine (ddC). *Ann Intern Med.* July 15, 1992;117(2):133–134.

25. Dezube BJ, Pardee AB, Chapman B, et al. Pentoxifylline (Trental) decreases tumor necrosis factor (TNF) and HIV replication in patients with AIDS. Presented at VIII International Conference on AIDS. Amsterdam, The Netherlands; July 1992.

26. Redfield RR, Birx DL, Ketter N, et al. A phase I evaluation of the safety and immunogenicity of vaccination with recombinant gp160 in patients with early human immunodeficiency virus infection. *N Engl J Med.* June 13, 1991;324(24):1677–1684.

27. Schwartz DH, Skowron G, Merigan TC. Safety and effects of interleukin-2 plus zidovudine in asymptomatic individuals infected with human immunodeficiency virus. *J AIDS.* 1991;4:11–23.

28. Bartlett JA, Blankenship KD, Greenberg M, et al. The safety of zidovudine and interleukin 2 in asymptomatic HIV infected patients. V International Conference on AIDS. Montréal, Québec, Canada; June 1989.

29. Rhame F. Immune serum. Presented at the 5th Annual Conference on Clinical Immunology. Chicago, IL; 1990.

30. Klimas NG, Fletcher MA, Walling J, et al. Phase 1 trial of adoptive therapy with purified CD8 cells in HIV infection. VIII International Conference on AIDS. Amsterdam, The Netherlands; July 1992.

31. Schmitt FA, Bigley JW, McKinnis R, et al. Neuropsychological outcome of zidovudine (AZT) treatment of patients with AIDS and AIDS-related complex. *N Engl J Med.* December 15, 1988;319(24):1573–1578.

32. Glatt AE, Chirgwin K, Landesman SH. Treatment of infections associated with human immunodeficiency virus. *N Engl J Med.* June 2, 1988;318(22): 1439–1448.

33. Lake-Bakaar G, et al. Gastropathy and ketoconazole malabsorption in the acquired immunodeficiency syndrome. *Ann Intern Med.* 1988;109:471–473.

34.   Jules-Elysee KM, Stover DE, Zaman MB, et al. Aerosolized pentamidine: effect on diagnosis and presentation of *Pneumocystis carinii* pneumonia. *Ann Intern Med.* May 15, 1990;112(10):750–757.

35.   The National Institutes of Health—University of California Expert Panel for Corticosteroids as Adjunctive Therapy for Pneumocystis Pneumonia. Consensus statement on the use of corticosteroids as adjunctive therapy for pneumocystis pneumonia in the acquired immunodeficiency syndrome. *N Engl J Med.* November 22, 1990;323(21):1500–1504.

36.   Division of AIDS. Important therapeutic information on prevention of recurrent *Pneumocystis carinii* pneumonia in persons with AIDS. Bethesda, MD: National Institute of Allergy and Infectious Diseases, National Institutes of Health; October 11, 1991.

37.   Bloom JN, Palestine AG. The diagnosis of cytomegalovirus retinitis. *Ann Intern Med.* December 15, 1988;109:963–969.

38.   Jacobson MA, Mills J. Serious cytomegalovirus disease in the acquired immunodeficiency syndrome (AIDS). *Ann Intern Med.* 1988;108(4):585–594.

39.   Palestine AG, Polis MA, De Smet MD, et al. A randomized, controlled trial of foscarnet in the treatment of cytomegalovirus retinitis in patients with AIDS. *Ann Intern Med.* November 1, 1991;115(9):665–673.

40.   Studies of Ocular Complications of AIDS (SOCA) and AIDS Clinical Trials Group. Mortality in patients with the acquired immunodeficiency syndrome treated with either foscarnet or ganciclovir for cytomegalovirus retinitis. *N Engl J Med.* January 23, 1992;326(4):213–220.

41.   Saag MS, Powderly WG, Cloud GA, et al. Comparison of amphotericin B with fluconazole in the treatment of acute AIDS-associated cryptococcal meningitis. *N Engl J Med.* January 9, 1992;326(2):83–89.

42.   Powderly WG, Saag MS, Cloud GA, et al. A controlled trial of fluconazole or amphotericin B to prevent relapse of cryptococcal meningitis in patients with the acquired immunodeficiency syndrome. *N Engl J Med.* March 19, 1992;326(12):793–798.

43.   Carr A, Tindall B, Brew BJ, et al. Low-dose trimethoprim-sulfamethoxazole prophylaxis for toxoplasmic encephalitis in patients with AIDS. *Ann Intern Med.* July 15, 1992;117:106–111.

44.   Kemper CA, Meng TC, Nussbaum J, et al. Treatment of Mycobacterium avium-complex bacteremia in AIDS with a four-drug oral regimen. *Ann Intern Med.* 116:466–472.

45.   Dautzenberg B, St. Marc T, Averous V, et al. Clarithromycin-containing regimens in the treatment of 54 AIDS patients with disseminated *Mycobacterium avium-intracellulare* infection. 31st Interscience Conference on Antimicrobial Agents and Chemotherapy. Chicago, IL; October 1991.

46.   Gordin F, Nightingale S, Wynne B, et al. Rifabutin monotherapy prevents or delays *Mycobacterium avium complex* (MAC) bacteremia in patients with AIDS. Presented at VIII International Conference on AIDS. Amsterdam, The Netherlands; July 1992.

47.   Cameron W, Sparti P, Pietroski N, et al. Rifabutin therapy for the prevention of M. avium complex (MAC) bacteremia in patients with AIDS and CD4 ≤ 200. Presented at VIII International Conference on AIDS. Amsterdam, The Netherlands; July 1992.

CARE AND MANAGEMENT OF PATIENTS WITH HIV INFECTION

Chapter 4: Legal Issues in the Treatment of Patients with HIV Infection

Janet B. Seifert, JD
Legal Medicine Center
Bethesda, MD

Frank T. Flannery, MD, JD
Chairman, Department of Legal Medicine
Armed Forces Institute of Pathology
Washington, DC

James G. Zimmerly, MD, JD, MPH
Legal Medicine Center
Bethesda, MD

CONTENTS

Introduction 141
Objectives 141
Recommended Preparation 141
Glossary 142
  I.   Overview of the Laws and Regulations Governing
      HIV-infected Persons 144
      A. Government Authority to Protect Citizens' Health 144
      B. Obligation to Report 144
      C. Criminal Liability 145
      D. Protection of Persons with HIV Infection and AIDS 146
      E. Significant Variation in Law Regarding HIV 146
      F. Disclosures of HIV Infection and AIDS 148
Review Questions (I) 150
  II. Testing and Treatment Issues 151
      A. Informed Consent 151
      B. Rationale for HIV Testing 152
      C. Reporting Test Results 154
      D. Warning Third Parties of HIV Infection Risk 154
Review Questions (II) 155
  III. Duty to Treat HIV-infected Persons 156
      A. Physician Obligation to Accept Patients 156
      B. Contractual Duties to Treat HIV-infected Persons 156
      C. Ethical Duties to Treat HIV-infected Persons 157
      D. Legal Duties to Treat HIV-infected Persons 157
Review Questions (III) 159
  IV. Confidentiality Issues and Disclosure of Patient
      HIV Infection to Third Parties 160
Review Questions (IV) 163
  V. Health Care Workers and Employees with HIV Infection 164
      A. Danger of HIV Infection from Health Care Providers 164
      B. Limiting the Risk of HIV Infection of Health Care
         Workers 164
      C. Employment Discrimination against HIV-infected
         Persons 165
      D. Limiting Risks to HIV-infected Employees and
         Coworkers 167
Review Questions (V) 170
Answers to Review Questions 172
References 173
Recommended Follow-up 176

INTRODUCTION

This chapter of *Care and Management of Patients with HIV Infection* is intended to provide health care workers with a summary of the laws and regulations that govern the care of HIV-infected patients and the employment of HIV-infected workers. This summary is provided for your information only and should not be relied upon for legal advice. The reader should consult his or her own attorney for legal advice concerning specific situations or legal matters.

OBJECTIVES

Objectives presented here are intended to focus the reader's attention on expected learning outcomes.

On completion of this chapter, the reader should be able to:

1.   Recognize the legal constraints on testing patients or health care workers for HIV.

2.   Describe the legal interests of HIV-infected patients that compete with those of health care workers.

3.   Describe the legal limits of refusing medical services to individuals or classes of persons.

4.   Explain the legal implication of HIV status as a handicap or disability.

5.   Identify the appropriate legal requirements of confidentiality in HIV testing and treatment.

6.   Describe the legal rights of HIV-infected health care workers.

RECOMMENDED PREPARATION

No specific preparation is necessary for this chapter. However, the reader is encouraged to become familiar with the terms and definitions in the following glossary and to review chapters 1 through 3 to gain a proper perspective for the legal issues involved in the care of HIV-infected patients.

GLOSSARY

Case law: legal principles applied to specific fact situations. Case law is drawn from judicial decisions in similar cases in a jurisdiction. Case law is used to make decisions based on precedent, which requires that similar cases be treated alike.

Civil liability: legal responsibility to compensate for losses or injuries caused by acts or failures to act. Compensation is awarded as money damages paid by the defendant to the injured party. By comparison, criminal liability is the legal responsibility imposed by the state for violation of the criminal laws. Consequences of criminal acts may include death, imprisonment, fines, and loss of property or privileges. Civil liability is limited to monetary damages; however, a single act may be both a criminal act and a civil liability failure (a tort).

Common law: the collection of legal principles and rules of law that are derived from decisions in cases; common law is also called case law. Much United States common law is derived from British common law.

Confidential communication: medical information given to health care providers in the course of diagnosis and treatment of an illness or injury. Providers are entrusted with the duty to keep the information from disclosure to third parties, subject to existing requirements of statute and case law.

Criminal liability: responsibility imposed when a criminal statute, regulation, or ordinance is violated. Once criminal liability is established, consequences provided by criminal statute or sentencing codes are imposed. Criminal liability is the legal consequence imposed by the state for violation of criminal law, an offense against the public interest in safety and liberty, and is not directed to compensating the losses of victims. Consequences of criminal acts may include death, imprisonment, fines, and loss of property or privileges.

Informed consent: a patient's agreement to permit diagnosis or treatment of an illness or injury based on the patient's knowledge of facts needed to choose whether or not to submit to the medical process considered. Informed consent is a patient's agreement to a medical procedure after risks, benefits, and alternatives have been discussed.

Invasion of privacy: any act that violates an individual's legally protected interest of privacy. Disclosure, without legal justification, of a medical condition could be such a violation. Invasion of privacy is a tort, for which civil liability damages are awarded to compensate for mental suffering or humiliation, or other losses of the person whose privacy was violated.

Ordinance: a rule established by the authority of the state, which is generally an enactment by the legislative body of a municipal corporation such as a city council or equivalent body.

Parens patriae: a term that refers to the role of the state as the sovereign and guardian of persons under the state's protection. It is the legal principle on which the state's power is based when it acts to protect the health, comfort, and welfare of persons who suffer from legal disabilities such as infancy or mental incapacity.

Physician-patient privilege: a rule of evidence by which communications made to a physician by a patient in the course of treatment may not be used as evidence in court. This privilege has not been recognized in all jurisdictions.

Police power: the power of the state to place restraints on certain personal freedoms and property rights of persons within the state for the protection of the public safety and health. Police power has certain limitations imposed by the United States Constitution and by state constitutions.

Regulation: a rule or order prescribed for the management of specific activities subject to government control. Regulations can be rules or orders issued by executive authority or by an administrative agency of government.

Statute: a written law enacted by the legislature to achieve a specified legislative objective. Statutes apply legislative prescriptions to some of the same fact situations dealt with by case law and administrative law. Generally, where a statute is applicable, former case law governing the situation is no longer operative.

⌐ I. OVERVIEW OF THE LAWS AND REGULATIONS GOVERNING HIV-INFECTED PERSONS

A. GOVERNMENT AUTHORITY TO PROTECT CITIZENS' HEALTH

The United States Constitution reserves the right of individual states to enact and enforce laws to protect the health and welfare of their citizens. This authority, known as "police power," also allows states to invest local bodies, such as county health departments, with regulatory and enforcement authority. Further justification for state action is provided by the *parens patriae* legal doctrine, expressing the role of the state as guardian. Under this doctrine, states may take reasonable measures to protect citizens' welfare.

B. OBLIGATION TO REPORT

Certain sexually transmitted diseases have been designated as reportable diseases and are considered to be of immediate public health importance. Physicians are required by statute to identify the disease and the patient and to submit this information to the local health department office.[1] Reportable disease entities may include tuberculosis, gonococcal infection, syphilis, AIDS, and other conditions that threaten public health.

Although there is no current consensus on the status of HIV infection as a reportable disease, all states require the reporting of AIDS cases. The term *HIV infection* describes the wide spectrum of disease caused by the human immunodeficiency virus (HIV). HIV infection includes the entire spectrum of the disease, starting with HIV exposure and infection and concluding with development of immunodeficiency symptoms and the ultimate diagnosis of AIDS. The term *AIDS* represents the latter stages of HIV infection, characterized by a T-cell count under 200 and the onset of opportunistic infections and cancers associated with the progression of HIV infection, as defined by the Centers for Disease Control (CDC).[2]

The particular immune system component subject to destruction by HIV is the CD4 lymphocyte, or T helper/inducer cell. One measure of determining the progression of HIV disease is to test for the number of CD4 cells per cubic millimeter of blood. The fewer CD4 cells present, the greater the progression of HIV disease. An HIV-positive diagnosis is based on finding HIV antibodies in the tested blood sample. An HIV-positive individual who also has one or more of the complications or opportunistic infections identified by the CDC is diagnosed as having AIDS. As more is learned about HIV disease, the CDC definition of AIDS may be revised. A possible diagnostic protocol would define AIDS as an immunological deficiency measured by a CD4 cell count below a specific value rather than by symptoms of one of the rare infections such as Kaposi's sarcoma or *Pneumocystis carinii* pneumonia.

Reports of contagious disease submitted by physicians, health care institutions, and laboratories are confidential and are not subject to public inspection. For example, the director of a medical laboratory may be required to report designated diseases within 48 hours of laboratory confirmation, as is the case in Maryland, but is prohibited from compiling reproducible lists of patients with positive test results. However, reports may be disclosed to other state agencies. Such agencies maintain confidentiality, but may require disclosure to prevent spread of infectious or contagious disease.[3] Regulations in some states, such as Arizona, Colorado, Idaho, Montana, South Carolina, and Wisconsin, also require laboratories to report positive HIV test results to a state agency. Other states, such as Georgia and Oregon, require epidemiological data, without patient identification.

Physicians may also be required to notify fire fighters, emergency rescue personnel, and funeral home personnel of their contact with patients who are diagnosed with certain contagious diseases.[4] Health care providers must consult their individual state's public health department or local statutes to determine if a separate law requiring notification exists.

C. CRIMINAL LIABILITY

As early as 1920, courts recognized that concealment and consequent transmission of a venereal disease could result in civil liability. Many jurisdictions have imposed criminal sanctions for the knowing exposure of another to a venereal disease. The status of liability or criminal penalty for endangering another by disease exposure may be found in individual state statutes or may be prescribed by case law decisions within a specific state.[5] Statutes already enacted that criminalize various forms of AIDS transmission include Fla Stat Ann §384.24 (prohibiting a person infected with HIV from having sexual intercourse without informing his partner of the infection); Idaho Code §39-601 (prohibiting a person with AIDS or an AIDS carrier from knowingly or willfully exposing another to HIV); Tenn Code Ann §68-32-104 (prohibiting AIDS carriers from donating blood); and Nev AB 550, ch 762, 1987 Laws (making practice of prostitution after a positive HIV test a crime of attempted murder).

Some prosecutors have already treated certain acts by AIDS carriers as violations of existing criminal laws. Several persons have been charged with such crimes as assault, attempted assault, reckless endangerment, and even attempted murder for allegedly biting or spitting at police or prison officers who had sought to restrain them while in custody. At least one man has been charged with attempted murder for selling blood when he knew he was seropositive.

Prosecutors have occasionally charged that sex acts by AIDS carriers amount to assault with a dangerous weapon, or attempted murder, and several servicemen have been court-martialed for risking transmission of HIV through sexual acts.

It is significant that actual transmission of HIV has not been shown in most of these prosecutions. Biting and spitting have not been identified as acts that can transmit AIDS, transmission of the AIDS virus through donated blood has been virtually eliminated through screening of the blood supply, and not all sex acts with an AIDS carrier transmit the virus. In these cases, states are criminalizing not harm but the risk of harm—and they are doing so in some situations where that risk is very slight.[5]

D. PROTECTION OF PERSONS WITH HIV INFECTION AND AIDS

Both federal and state laws address some of the problems that arise in providing health care for persons with AIDS or HIV-seropositive status.[6] (Under the law, all persons who are seropositive for HIV are entitled to the same protection, whether or not they manifest clinical AIDS.) These laws and the case decisions interpreting them affect the basic rights and duties of health care professionals and HIV-infected persons. Many of the legal issues that have an impact on HIV-infected patients are the same as those for all patients. The duty to treat by health care providers, the requirement or permission to test for contagious diseases, the duty to report specified diseases, and the duty to contact those who may be endangered by an infected person are all legal issues that have been addressed in regard to other contagious diseases. The rights of HIV-infected health care providers are subject to the same laws that safeguard the rights of anyone who may be discriminated against or otherwise treated unfairly in the workplace because of their disease or handicap or because they are perceived as having a contagious condition.[7]

E. SIGNIFICANT VARIATION IN LAW REGARDING HIV

To discover exactly what is permitted and what is required in any jurisdiction with regard to HIV-infected persons involves an examination of that jurisdiction's laws and cases and the regulations of the health authorities, as well as the national recommendations of the CDC or the Occupational Safety and Health Administration (OSHA). Specific duties and responsibilities are best provided by legal counsel in the jurisdiction where the questions arise, since major variations in laws dealing with AIDS exist among jurisdictions.

State law may require that health care workers provide emergency care to HIV-infected patients under certain circumstances.[8] In addition, the "antidumping" provisions of the Social Security Act require hospitals receiving Medicare and

Medicaid reimbursement that operate emergency rooms to provide needed emergency treatment to persons who present themselves for care.[9]

State laws governing the routine screening of patients for HIV infection vary significantly from state to state. A routine screening program may be permissible without violating antidiscrimination laws, provided that the screening is not used for purposes that would violate federal or state laws regarding the disabled or the civil rights of patients. For example, there are CDC guidelines for a provider who wishes to implement a routine screening program that may help prevent transmission of AIDS to health care providers in environments such as emergency departments or operating rooms.[10] Although adherence to guidelines cannot ensure that a program will be immune to legal challenge, it will protect the provider's interests. The following are important issues in routine screening:

- consent for testing;

- disclosure to patients of test results with counseling of HIV-positive patients by properly trained personnel;

- assurance of confidentiality to limit the knowledge of test results to those directly involved in the care of the infected patient or to those designated by law to have knowledge of such test results;

- assurance that identification of infected patients does not result in denial of care or the provision of substandard care; and

- maximum use of the program to reduce health care workers' exposure to the fluids of infected patients with minimum effect of such modified procedures on patients.

State law regarding informed consent to medical care in general applies to procedures, including testing, performed on HIV-infected patients. State law may require that patients be told that a test will be performed and that information be provided about the purpose of the test and the use of test results.[11] The CDC recommends that universal precautions be used for all patients whether or not infected with HIV,[10] although health care providers may still feel more protection is afforded by being aware of those patients who have tested positive for HIV.

Protecting the interests of health care providers while safeguarding the rights of patients has been addressed by federal law, as well as by differing jurisdictional laws of the 50 states. The Federal Rehabilitation Act requires employers accepting federal contracts to take affirmative action to employ and advance qualified handicapped individuals and prohibits discrimination against qualified handicapped individuals. Since AIDS is considered a handicap or disability under the Federal Rehabilitation Act and the Americans with Disabilities Act of 1990, all their provisions apply to HIV-infected individuals.

The Intergovernmental Health Policy Project of George Washington University has monitored state laws with regard to AIDS. Such legislation deals with a variety of issues, such as voluntary AIDS testing, discrimination against those with AIDS or HIV-positive status, HIV in the schools, and AIDS research. The project reports that a number of states, including California, Maine, Massachusetts, Missouri, New Jersey, and Oregon, have specifically declared AIDS to be a protected handicap under state law. Colorado, Connecticut, Delaware, Illinois, Maryland, Minnesota, New Hampshire, New Mexico, Rhode Island, and Texas have concluded, generally, that AIDS is a handicap for which protection will be granted under state law.

F. DISCLOSURES OF HIV INFECTION AND AIDS

Once an individual is known to be infected with HIV, a duty may arise to notify third parties at risk. This notification or warning may not be the duty of the health care provider but of state authority, as for reportable diseases.

When reporting of HIV infection is not required under state reporting laws, other state and federal laws apply to balance the interests of the HIV-infected person against the interests of persons who may be at risk of infection from that person as well as the interests of the public. Although there is no current consensus on the reportability of HIV infection, all states require that AIDS cases be reported to the appropriate public health authority.[12] A health professional who fails to report a case of AIDS is subject to and may be held liable to a plaintiff who contracts the disease, if failure to report causes the plaintiff to contract the disease.[12]

Except for required notification, it is the health care provider's ethical and legal duty to preserve the confidentiality of medical information. State statutes define the physician-patient privilege,[12] and professional and health facility licensure laws also require medical information confidentiality.[12]

Virtually every American jurisdiction has recognized the privilege of confidentiality through legislation or through case law. State statutes and accrediting agencies have imposed parallel obligations on health care facilities.[12] State licensing laws extend to health care professionals the duty to maintain the confidentiality of medical information.[12] The general rationale for requiring confidentiality is the public interest in encouraging patients to furnish complete information needed to diagnose and provide appropriate care. Sometimes disclosure of HIV infection, in spite of the patient's interest in confidentiality and privacy, must be made to safeguard an even more important interest, such as life or health, of another individual. To be legally appropriate, the disclosure must be based on valid risk data. Disclosure based on speculative or unscientific beliefs of risk are not protected. The following are some examples of statutes that provide for notification of third parties of a subject's positive test results:

- an Arkansas law by which a victim of a sex offense may be told the results of the offender's HIV test[13];

- a Louisiana law requiring a doctor to notify a hospital or nursing home on admission of a patient known to be HIV infected[14];

- a Maryland law which allows notification of sexual and needle-sharing partners[15]; and

- laws in other states which allow notification of school authorities, parents, and spouses.[16]

In addition to safeguarding medical information, additional protection has been recognized for information about treatment for AIDS. These added protections have been developed because of the special public interest in encouraging individuals to seek and receive treatment. This rationale also applies to persons infected with HIV. Although there is no cure for AIDS, confidentiality protection encourages individuals to submit to voluntary testing, counseling, treatment, and research. There is both individual and community benefit if HIV-infected persons can be treated and experimental drugs, therapies, and vaccines can be tested.

Where no risk is shown to outweigh privacy interests, case decisions and statutes have been used to protect the confidentiality of HIV antibody test results. An example is protection of identity of HIV-positive blood donors.[12] California, Florida, Hawaii, Kentucky, Maine, Massachusetts, Wisconsin, and New York City, among others, also have recognized and protected confidentiality of HIV records.[12]

Medical information is routinely disclosed under a standard general release form signed by the patient. Such a release is applicable to insurance companies, third-party payers, and a number of other agencies and organizations. A standard release form is generally not sufficient to authorize disclosure of information pertaining to AIDS or HIV-positive status because many statutes have been enacted and special protection recognized for HIV-positive persons and their privacy interests. Request for execution of a specific release of HIV test status information is appropriate.

REVIEW QUESTIONS (I)

DIRECTIONS. Circle the letter corresponding to the correct response in each of the following.

1. Which of the following is *not* a legal source for health care providers' duties toward HIV patients?

   a. federal regulations
   b. state laws
   c. the United States Constitution
   d. the Library of Congress regulations

2. Which of the following does *not* provide authoritative advice regarding medical treatment of HIV-infected patients?

   a. federal law
   b. legal counsel
   c. state law
   d. all of the above

3. Discrimination against the handicapped and disabled, including HIV-infected persons, is forbidden by federal law.

   a. true
   b. false

4. Laws regarding treatment of AIDS patients are significantly different from laws governing treatment of HIV-positive patients.

   a. true
   b. false

Check your responses on page 172.

II. TESTING AND TREATMENT ISSUES

While the AIDS epidemic is relatively new, the legal issues presented by this disease entity are not. Our legal system has struggled for years to balance the individual's right to privacy with the public's right to protection by identification of infectious disease carriers. Guidelines for the release of test results that indicate possible infection with HIV are therefore inextricably linked to concerns of confidentiality. Release of positive test results can trigger discrimination from more than one source: because the disease itself engenders fear and rejection, and because of discrimination against the behaviors associated with HIV acquisition such as homosexuality and intravenous drug use.

A. INFORMED CONSENT

Voluntary screening to ascertain the patient's HIV antibody status is performed at the request of the patient or at the recommendation of the physician. Health care personnel are commonly required to obtain the patient's informed consent before testing. This doctrine is rooted in the principle that adults of sound mind have a right to determine what will be done with their own bodies. An exception to this requirement is the treatment of patients in an emergency setting, where testing or treatment is required for the preservation of the life or health of the patient.

Withdrawal of a blood specimen for determination of HIV antibody status does not represent the traditional surgical procedure entailing a physical invasion. Nonetheless, unlike ordinary blood tests, a positive HIV test result may have far-ranging negative implications. Some state legislation requires patient consent before testing.[17] Informed consent to testing involves providing information about the mechanics of testing and its uncertainties, and about the duplicating of a positive or negative result. Massachusetts, for example, expressly forbids health care facilities, physicians, or other health care providers from conducting HIV testing without first obtaining written informed consent to conduct the test.[12]

The extremely negative consequences which can result from a positive HIV test are the basis for requiring a patient's informed consent before performing an HIV test. To offer or urge HIV testing and to counsel before and after the test regarding the results recognizes the important interests of the tested individual. Nonconsensual testing has been proposed in many contexts, but has only been found justified where serious and imminent risks to the life or health of others are at issue. The few examples are prisoners, military service members, convicted prostitutes, applicants for immigration, and police officers or fire fighters who have been exposed to blood or body fluid from an individual suspected of being HIV infected. Health care workers should become familiar with relevant statutes in their jurisdiction. Even in the absence of such legislation, a patient's consent may be obtained, and counseling should be provided both before and after the results are known.

B. RATIONALE FOR HIV TESTING

HIV testing may offer multiple potential benefits to the individual and the public health. First, an individual testing HIV positive will have the opportunity to receive medical care, which can improve both the quality and quantity of his or her life. Second, public health may be protected through the education of HIV-infected persons with subsequent reduction in risk behaviors and prevention of further infections, and through the identification, testing, treatment, and counseling of their sexual or needle-sharing contacts. However, the implementation of testing programs must balance these potential benefits to individual and public health against the social and psychological consequences of HIV testing and the significant financial cost associated with widespread testing. Therefore, certain populations may be targeted for testing on the basis of real or perceived risk for the acquisition of HIV. These populations frequently include persons with a history of risk behavior (e.g., homosexuality, heterosexual contact with someone at risk for HIV, heterosexual contact with multiple partners, or history of intravenous drug use), and may be extended to include all hospital patients, health care workers, and other groups.

Most experts agree on the need to offer voluntary HIV testing to persons with a history of risk behavior. However, the routine testing of other populations generates more controversy. The CDC recently completed a study of routine HIV testing among hospitalized patients, and suggested that 110,000 new HIV infections could be diagnosed through the routine HIV testing of all hospitalized patients in the United States between the ages of 15 and 54. Of note, establishing these 110,000 diagnoses would require performing a large number of HIV antibody tests at a significant annual cost. In light of the projected extraordinary expense, the CDC concluded that routine HIV testing may be most cost efficient in hospitals with one new AIDS case per 1,000 admissions.

The routine testing of health care workers has been advocated both from the perspective of a health care worker's risk in providing care to HIV-infected patients and from the perspective of the need to protect noninfected patients from HIV-infected health care workers. Health care workers may be at risk for acquiring HIV from their infected patients after a needle-stick or other sharp instrument injury, or from exposure to HIV-infected blood on nonintact skin or mucous membranes. The risk to health care workers has been recognized as real, but fortunately the relative risk is quite low. The implementation of universal blood and body fluid precautions and the proper disposal of needles and sharp instruments have served to minimize the number of exposures to HIV-infected patients. However, some organizations still propose routine testing of all hospital admissions for the protection of the health care workers providing their care.

The need for protection of patients from HIV-infected health care workers has stirred great interest since the report of a Florida dentist who reportedly transmitted HIV to five patients. This report was followed by a flurry of calls for the routine testing of all health care workers, severe restrictions on those health care workers who tested HIV positive, and criminal penalties for those HIV-infected health care workers who fail to abide by their restrictions. Since this isolated report, the careful epidemiologic investigation of many other HIV-infected health care workers performing invasive procedures has been completed, including the HIV testing of over 15,000 of their patients. No other case of HIV transmission from health care worker to patient has been documented.

On the basis of these observations, the risk of HIV transmission in the health care setting is extremely low, and therefore the legal justification for compulsory screening is weak. Both private institutions and public hospitals could also find that compulsory screening of all patients would be challenged as an infringement of individual privacy and personal liberties without medical or social justification. Mandatory testing of health care workers has been the subject of much scientific and legal dispute. A facility policy in Nebraska requiring testing for mental health facility employees was opposed by the employees. The federal court concluded that the risk of HIV transmission from health care workers to their patients was minuscule, and the policy had no rational basis.[18]

Proposals for compulsory or nonconsensual testing or for management of testing and use of test result data have been offered in a number of areas, such as marriage license applications, arrests for sexual or drug offenses, prisoners, hospital patients and employees, immigrants, mental health facility residents and employees, and military members. Some have been enacted into law in Illinois, Colorado, Utah, Washington, Michigan, California, Rhode Island, and Massachusetts.[11] The George Washington University Intergovernmental Health Policy Project continues to monitor state-by-state AIDS and HIV legislative activity.

Generally, it is acknowledged that the public health goal of preventing AIDS transmission is not furthered by group-based testing, since knowledge of HIV status is more likely to discourage those seeking care and to invite discrimination by others. The compulsory and even nonconsensual testing of suspected HIV-positive individuals in the interests of persons exposed to a risk of HIV transmission is more favored by recent laws. A number of states have enacted laws which permit testing when a person, such as a fire fighter, health care worker, or police officer, has suffered an exposure event.[11] Exposure testing of this type depends on an ascertainable exposure to an identifiable person. Such laws have been adopted in Washington, Wisconsin, and California.[11]

C. REPORTING TEST RESULTS

Traditionally, certain infectious diseases have been designated as reportable diseases and are considered to be of immediate public health importance. Depending upon the law of each jurisdiction, physicians may be required by statute to inform the local health department of disease and patient. For example, reportable diseases in the state of Maryland include diagnoses of gonococcal infection, syphilis, and confirmed cases of AIDS.[19] An HIV-positive individual who also has one or more of the complications or opportunistic infections identified by the CDC is diagnosed as having AIDS. Although all states require the reporting of AIDS cases, not all states require the reporting of positive HIV test results. In certain states, such as Arizona, Colorado, Idaho, Montana, South Carolina, and Wisconsin, patients with a positive HIV antibody test must be reported.[12] As more has been learned about HIV disease, the CDC definition of AIDS has been revised.[2] Practitioners should obtain the specific reporting requirements in their jurisdictions, and monitor changes as requirements are revised.

D. WARNING THIRD PARTIES OF HIV INFECTION RISK

Whether practitioners are receiving screening test results or actually treating AIDS patients, they may face the issue of a duty to warn third parties and potential contacts of HIV-infected individuals in order to protect them against infection. Both old and new court decisions have recognized a duty to warn family members about the transmission risk of certain contagious diseases such as scarlet fever.[20] Courts have also recognized a psychotherapist's general duty to warn an intended victim when the patient makes known his intention to harm that third party.[21] Reasoning by analogy, sexual partners of HIV-infected patients can be endangered by continued relations, and therefore it could be inferred that there may be a duty to inform such parties of the risk of contracting HIV infection. Many states now require the notification by health care providers of spouses of HIV-infected persons, after unsuccessful counseling of the HIV-infected patient to do so.[22]

Balancing warning disclosure against patient confidentiality is often difficult. Whether health care personnel will be liable for damages in cases of failure to warn third parties is not settled law at this time. In the absence of a clear legal duty to disclose test results, it is appropriate to inform and persuade infected individuals that they may have a duty to inform other persons who may be at risk.

REVIEW QUESTIONS (II)

DIRECTIONS. Circle the letter corresponding to the correct response in each of the following.

1. Informed consent for HIV testing

    a. is legally mandated in every state.
    b. is rooted in the principle that individuals have the right to determine what will be done with their own bodies.
    c. is not very important.
    d. is not necessary in Massachusetts.

2. Voluntary HIV testing

    a. requires consent and consultation with the patient's attorney.
    b. should be performed only after obtaining the patient's informed consent.
    c. requires that patients be identified to public health authorities.
    d. yields highly unreliable results.

3. AIDS is a reportable disease.

    a. true
    b. false

4. In some states, prison inmates and applicants for immigration and naturalization may be subjected to compulsory HIV testing.

    a. true
    b. false

Check your responses on page 172.

III. DUTY TO TREAT HIV-INFECTED PERSONS

Under the common law rule, a health care provider may refuse to enter into a treatment agreement with a patient suffering from any condition that the health care provider does not wish to treat. The provider may even withdraw from treating the patient, provided the patient's condition is stable and the patient is given adequate opportunity to locate alternative health care providers.

The refusal of some health care providers to treat patients infected with the AIDS virus is one of the many painful symptoms produced by the fear of this fatal disease. The AIDS epidemic has caused a reexamination of both the legal and the ethical issues surrounding a health care provider's duty to treat. A workable policy recognizes and provides for the safety concerns of the health care professionals and ensures that access to adequate health care is available to patients regardless of their diagnosis.

A. PHYSICIAN OBLIGATION TO ACCEPT PATIENTS

Historically, the physician's duty to treat existed only after the creation of a physician-patient relationship. Since the relationship was consensual, there was no duty to treat until the physician had agreed to treat the individual patient. Even after there was a duty, the physician's obligation was limited to treating the patient for the specific conditions for which the physician had accepted the patient. Physicians traditionally have had the right to limit the scope of their medical practice.

In determining whether a duty to treat exists, one must consider the nature of the physician's practice. The physician in private practice has greater flexibility in deciding which patients to accept and which to reject. From a medical practice perspective, a private physician is ethically and morally free to choose whom to treat. Until physicians agree to enter into a physician-patient relationship, they are free to limit their medical practice in any manner. Health care providers may exclude certain diseases or medical conditions from their practice at any time, although they may choose to continue treating particular patients. To state that a physician does not treat AIDS is not to say that the physician does not treat patients who have AIDS.

B. CONTRACTUAL DUTIES TO TREAT HIV-INFECTED PERSONS

The legally-supported choices of a private practitioner to refuse to accept any patient is modified when the physician is under contract, to either a group health plan or to a hospital, to provide care for all patients referred to that health care facility. Under these contractual circumstances, the health care provider may not refuse care to any category of patients. If an emergency department physician, under contract with the hospital to provide services to all emergency patients, refuses care, that physician violates a contractual duty to both the hospital and to the patients who arrive at the emergency department expecting care.

C. ETHICAL DUTIES TO TREAT HIV-INFECTED PERSONS

The vast majority of health care providers recognize a personal obligation to treat patients regardless of their disease, even at risk to themselves. However, at the national level, the American Medical Association's code of ethics is not completely clear on the subject. The 1846 code contained a provision that admonished health care providers that "when pestilence prevails, it is their duty to face the danger, and to continue their labors for the alleviation of the suffering, even at the jeopardy of their own lives." However, since 1912, the AMA's code of ethics has also contained the statement, "A physician shall in the provision of appropriate patient care, except in emergencies, be free to choose whom to serve . . . ." Recently, the AMA's Council on Ethical and Judicial Affairs has taken the position that physicians may not ethically refuse to treat AIDS patients solely because of seropositivity.

While several professional health care organizations have adopted policies affirming the health care provider's ethical obligation to treat AIDS patients, these policies have not been uniformly adopted by state medical organizations, which control professional conduct within their boundaries. The primary focus of traditional medical ethics is the duty the physician owes to the medical profession, as well as to the patient. A breach of a state code of professional ethics may carry no formal sanctions other than loss of membership in the association, although it could also result in loss of licensure.

D. LEGAL DUTIES TO TREAT HIV-INFECTED PERSONS

Because a few health care providers have hesitated to treat HIV-infected patients, the federal government and several states have enacted legislation to ensure that all patients receive the requisite medical care. Certain of these statutes have been interpreted as covering persons with AIDS, since these patients are considered to be handicapped within the meaning of the Federal Rehabilitation Act and the Americans with Disabilities Act. Section 504 of the Federal Rehabilitation Act of 1973 prohibits discrimination by any program or activity that receives federal financial assistance. Most states have similar antidiscrimination laws that protect the handicapped, and many states have now concluded that AIDS constitutes a handicap for purposes of state antidiscrimination statutes.

The United States Supreme Court's decision in *School Board of Nassau County, Florida v. Arline*[23] defines the Federal Rehabilitation Act of 1973's use of the term *handicap* broadly enough to include persons who are HIV infected, although that case dealt with a person with tuberculosis, not HIV infection or AIDS. In addition, recent federal decisions have held that because Medicare and Medicaid funds constitute federal assistance, for purposes of the Rehabilitation Act, physicians and hospitals are subject to federal law prohibiting handicap discrimination. If they refuse to treat AIDS patients, they may be liable under the act.[24] While the hospital-employed physician might avoid personal liability under Section 504 of the Federal Rehabilitation Act of 1973, because he is not in a position to accept or reject federal monies, the hospital cannot avoid sanctions if it accepts Medicare and/or Medicaid funds.[25] The Americans with Disabilities Act prohibits discrimination in employment, public services, and public accommodations.[26]

In summary, the health care provider's duty to treat HIV-infected patients varies from jurisdiction to jurisdiction and depends significantly on the nature of the health care provider's practice and affiliation agreements. In a growing number of localities within the United States, physicians have a legal and ethical obligation to treat patients without discrimination as to disease. This obligation is tempered by the specialty of the physician and the environment in which that physician practices. While the private-practice physician in some states may refuse to treat HIV-infected patients without being in violation of any ethical guidelines, in other states ethical directives would apply. Physicians who are hospital-based or working under an employment contract with a group health plan must examine that contract to determine whether any patients may be rejected from their personal care. Hospital bylaws may impose additional obligations on health care providers when they treat HIV-infected patients in a hospital setting.

Statutes are constantly being revised and new court decisions issued regarding HIV infection. The best solution is to combine ethical principles with sound patient care practices. When dealing with any patient with a known or suspected infectious disease, risks to everyone associated with the patient are reduced by enforcing appropriate infectious disease safety protocols.

REVIEW QUESTIONS (III)

DIRECTIONS. Circle the letter corresponding to the correct response in each of the following.

1. All health care providers must treat HIV-infected patients in every jurisdiction or risk loss of medical licensure.

   a. true
   b. false

2. AIDS has been considered to be a handicap or disability under certain federal and state statutes.

   a. true
   b. false

3. Under Section 504 of the Federal Rehabilitation Act of 1973,

   a. all patients with AIDS must be offered employment.
   b. health care workers with AIDS must be given a paid leave of absence.
   c. patients with AIDS may not be discriminated against.
   d. patients with AIDS may not be employed in the health care industry.

4. The duty to treat HIV-infected patients is purely a moral or ethical issue and does not involve the law.

   a. true
   b. false

5. AIDS patients are exceptions under federal and state regulations dealing with discrimination.

   a. true
   b. false

Check your responses on page 172.

IV. CONFIDENTIALITY ISSUES AND DISCLOSURE OF PATIENT HIV INFECTION TO THIRD PARTIES

State governments have enacted laws to safeguard confidentiality of test results to encourage voluntary testing. Some state laws, such as Massachusetts's, bar release of test results without the consent of the subject.[27] Other state laws, such as those of Missouri, New York, Florida, and California, permit limited disclosure of positive results without consent to notify spouse or HIV-transmission activity partners.[28] Some states offer anonymous test sites, which guarantee confidentiality by having no identifiable subject records.

There may be a clear statutory duty to report HIV antibody test results. Even in the absence of statute, court decisions have recognized that societal interests could take precedence to permit disclosure of a contagious disease such as syphilis, where failure to disclose could lead to disease transmission. Without statutory authority or a compelling societal interest, disclosure of a patient's HIV antibody status may not be permissible and may subject the physician to liability. Because unauthorized disclosure can prove detrimental and subject a patient to various forms of discrimination, some states have enacted legislation that specifically prohibits disclosure of HIV test results.[29] Practitioners should become aware of the statutory provisions regarding disclosure of HIV test results in their particular jurisdiction.

Consent to testing and acceptance of disclosure of test results is primarily the burden of the test subject. The social aspects of positive HIV testing significantly affect the individual's privacy interests. Any mandatory testing plan is enacted with the intention of disclosure of test results to third persons. Numerous people may share the knowledge of the subject's HIV status—the party fearing transmission from exposure, public health officials, contact-tracing personnel, employers, insurers—many of whose interests directly conflict with the subject's. Protection of test subjects' privacy interests and their employment and access to services has been furthered by federal and state laws prohibiting disclosure, or discrimination after disclosure, of HIV-positive or AIDS status.

The subjects of confidentiality and disclosure raise serious questions for health care personnel. In the absence of clear statutory guidance, existing law leaves many important questions unanswered. At a minimum, it is appropriate to advise infected individuals to disclose their status to third parties who may be at risk of contracting the disease. Pertinent advice regarding avoidance of transmission would also seem to be required. The known failure of an infected individual to disclose his or her status to third parties continues to present a dilemma. On the one hand, a physician's failure to disclose this information to other health care workers, the patient's spouse, or others at risk could conceivably subject him to liability for failure to warn. On the other hand, a careless or overly broad disclosure of such information could conceivably subject the same physician to liability for causing the patient serious economic or psychological harm.

Confidentiality of medical data is protected by common law and by Constitutional rights to privacy, as well as confidentiality statutes enacted by states and state health facility licensure laws. There are exceptions to the right of privacy or confidentiality. Such situations involve a more important interest than the individual right of privacy. For example, disclosure is permitted to hospital personnel involved in medical treatment for their protection and for the patient's welfare. Certain public interests are also considered to take priority over an individual's right to privacy. Among these public interests are the reporting of contagious diseases, child abuse, and medical evidence of criminal acts, as well as the potential threat to another person from the conduct of a patient.

Disclosures which are exceptions to the rule of confidentiality are subject to specific requirements that limit how and to whom disclosure is made. Disclosure of accurate information to a proper authority or agency and disclosure of only information which is appropriate will be protected from assertions of defamation, invasion of privacy, or breach of confidentiality. Disclosure of erroneous test results, disclosure of true but private medical test findings, or proper disclosure but to an improper party, can result in legal liability for the harm to employment status, mental state, and privacy itself caused by the report.

An example of the balancing of interests that must be made is the tension between confidentiality of HIV test results and public danger from HIV infection. Proponents of limiting disclosure to treating health care personnel are countered by those who urge that positive HIV test results be reported to public health authorities. State law can vary on accessibility of such results, and proposals are numerous in many states to deal with the privacy interests of HIV-infected individuals which compete with the public health interests of the uninfected population.

Laboratories must report positive HIV tests to public health agencies in some jurisdictions.[30] Failure to report subjects the laboratory supervisor to fines or imprisonment and may also result in liability to third parties.

Recommendations relating to laboratory data in HIV testing include[31]:

- No HIV testing should be performed without verification of informed consent.

- Verbal requests for HIV antibody testing should not be accepted. Only those requests that can be shown to have originated with appropriate informed consent should be accepted for analysis.

- Informed consent documents should be maintained by the requesting clinician. The laboratory should receive verification of consent that bears the signature of the physician, but not the signature of the patient.

- Whenever and wherever practical and when allowed by state law, patient identification should be accomplished without the use of names. Special request forms should be developed that provide laboratory staff with only alphanumeric code numbers.

- All records bearing identifiable patient information should be maintained in secured files. Access should be restricted to a need-to-know basis only. Access logs should be maintained and periodically reviewed.

- The laboratory should provide the practitioner with necessary documents to ensure compliance with public health reporting regulations. All information should be completed by code number, and the attending physician should provide patient-specific data. Envelopes should be provided in pre-addressed form, ready for mailing.

Procedures to maintain confidentiality in insurance claim processing must also be considered by the clinician. This information also should be reviewed with the patient along with the specific meaning of release of information statements that accompany most insurance forms. The patient then should decide if insurance billing is desired for this particular test. All documents associated with insurance claim processing should be secured.

REVIEW QUESTIONS (IV)

DIRECTIONS. Circle the letter corresponding to the correct response in each of the following.

1. A physician's duty to warn potential contacts of HIV-infected individuals is

    a. absolute.
    b. always governed by statute.
    c. not well settled.
    d. well known.

2. Appropriate counseling of an HIV-infected person about disclosures is

    a. unnecessary until AIDS is diagnosed.
    b. required only for married partners.
    c. to specifically inform all possible contacts of the infection.
    d. that all notification will be done by health department personnel.

Check your responses on page 172.

V. HEALTH CARE WORKERS AND EMPLOYEES WITH HIV INFECTION

A major health care employment issue is whether employers, particularly health care employers, may screen employees for HIV infection and refuse to employ, may terminate employment, or may limit employment of people who are seropositive. The CDC estimates that 5.5% of all HIV-positive people are employed in the health care field, making health care services one of the largest single industry groups affected by this issue.

A. DANGER OF HIV INFECTION FROM HEALTH CARE PROVIDERS

Since there is a very remote possibility of HIV transmission during a surgical procedure, health care workers who are known to be HIV infected might be advised to refrain from participating in certain surgical procedures. Not only would the health care provider risk personal liability by continuing to operate in such circumstances, the hospital may be found liable for permitting a health care provider with HIV infection to continue to operate. The patient will argue that performance of surgery by a surgeon with a communicable disease exposes the patient to added and unnecessary risk, without informed consent to assume that risk. While patients accept the risk of certain infections attendant to surgery, the risk of receiving an infection directly from a surgeon is not regarded as a normal risk associated with surgery. Hospitals can be liable for negligence in allowing infected health care providers to continue to function. Courts have long held hospitals liable for injuries caused by the illness of health care providers.

B. LIMITING THE RISK OF HIV INFECTION OF HEALTH CARE WORKERS

When a health care provider is found to be seropositive, or develops AIDS, the hospital may review that person's staff privileges or scope of employment and determine whether or not the medical condition interferes with the ability to perform on the job and whether the condition creates a health risk to patients. The health care provider's performance should be regularly monitored and evaluated in terms of protecting patients.

There is no generally accepted medical evidence that HIV can be transmitted through normal day-to-day contact in typical private workplace settings. The CDC has issued guidelines that recognize that, with the exception of health care workers and personal service workers (e.g., tattoo artists) who use instruments that pierce the skin, no testing or restriction is indicated for workers known to be infected with HIV but are otherwise able to perform their jobs. Since present medical evidence indicates that HIV-infected individuals pose virtually no threat of infection to fellow workers, HIV-positive persons in most settings must be permitted to continue their employment as long as they are able to perform their jobs. Termination of employment would be a violation of federal and certain state statutes. Such workers are also entitled to protection from harassment by co-workers and/or supervisors and managers under federal antidiscrimination statutes.

The CDC has recognized that certain direct patient care areas such as surgery may create an increased risk of transmission of HIV from physician to patient. While the CDC does not recommend that HIV-positive individuals be routinely restricted from performing surgery, it does recommend that restrictions be determined on a case-by-case basis. The health care provider could be given other duties in the hospital that involve lesser degrees of direct patient care, or could be required to use extra safety precautions while working with patients. Duty reassignment or restriction must be based on valid risk of HIV transmission. By allowing the HIV-infected provider to continue employment with this accommodation, patients' health interests are protected and the provider's employment is maintained. The Americans with Disabilities Act does not require that patients be put at risk to allow HIV-infected personnel to continue employment.

C. EMPLOYMENT DISCRIMINATION AGAINST HIV-INFECTED PERSONS

The Federal Rehabilitation Act of 1973 prohibits discrimination against qualified handicapped individuals by agencies that receive federal financial assistance.[32] This includes almost all hospitals. The statute defines handicapped as including an individual who has a record of, or is regarded as having, a physical or mental impairment that substantially limits one or more major life activities. Since employment is considered to be a major life activity under the statute, a worker would be substantially limited if he or she experienced difficulty in obtaining or maintaining employment because of a handicapped condition, namely, HIV seropositivity.

State agencies administering handicapped or disability discrimination laws also maintain that an individual is entitled to be free from discrimination as long as he or she can perform the job without reasonable probability of substantial injury to self or others, or can do so with reasonable accommodation not imposing undue hardship on the employer. State statutes also protect the HIV-infected patient from discrimination in the workplace.

The United States Supreme Court has held that the victim of a contagious disease may be covered by the Federal Rehabilitation Act. Although a case dealing with an HIV-infected person under the Federal Rehabilitation Act has not been brought, it is highly likely that a patient with AIDS or HIV infection would be considered handicapped under the Rehabilitation Act. In the *Arline* case, the court held that a person who poses a significant risk of communicating an infectious disease to others in the workplace would not be otherwise qualified for his or her job if reasonable accommodation would not eliminate that risk. Another case, *Leckelt v. Board of Commissioners of Hospital District No. 1*,[33] arose in Louisiana. A hospital employee was terminated for failure to comply with hospital policies regarding disclosure of HIV exposure. Discrimination was not found by the court because the employee was not fired for HIV status, but for failure to comply with hospital rules, which made him "not otherwise qualified," as the law requires.

The Americans with Disabilities Act of 1990 (ADA)[26] prohibits discrimination on the basis of disability in employment, public services, transportation, public accommodations, and telecommunications. All employers must comply by July 1994, with small groups phased in over time. The ADA extends protection to many disabled who are not protected by state antidiscrimination laws, and it is not limited to government employment and contracting; it applies to private employers as well.

In determining whether there is a significant risk of contagion to others, the employer must consider reasonable medical judgments by public health officials about the following factors:

- the nature of the risk (how the disease is transmitted);
- the duration of the risk;
- the severity of the risk (the potential harm to third parties); and
- the probability that the disease will be transmitted.

The health care employer reviewing an employee or applicant with AIDS, ARC, or HIV seropositivity, who is otherwise qualified for the position, must consider two factors. The first is whether the individual is able to perform the essential functions of the job in question, and if not, whether the person could perform the job with reasonable accommodation by the employer. The second is whether the individual poses a significant risk of infecting others in the work-place, and if so, whether that risk could be eliminated with reasonable accom-modation on the part of the employer. The safety of coworkers and patients has long been recognized as a legitimate concern under federal and state discrimi-nation statutes.

Since, according to present medical theory, there is virtually no risk of HIV transmission in non–health care workplace settings, any termination of employ-ment in that environment would be difficult for an employer to defend. Similarly, it would be difficult for a health care employer to justify any mandatory screen-ing of health care workers for presence of antibodies to the virus. This is particularly true since the CDC generally disapproves of such general screening programs and recommends that universal blood and body fluid precautions be employed for all patients to minimize the transmission risk of any infectious disease.

D. LIMITING RISKS TO HIV-INFECTED EMPLOYEES AND COWORKERS

Depending on the requirements of the particular employee's job, even after the employer has made reasonable accommodation, the risk of danger to the HIV-infected employee may justify certain employment restrictions, such as reassignment out of a patient care area and away from dealing with certain patients whose diseases may be communicable. It may be prudent, for instance, to restrict an HIV-infected employee from dealing with certain infectious diseases because the employee's impaired immune system increases the risk of acquiring or experiencing severe complications of infectious diseases. However, an employer would not be justified in not hiring or terminating employment of employees based on anticipated future absenteeism. Since asymptomatic people who are HIV-positive may be disease-free for many years, they would be unjustly precluded from working for a substantial period of time. CDC guidelines for limiting transmission of HIV infection in the health care setting are published and updated to reflect current medical knowledge of HIV.[34]

State health departments must either adopt CDC guidelines for AIDS transmission prevention in health care by 28 October 1992, or adopt their own equivalent measures. CDC has proposed requiring infected professionals to get permission from review panels before performing certain invasive procedures, and to inform patients of their HIV status.

Employers have a general duty to provide a safe working environment; under the Occupational Safety and Health Act (OSHA), employers have a responsibility to eliminate or minimize employee exposure to HIV. OSHA's standards dealing with AIDS in the workplace are covered in regulations entitled "Occupational Exposure to Bloodborne Pathogens."[35] An OSHA program of inspection and enforcement monitors the use of infection control precautions in the health care setting.[36] These precautions follow the universal blood and body fluid precautions for infection control that have been recommended by the CDC. By following these recommendations the employer complies with the duty to provide a workplace free from hazards which would cause death or serious bodily injury.

The OSHA standards dealing with exposure to bloodborne pathogens apply to all occupational exposure to blood or other potentially infectious materials. Bloodborne pathogens are defined as pathogenic microorganisms present in human blood and which cause disease in humans. These pathogens include, but are not limited to, hepatitis B virus (HBV) and human immunodeficiency virus (HIV).

The regulations, published in 29 Code of Federal Regulations §1910.1030, became effective March 6, 1992. The scope of the standards includes definitions of materials, incidents, controls, procedures, personnel, exposure, protective equipment, and facilities. The standards set by the final regulations require exposure control; set methods of compliance; define HIV and HBV research laboratories and production facilities; require hepatitis vaccination and post-exposure evaluation and follow-up; specify mandatory communication of hazards to employees through signs and labels and information and training; prescribe record keeping of medical and training records; and provide for protected availability and transfer of records.

In exposure control, employers are required to establish an exposure control plan which includes exposure determinations, schedule and method of implementation, and a procedure for evaluation of exposure incidents. Exposure determination must list job classifications for which all employees have occupational exposure, job classifications for which some employees have exposure, and all tasks or procedures in which employee exposure may occur.

For methods of compliance, general use of universal precautions is required, as well as use of engineering and work practice controls, personal protective equipment, and housekeeping practices to limit or minimize occupational exposure. The regulations specify for HIV and HBV research laboratories and production facilities use of standard and special practice in isolation and housekeeping training.

Hepatitis vaccination and postexposure evaluation and follow-up are mandated in the standards. Confidential medical evaluation and follow-up must include documentation of route and circumstances of exposure and identification and documentation of the source individual, unless infeasible or prohibited by law. Testing of the source individual's blood is specified, with consent, or without consent if allowed by law. Results of source individual testing are to be made available to the exposed employee, along with counseling regarding the legal limits on disclosure of the identity and status of the individual. The standards and copies of medical exposure evaluations are required to be given to the exposed employee, including a health care professional's opinion and recommendations for postexposure evaluation and follow-up.

Mandatory communication of hazards to employees through signs and labels and information and training are specified. Prescribed record keeping of medical and training records include sequestered and confidential measures to protect employees' privacy interests.

OSHA inspections focus on certain areas of high risk, including emergency departments, other direct patient care areas, laboratories, x-ray, laundry, and housekeeping. Failure to provide a safe workplace can result in fines for each violation.

Under the Occupational Safety and Health Act and analogous state statutes, employers may not discriminate against employees who make bona fide safety complaints.[37] Regulations for implementing this statute ban discrimination against individuals who in good faith refuse to expose themselves to conditions they reasonably believe are dangerous.[38] Under the National Labor Relations Act, if an employer fails to communicate adequately the lack of danger from working with HIV-infected coworkers, that employer may have limited ability to discipline or discharge workers who believe erroneously, but in good faith, that they are being exposed to a health hazard.

Health care workers who become infected with HIV on the job may have a claim for compensation under applicable state workers' compensation acts. The various workers' compensation acts were set up as no-fault recovery systems intended to remove from the traditional tort system all injuries sustained in industrial accidents. However, a health care worker who contracted AIDS on the job could still attempt to bring a traditional civil liability action against the health care employer. Grounds for such an action would be that the employer was negligent in failing to identify hospital patients infected with HIV and that such failure constituted sufficiently reckless misconduct to remove the job-related disease from the workers' compensation act, thus removing the employer's statutory immunity from suit. Hospitals can further protect employees, and employees can protect their own interests, by purchase of group or individual disability coverage.

To minimize work force disruption over the presence of HIV-infected individuals and to preserve the ability to respond to violations with appropriate discipline, employers must educate both managers and the general work force with the medical facts about HIV infection as they are presently understood. The employer should emphasize that there is no significant risk of AIDS virus transmission in the ordinary course of work. Further, employers should stress that any harassment, discrimination, or refusal to work with individuals infected with the virus or believed to be infected will result in appropriate disciplinary action.

REVIEW QUESTIONS (V)

DIRECTIONS. Circle the letter corresponding to the correct response in each of the following.

1. Health care employers are required to employ a person who is HIV-seropositive; however, there is no legal requirement to continue to employ a person once he or she has developed ARC or AIDS.

    a. true
    b. false

2. Occupational Safety and Health Act regulations require that

    a. employees working in a health care setting be regularly screened for HIV seropositivity.
    b. HIV-seropositive patients be isolated in designated hospital wards.
    c. hospital employees who are seropositive be removed from positions requiring direct contact with patients.
    d. universal infection control precautions be employed in all cases.

3. Hospital employees who contract AIDS as a result of an on-the-job injury may receive monetary compensation through

    a. hospital disability insurance programs.
    b. state workers' compensation act.
    c. tort litigation against the health care employer for failing to warn of the existence of a known infected patient.
    d. all of the above.

4. CDC recommendations include

    a. informing patients of the seropositivity of their surgeons.
    b. monitoring the risks of procedures performed by HIV-seropositive surgeons.
    c. permitting HIV-seropositive surgeons to perform only procedures in which blood transfusions are not likely.
    d. revoking the surgical privileges of any HIV-seropositive surgeon.

5. OSHA guidelines require that hospitals

   a. establish educational and training programs about infection control precautions.
   b. provide employees appropriate personal protective equipment.
   c. provide testing and other services to employees who sustain exposures.
   d. adopt standard operating and monitoring procedures designed to reduce exposures.
   e. all of the above.

Check your responses on page 172.

ANSWERS TO REVIEW QUESTIONS

I		IV	
1.	d	1.	c
2.	d	2.	c
3.	a		
4.	b	**V**	

II

		1.	b
		2.	d
1.	b	3.	d
2.	b	4.	b
3.	a	5.	e
4.	a		

III

1.	b
2.	a
3.	c
4.	b
5.	b

REFERENCES

1. For example: Maryland, MD Ann Code Health Gen §18-201 et seq.

2. Centers for Disease Control. 1993 revised classification system for HIV infection and expanded surveillance case definition for AIDS among adolescents and adults. *MMWR*. December 18, 1992;41(RR-17).

3. For example: Maryland, MD Ann Code Health Gen §4-305, in which disclosure is permitted where organ donation is involved.

4. For example: Maryland, MD Ann Code Health Gen §18-213.

5. Discussion and analysis of such law is provided in: Sullivan and Field. AIDS and the coercive power of the state, 1988, 23 *Harv CR-CL L Rev*. 139.

6. The most significant federal law is the Americans with Disabilities Act of 1990, 42 USCS §12101 et seq; for state legislation, see: Gostin LO. Public health strategies for confronting AIDS: legislative and regulatory policy in the United States. *JAMA*. 1989;261:1621–1630.

7. ADA, 42 USCS 12101 et seq.

8. Dickens BM. Legal rights and duties in the AIDS epidemic. *Science*. 1988; 239:580–586.

9. 42 USCA §1395dd (Suppl 1987).

10. Centers for Disease Control. Recommendations for prevention of HIV transmission in health-care settings. *MMWR*. 1987;36(2S).

11. Eisenstat S. An analysis of the rationality of mandatory testing for the HIV antibody: balancing the governmental public health interests with the individual's privacy interest. 1991, 52 *U Pitt L Rev*. 327.

12. McDonald BA. Ethical problems for physicians raised by AIDS and HIV infection: conflicting legal obligations of confidentiality and disclosure. 1989, 22 *UC Davis L Rev*. 557.

13. Ark Code Ann §16-82-101 (c).

14. LA Stat Ann 40 §1300.11 et seq.

15. MD Ann Code Health Gen §18-337.

16.   Smith JM. AIDS symposium: legal issues confronting families affected by HIV. 24 *J Marshall L Rev.* 543, at FN67.

17.   See, for example, California Health and Safety Code §199.22 (West 1987).

18.   *Glover v. Eastern Nebraska Office of Retardation*, 686 F.Supp. 243 (D. Nebraska 1988).

19.   MD Ann Code Health Gen §18-205.

20.   *Skillings v. Allen*, 143 Minn. 323, 173 NW 663 (1919). See also *DiMarco v. Lynch Homes*, 1990 WL 197807 (Pa. 1990) [a physician's failure to adequately warn a patient of the risk of third-party transmission of a communicable disease could result in liability of that physician to the third party].

21.   *Tarasoff v. Regents of the University of California*, 131 Cal. Rptr. 14, 551 P.2d 334 (1976).

22.   MD Ann Code Health Gen §18-337, for example. See note 15.

23.   *School Board of Nassau County, Florida v. Arline*, 107 S. Ct. 1123 (1987).

24.   *United States v. Baylor University Medical Center*, 736 F.2d 1039, 1042 (5th Cir. 1984), cert. denied, 469 U.S. 1189 (1985).

25.   *Glanz v. Vernick*, 1991 WL 15130 (D. Mass).

26.   42 USCA 2000e et seq; Regulations 29 CFR 1601.1.

27.   Mass Gen Laws Ann, ch 111, §70F.

28.   MO ST §191.656; NY Pub Health §2780(10); FL ST §381.004; CA Health and Safety Code §199.25.

29.   See, for example, California Health and Safety Code §199.21 (c).

30.   For example, MD Ann Code Health Gen §18-207.

31.   Wecht CH. Considerations and potential pitfalls in AIDS lab testing. *Journal of Legal Medicine.* 1988;9(4):623–635.

32.   Rehabilitation Act of 1973 (29 USCA §701 et seq).

33.   Vash LA. *Leckelt v. Board of Commissioners of Hospital District No. 1*, 909 F.2d 820 (5th Cir. 1990) [forced disclosure for HIV infected health care workers]. *Tul L Rev.* June 1991;1722(65).

34.   See Centers for Disease Control. Guidelines for preventing the transmission of tuberculosis in health-care settings, with special focus on HIV-
related issues. *MMWR*. 1990;39(RR-17).

35.   29 USCA §651–678; 29 CFR Part 1910.1030.

36.   52 *Federal Register* 41818-01 (October 30, 1987).

37.   29 USCA §660 (c)(1).

38.   29 CFR §1977.12 (b)(2).

RECOMMENDED FOLLOW-UP

In addition to the material listed in the References section, the reader may wish to consult the following sources:

Barnes M, Rango NA, Burke GR, Chiarello L. The HIV-infected health care professional: employment policies and public health. *Law Med & Health Care*. Winter 1990;311(18).

Barney JH. A health care worker's duty to undergo routine testing for HIV/AIDS and to disclose positive results to patients. *La L Rev*. March 1992; 933(52).

Closen ML. Mandatory disclosure of HIV blood test results to the individuals tested: a matter of personal choice neglected. *Loy U Chi L J*. Winter 1991;445(22).

Eisenstat S. An analysis of the rationality of mandatory testing for the HIV antibody: balancing the governmental public health interests with the individual's privacy interest. *U Pitt L Rev*. Winter 1991;327(52).

Fitzpatrick RB, Benaroya EA. Americans with Disabilities Act and AIDS. C669 ALI-ABA 555, December 5, 1991.

Lieberman KC, Derse AR. HIV positive health care workers and the obligation to disclose: do patients have a right to know? *J Leg Med*. September 1992;333(13).

Margolis RE. Hospitals may not discriminate against AIDS-infected health care workers. *HealthSpan*. May 1992;16(9 No. 5).

Margolis TE. Health care workers and AIDS: HIV transmission in the health care environment. *J Leg Med*. September 1992;357(13).

Reed BS. Testing health care workers for aids. *J Contemp Health L & Policy*. Spring 1992;237(8).

Vash LA. *Leckelt v. Board of Commissioners of Hospital District No. 1*: Forced disclosure for HIV infected health care workers. *Tul L Rev*. June 1991; 1722(65).

CARE AND MANAGEMENT OF PATIENTS WITH HIV INFECTION

Chapter 5: The Role of the Physician in the Care of Patients with HIV Infection

Ross E. McKinney, Jr, MD
Assistant Professor of Pediatrics and Microbiology
Duke University Medical Center

Harry A. Gallis, MD
Associate Professor of Medicine
Duke University Medical Center

CONTENTS

Introduction   181
Objectives   181
Recommended Preparation   182
   I.   Overview: The Physician and the Patient with HIV Infection   183
  II.   Initial Evaluation of a Patient with HIV Infection   185
 III.   Case Studies of Patients with HIV Infection   187
      A. Case 1: A 30-year-old Carpenter with Adenopathy   187
      B. Case 2: A 26-year-old Woman with Weight Loss,
          Fatigue, and Amenorrhea   193
      C. Case 3: A Newborn Child of an HIV-positive Mother   200
      D. Case 4: A 40-year-old Postman with Skin Lesions   207
Summary   215
References   215
Recommended Follow-up   215
Continuing Medical Education Posttest   216
Continuing Medical Education Posttest Answer Sheet   223

INTRODUCTION

This is chapter 5 of *Care and Management of Patients with HIV Infection*. This chapter is recommended for physicians who desire a review of their role in treating patients with HIV infection and AIDS. The prevalence of HIV infection has increased dramatically in most areas of the United States within the last five years. Hence, it is likely that all physicians will encounter situations involving HIV testing, counseling, referral to other physicians, and the direct care of patients with asymptomatic and symptomatic HIV disease. The purpose of this chapter is to give the physician basic information regarding the more important issues related to HIV, primarily through case study examples.

OBJECTIVES

Objectives presented here are intended to focus the reader's attention on expected learning outcomes.

On completion of this chapter, the reader should be able to:

1. Identify groups of patients at risk for HIV infection.

2. Describe the therapy plan for a patient who presents with lymph-adenopathy alone.

3. Recognize the association of autoimmune cytopenias, such as thrombocytopenia, and HIV disease.

4. Describe the counseling procedures for a patient in the early stages of HIV infection.

5. Outline the differential diagnosis of early HIV.

6. Summarize the implications of pregnancy in the treatment of an HIV-infected patient.

7. Identify the rate of transmission of HIV infection to newborns and its implications for therapeutic abortion.

8. Review the management of varicella exposure in a nonimmune person with HIV infection.

9. Describe some of the problems associated with intravenous drug abuse, particularly in pregnant women.

10. Explain the need to evaluate a patient with infection for sexually transmitted diseases and tuberculosis.

11. Identify the effects of pregnancy on the course of HIV disease.

12. Describe the difficulties in making a diagnosis of HIV infection in newborns.

13. Review problems and life-expectancy information for children with HIV infection.

14. Summarize the treatment options for HIV-infected children, including

    - antiretroviral therapy,
    - opportunistic infections,
    - early treatment for fevers, and
    - vaccination issues.

15. Describe the clinical picture and treatment options for a patient with

    - Kaposi's sarcoma,
    - cytomegalovirus retinitis, and
    - toxoplasma encephalitis.

16. Present approaches to a patient who does not comply with the treatment regimen.

RECOMMENDED PREPARATION

Since this chapter contains a continuing education posttest that is comprehensive of chapters 1 through 4 as well as chapter 5, the reader is encouraged to review the first four chapters, which cover the pathophysiology, diagnosis, and treatment of acquired immunodeficiency syndrome and its associated infections.

I. OVERVIEW: THE PHYSICIAN AND THE PATIENT WITH HIV INFECTION

The practicing physician will encounter many different situations involving HIV infection. These situations include counseling individuals at low risk who request an HIV test, following individuals known to be infected with HIV, treating patients presenting with pneumocystis pneumonia, and dealing with the chronic and devastating features of the terminal phases of AIDS. Since this disease is so complex, both in terms of management and in terms of the emotional toll, the physician must work closely with patients and others involved in their care.

Although many different individuals are involved in the care of HIV-related illnesses, two broad groups predominate: caregivers in the home (lovers, spouses, parents, volunteers) and health care professionals (a complex partnership of specialists and primary care physicians, nurses, physicians' assistants, nurse practitioners, social workers, and clinical pharmacists).

Primary care physicians who encounter or follow HIV-infected patients will therefore be called upon to counsel patients about prognosis and the risk of various sexual behaviors, to give advice about beginning therapy with anti-retroviral drugs, to diagnose a variety of opportunistic infections, to collaborate with AIDS specialists in long-term care, to monitor side effects and toxicities of drugs, and to give sensitive care to dying people. The physician's greatest reward in this unpleasant task is the quality of the interaction.

With the miracles of modern medicine, health care professionals seem to have become complacent about the risks of health care delivery. At one time, it was accepted that special risks existed. Prior to the 1950s, it was known that caring for patients with diseases such as tuberculosis, polio, diphtheria, and typhoid fever carried some risk. Clearly this was an occupational exposure that was noted and accepted. Even in the era of antibiotics and "miracle drugs," some risks persist. The most common example is hepatitis B (200,000 health care professionals were infected in 1986–87). Even though the case fatality rate is lower, more health care professionals will die each year from hepatitis B than from occupationally acquired AIDS. Nonetheless, the perceived risks of occupational exposure to HIV have led to prejudicial attitudes in the care of AIDS patients. In areas of moderate to high prevalence of the disease, these prejudices and fears have generally waned with increased experience on the part of the health care providers.

The actual risk from needle-stick exposure or blood spatter appears to be less than 1%.[1] If infection control policies had been strictly enforced, many of these exposures would not have occurred. No barrier method is currently foolproof, but the risk can be minimized with appropriate infection control policies and a full understanding of the modes of HIV transmission.

Unless we acknowledge that risk exists and that current technology cannot eliminate this risk, fear will remain high. It is reassuring, however, that after 12 years of this epidemic the number of health care workers infected has remained small. Adherence to current infection control policies is likely to keep this number low, but continued education and open discussion of fears will be needed to ensure adequate health care delivery.

II. INITIAL EVALUATION OF A PATIENT WITH HIV INFECTION

The role of the physician in the treatment of those infected with HIV is complex. Physicians should have a high index of suspicion of early manifestations of HIV disease. Physicians should learn to elicit a thorough sexual and drug history, focusing particularly on high-risk behaviors by the patient and his or her partner(s). With this knowledge the physician can help the patient decide whether to be tested for HIV infection. The physician can also take this opportunity to counsel the patient on modifications of high-risk behavior. It is extremely important that physicians counsel all patients, whether HIV-infected or not, with regard to preventive techniques. It is worthwhile to point out, for example, that unprotected intercourse may be lethal for the infected person's partners. This point is particularly worth making to adolescents. In contrast, there is no reason to emphasize the route of HIV transmission if someone already feels guilty about infecting their partner.

Once a diagnosis of HIV infection is made, the physician must be prepared to deal with a patient who is facing an inevitably fatal disease. Even though AIDS may not manifest itself for a decade or more, the patient's first thought is that he or she is soon going to die. Reviewing the long natural history of HIV disease can help remedy this, but the patient still must live under the weight and foreknowledge of probable premature death. The patient's anxiety level around the time of diagnosis is extreme: every ache, cough, or sniffle is thought to be the first sign of AIDS. The physician must be there to evaluate, reassure, or diagnose.

Confidentiality becomes a prime concern. The patient's livelihood, housing, and insurance may be at risk. The prejudices already experienced by those with high-risk behaviors are compounded. Federal legislation exists (the Americans with Disabilities Act) to protect patients from losing their jobs and housing, but even with improved legal protections, confidentiality is still critical. Procedures for maintaining patient confidentiality should be periodically reviewed with office staff.

Telling loved ones about HIV can be very painful. The family or spouse may not be aware of the patient's life-style, and the physician may be called upon to help inform them. Issues of confidentiality are frequently difficult to navigate when, for example, a bisexual male may have exposed his wife and refuses to divulge this to her. Similar issues may arise related to promiscuity or drug use. Most states have laws that govern the reporting of AIDS cases and identification of sexual contacts. This information is available through state medical societies and state communicable disease offices.

When the patient requires hospitalization during the course of the disease, the physician may also be needed to mediate interaction with hospital personnel. Most hospitals are quite experienced in HIV care and have established procedures. The physician may wish to consult a hospital social worker early during the course of admission or consult a physician experienced in various aspects of AIDS care. These individuals can provide useful information about insurance, post-hospital care, outpatient intravenous therapy, support groups, and hospices.

The next section of this chapter will lead the physician through several practical issues relating to HIV infection. It is intended to supply information concerning several common scenarios in which many misconceptions still exist.

III. CASE STUDIES OF PATIENTS WITH HIV INFECTION

Since treatment of HIV infection and its subsequent medical conditions is complex, the following case histories are provided for adult and pediatric patients, both early in the course of the disease and as the disease progresses. After laboratory or physical findings are presented, questions are provided to help you analyze the data. You are encouraged to think through the answers first before proceeding with the text.

A. CASE 1: A 30-YEAR-OLD CARPENTER WITH ADENOPATHY

HISTORY OF PRESENT ILLNESS

P.A. is a 30-year-old single, white male carpenter from the Washington, DC area who presents complaining of a three-week history of painless bilateral axillary lymphadenopathy. He otherwise feels well, with a normal appetite, stable weight, and no fevers.

PAST MEDICAL HISTORY

Unremarkable. His only past hospitalization was for a tonsillectomy and adenoidectomy in 1969. His only physician contacts have been in sexually transmitted disease clinics, where he has been treated several times for gonorrhea and nonspecific urethritis.

SOCIAL HISTORY

P.A. absolutely denies the use of intravenous drugs. He admits to an "active" social life since a divorce four years ago, but he denies homosexual behaviors. On further questioning, he estimates that he has five to seven new sexual partners each month, usually women that he "picks up" in bars. Some of these women have been prostitutes. He has not traveled out of the Maryland-Virginia region in several years.

PHYSICAL EXAM

P.A. is a healthy-appearing, slightly overweight male.

Vital Signs: T 37.0°   BP 125/70   PR 76   RR 16

Skin: Scattered petechiae on the face, hands, and lower extremities.

Neck: Bilateral posterior cervical adenopathy, with many 15 × 10 mm nodes.

Thorax: Bilateral axillary adenopathy, with 30 × 20 mm node clusters which are not tender to palpation.

Abdomen: Spleen tip palpable 2 cm below the left costal margin. Multiple inguinal nodes, 15 × 10 mm bilaterally.

SELF-STUDY QUESTION

1. Other than HIV infection, initial differential diagnosis for P.A.'s illness includes all of the following *except*

    a. Crohn's disease.
    b. infectious mononucleosis.
    c. lymphoma.
    d. systemic lupus erythematosus (SLE).

DISCUSSION

The initial differential diagnosis includes several possibilities:

*   HIV infection

*   Infectious mononucleosis (Epstein-Barr virus, cytomegalovirus, or *Toxoplasma gondii*)

*   Neoplasm, particularly lymphomas and leukemias

*   Autoimmune diseases such as systemic lupus erythematosus

Other infectious processes that might produce generalized adenopathy, like disseminated bacterial infections, are unlikely in a well-appearing, afebrile adult.

SELF-STUDY QUESTION

2. Diagnosis could be clarified by ordering a

    a. head CT scan.
    b. HIV ELISA.
    c. serum magnesium level.
    d. upper GI radiograph.

LABORATORY RESULTS

Complete Blood Count

Hemoglobin: 12.3 g/dL

Hematocrit: 37.0%

White Blood Count: 4,500/mm^3

Differential

Segs:	76%
Lymphs:	14%
Monos:	3%
Eosin:	7%

Platelet Count: 20,000/mm^3

Sedimentation Rate: 15 mm/hr

Mono Spot Test: Negative

Urinalysis: Normal

Chest X-Ray: Normal bones. Cardiovascular silhouette normal in size and shape. Moderate bilateral hilar adenopathy. Lung fields clear.

SELF-STUDY QUESTIONS

3. How do these laboratory results affect the initial diagnosis?

    a. Hilar adenopathy is consistent only with lymphoma and HIV infection.
    b. Negative mono spot test reduces the probability of Epstein-Barr virus disease.
    c. Normal sedimentation rate rules out SLE.
    d. The thrombocytopenia rules out HIV infection.

4. Additional titers should be ordered for all of the following *except*

    a. anti-dengue antibodies.
    b. anti-EBV antibodies.
    c. anti-platelet antibodies.
    d. CMV.

DISCUSSION

These results include several interesting findings. P.A. is thrombocytopenic and mildly anemic. He is also lymphopenic, with an absolute lymphocyte count of 630. The hilar adenopathy could be consistent with any of the diagnoses listed above. The negative mono spot and normal sedimentation rate tend to reduce the probability of Epstein-Barr virus disease or systemic lupus erythematosus.

After getting the results of the screening labs, a number of other tests are ordered. The results are available a few days later.

LABORATORY RESULTS

FANA (Fluorescent Anti-nuclear Antibodies): Negative

Whole Hemolytic Complement (CH50): Normal

HIV Antibodies by ELISA: Positive

HIV Antibodies by Western Blot: Positive

PPD Skin Test: Negative

EBV Titers

   IgG to Virus Capsid Antigen: 1:320

   IgM to Virus Capsid Antigen: <1:10

   Anti-EBNA: 1:5

   Anti-Early Antigen: <1:5

   Interpretation: Consistent with previous EBV disease.

CMV Titer: 1:256

Toxoplasma gondii **Titer:** Negative

VDRL: Negative

FTA-Abs: Positive

Lymphocyte Subtyping

CD4: 20%   Absolute CD4 Count $126/mm^3$

CD8: 60%   Absolute CD8 Count $378/mm^3$

T4/T8 Ratio: 0.33

Anti-platelet Antibodies: Positive

SELF-STUDY QUESTIONS

5. On the basis of these laboratory results, you can conclude that

    a. further tests are needed.
    b. the patient has active CMV disease.
    c. the patient has HIV infection.
    d. the patient has HIV infection and autoimmune thrombocytopenia.

6. P.A.'s CD4 lymphocyte count indicates that all of the following are true *except*

    a. he is at high risk for *Pneumocystis carinii* pneumonia.
    b. he has less than six months to live.
    c. he would benefit from starting antiretroviral therapy.
    d. his HIV infection is more advanced than his symptoms indicate.

7. On the basis of his CD4 lymphocyte count, you should

    a. begin IVIg injections.
    b. begin prophylaxis for *Pneumocystis carinii* pneumonia.
    c. give him varicella vaccine.
    d. withhold zidovudine therapy.

8. What, if anything, would you do about P.A.'s FTA-Abs and VDRL?

    a. No treatment is required.
    b. The patient will require more aggressive therapy than usual.
    c. Treatment should be given only if the patient has not had previous treatment.
    d. Treatment should be repeated regardless of previous treatment history.

9. Treatment options for P.A.'s immune thrombocytopenia include all of the following *except*

    a. acyclovir.
    b. high-dose immunoglobulin.
    c. splenectomy.
    d. zidovudine.

DISCUSSION

These results confirm the patient's primary diagnosis: HIV infection. The HIV ELISA and Western Blot are very accurate tests, with an excellent predictive value in patients in whom HIV is suspected. P.A. has a negative skin test for tuberculosis. Patients should have a PPD on initial evaluation. However, false negative skin tests can occur in patients with low CD4 counts (< 300). P.A.'s CD4 lymphocyte count suggests that his HIV is more advanced than his symptoms would indicate. Adult patients whose CD4 counts are below 200 are at an increased risk for *Pneumocystis carinii* pneumonia (PCP) sufficient to warrant prophylaxis, either with trimethoprim/sulfamethoxazole (TMP/SMX) [the preferred option if the patient can tolerate it], or with aerosolized pentamidine. Research on PCP prophylaxis is continuing, and other alternatives like dapsone and atovaquone may become more widely used if they prove to be effective.

P.A. has a positive FTA-Abs and negative VDRL. This pattern is consistent with a previous exposure to syphilis. A positive FTA-Abs and positive VDRL would have indicated recent or active disease, requiring treatment if not previously administered.

P.A.'s immune thrombocytopenia (confirmed by the anti-platelet antibodies) is a fairly common finding in HIV. The reason for the high incidence of auto-antibodies in HIV-infected people is not yet established, although B-cell regulation is probably faulty. Therapeutic options include corticosteroids, high-dose intravenous immunoglobulin (IVIg), zidovudine, intravenous RhoGAM (currently on research protocol), and splenectomy. The relative risks and benefits of each option are still being studied.

Zidovudine is the only currently licensed antiretroviral agent with an FDA-approved indication as first-line therapy for the treatment of HIV infection. P.A.'s low CD4 lymphocyte count warrants treatment with zidovudine at this point in his course. Most clinicians would begin a regimen of:

1. Zidovudine—100 mg q4h 5 times a day (the nighttime dose can be skipped).

2. Trimethoprim/sulfamethoxazole—one double-strength tablet (160 mg TMP/800 mg SMX) three times weekly *or* aerosolized pentamidine (300 mg once a month)

Because of the hematologic toxicity of zidovudine, the patient's blood counts should be monitored closely, especially the hemoglobin and neutrophil count. Since P.A. is thrombocytopenic, his platelet count should also be watched carefully.

The time to initiate *Pneumocystis carinii* prophylaxis is subject to physician judgment. Most physicians begin when one or more of the following conditions are met:

- The absolute CD4 count is less than 200
- The percentage of CD4 lymphocytes is less than 20%
- The patient has any AIDS-defining condition

The choice between TMP/SMX and aerosolized pentamidine for PCP prophylaxis depends on the patient's preferences and ability to tolerate TMP/SMX. Many HIV-infected individuals have severe cutaneous and/or systemic reactions to TMP/SMX. The treatment is much cheaper than aerosolized pentamidine, and there are now studies which clearly indicate that TMP/SMX is more effective when tolerated. In addition, the pharmacokinetics of aerosolized pentamidine have not been studied sufficiently to develop dosing schedule guidelines for children.

B. CASE 2: A 26-YEAR-OLD WOMAN WITH WEIGHT LOSS, FATIGUE, AND AMENORRHEA

HISTORY OF PRESENT ILLNESS

Jennifer is a 26-year-old white, previously healthy, waitress from rural North Carolina who presents with an eight-week history of fatigue and a ten-pound weight loss. The latter is due in part to nausea, anorexia, and occasional morning vomiting. She is sexually active, and reports multiple sexual partners (mostly truck drivers). A gravida 0, she suspects she could be pregnant since her last menstrual period was 12 weeks earlier. She takes oral contraceptives, but admits that she has been forgetful about them lately. She denies that she has used intravenous drugs, although she has a history of *Serratia* endocarditis 18 months ago. At that time she was tested for HIV and was seronegative by ELISA.

Jennifer recalls that roughly a year ago she had an episode of fever, sore throat, and fatigue. She went to the local emergency room where she was told she had infectious mononucleosis. The physician told her to return to the local health department for follow-up, but she began to feel better in a few weeks and never went back.

PAST MEDICAL HISTORY

Jennifer has been treated multiple times for sexually transmitted diseases (gonorrhea, chlamydia, syphilis), and she takes acyclovir regularly when the early symptoms of genital herpes simplex recur.

SOCIAL HISTORY

Jennifer lives by herself in an apartment a block from her work, a truck stop near I-95. She is of low normal intelligence and does not drive a car. She is estranged from her parents, allegedly because of her mother's disapproval of Jennifer's lifestyle. There is no steady boyfriend. She states that if she is pregnant, she has no idea who the father is.

PHYSICAL EXAM

Jennifer is a thin, pale, worn-appearing woman.

Weight: 47 kg (103 lbs) Height: 160 cm (5'3")

Vital Signs: BP 120/75 PR 88 RR 20

HEENT: Within normal limits.

Lymph Nodes: 10–15 mm nodes in the posterior cervical, axillary, and inguinal regions.

Chest: Breasts tender, appear mildly engorged.

Lungs and Cardiovascular: Normal.

Abdomen: Liver palpable 2 cm below the right costal margin. Spleen tip palpable.

Neuro: Grossly intact. Mental status exam demonstrates limited intellectual capability.

Pelvic: Normal external genitalia. Vaginal and cervical mucosa have a mildly blue coloration (Chadwick's sign). The uterus is enlarged to the level of the pubis (consistent with 12 to 14 weeks gestational age).

Skin: Scars on the arms, hands, and feet consistent with intravenous drug use.

LABORATORY TESTS

Complete Blood Count

Hemoglobin: 10.1 g/dL

Hematocrit: 30.0%

White Blood Count: 6,300/mm^3

Differential

Segs:	60%
Lymphs:	37%
Monos:	2%
Eosin:	1%

Platelet Count: 270,000/mm^3

Urinalysis: Normal

Urine Pregnancy Test: Positive

Chemistries

Electrolytes: Within normal limits

Glucose (non-fasting): 150

AST (SGOT): 50 U

ALT (SGPT): 65 U

Bilirubin: 0.2 mg/dL

DISCUSSION

The laboratory results confirm that Jennifer is pregnant. As you discuss the results of her pregnancy test, Jennifer is clearly pleased. Since there are several other laboratory results pending, you tell Jennifer that you will see her again in a week, during which time she should consider whether she wants to continue her pregnancy, and whom she would like to go to for her obstetrical care. Because of her pregnancy and anemia, a multivitamin with iron is prescribed. A PPD skin test is placed, and Jennifer is instructed to come by your office in 48 hours to have it read.

The infectious mononucleosis-like syndrome experienced by Jennifer a year ago could have been the acute HIV syndrome. Unless serum is available from before that episode it will not be possible to be certain whether the episode was HIV related or due to one of the other causes of infectious mononucleosis like EBV or CMV.

SELF-STUDY QUESTION

10. In addition to Jennifer's pregnancy, you should plan to evaluate her for all of the following *except*

    a. hepatitis A.
    b. hepatitis B.
    c. rubella immune status.
    d. venereal diseases (syphilis, gonorrhea).

FURTHER LABORATORY RESULTS

HIV Serology

ELISA: Positive

Western Blot: Positive

Rubella Serology: Seropositive

Cytomegalovirus Serology: Seropositive

VDRL: Negative

Hepatitis B Serological Testing

Hepatitis B Surface Antigen: Negative

Hepatitis B Surface Antibody: Positive

Cervical Cultures

Gonorrhea: Negative

Chlamydia: Negative

Lymphocyte Subtyping

CD4: 40%   Absolute CD4 Count: 932/mm^3

CD8: 50%   Absolute CD8 Count: 1,166/mm^3

T4/T8 Ratio: 0.8

PPD: Read as negative.

SELF-STUDY QUESTIONS

11.   In counseling Jennifer about her pregnancy, you should inform her that

    a.   her fetus is almost certainly HIV infected already.
    b.   HIV infection is less likely if the baby is delivered by cesarean section.
    c.   no single factor or factors predict the risk of HIV transmission to her fetus.
    d.   the risk of her fetus being infected is about 20% to 30%.

12.   All of the following support a history of drug abuse in this patient *except*

    a.   antibodies to hepatitis B surface antigen.
    b.   CMV seropositivity.
    c.   history of *Serratia* endocarditis.
    d.   needle tracks.

13.   Which therapy is appropriate for Jennifer now?

    a.   intravenous pentamidine.
    b.   no treatment.
    c.   sulfa drugs.
    d.   zidovudine.

DISCUSSION

Jennifer's situation illustrates several important points. She is HIV infected, as demonstrated by the ELISA and Western Blot, and has only mild symptoms (lymphadenopathy, splenomegaly, and perhaps very mild hepatitis), but may still transmit the virus to her fetus. The current estimates are that 20% to 30% of pregnancies in HIV-infected women will result in an HIV-infected newborn. In order to estimate the probability of HIV transmission during any given pregnancy, studies of a variety of maternal factors (age, race, route of HIV acquisition, state of HIV disease, etc.) have been performed. The factors which seem to relate most closely to transmission are the severity of maternal disease, as indicated by a low CD4 count and a history of chorioamnionitis. Some studies suggest a higher rate of transmission to premature infants. Given the substantial nature of a 30% transmission rate and the low quality of life for HIV-infected infants, many physicians have advocated termination of pregnancy in HIV-infected women. This is, however, obviously a choice the patient has to make.

Although Jennifer denied intravenous drug use, the physical exam, presence of antibodies against hepatitis B surface antigen, and history of "unusual organism" endocarditis, are all very strong evidence that she is in fact using drugs. Because of the implications of IV drug use for the pregnancy and for her future functioning as a parent (particularly as a single mother), it is important to address this issue directly with the patient. It may be necessary to discuss screening Jennifer's urine for drugs of abuse.

Pregnancy probably does not accelerate the course of HIV disease. Early studies suggested that pregnancy hastened the progression to ARC or AIDS. These studies tended to focus, however, on women who were recognized to be infected either because their children became ill with HIV, or because the mothers were themselves found to be symptomatic. More recent prospective evaluations suggest that pregnancy has no effect on the natural history of progression to AIDS. Thus, for the relatively asymptomatic woman, concern about damaging the mother's health is not by itself an indication for termination of the pregnancy.

The lack of research about HIV infection in pregnant women and concerns regarding the impact of drugs on the fetus have made it very difficult to propose a rational plan for treating HIV-infected pregnant women. Jennifer is fortunate that her disease is quite mild. With a CD4 count of 932 there is no urgency to begin PCP prophylaxis. Her weight loss is more likely to be related to her pregnancy than to her HIV infection.

Zidovudine usage in pregnancy is currently under study. The research studies are far too preliminary to make any strong recommendations. The objectives of zidovudine use in pregnancy are 1) to treat the pregnant woman's HIV infection, and 2) to prevent HIV transmission to the fetus. Since there are as yet no data regarding the latter objective, the primary indication for zidovudine during pregnancy is to treat a woman who requires therapy (very immunosuppressed or with symptomatic HIV disease). No other antiretroviral drugs are any closer to FDA approval for pregnant women. Treatment of opportunistic infections is also a problem. While acyclovir is probably safe during pregnancy, pregnancy continues to be a relative contraindication to acyclovir use.

Pneumocystis prophylaxis and treatment are also problems. Sulfa drugs should be avoided during the late stages of pregnancy because they displace bilirubin from albumin and may thus contribute to kernicterus in the newborn infant. Intravenous pentamidine's propensity to cause hypoglycemia and hypotension could be devastating to a fetus, but these side effects have not been a problem for aerosolized pentamidine. Thus, although studies on pregnant women have not been done, if pneumocystis prophylaxis is necessary, aerosolized pentamidine would seem to be a reasonable option. There are no clear recommendations for treatment of an active case of *Pneumocystis carinii* pneumonia in a pregnant woman, although most physicians would probably begin the patient on TMP/SMX and use pentamidine only if TMP/SMX appeared to be failing.

RETURN APPOINTMENT (SEVEN DAYS LATER)

When Jennifer returns to the office, she immediately makes it clear that she intends to carry the child to term. She spent the weekend with her sister, with whom she continues to be on good terms, and with her sister's children. She thought having children looked like fun, despite one of the children having chickenpox. When you inquire, Jennifer has no history of previous chickenpox herself.

When Jennifer is confronted with the issue of drug abuse, she admits that she has intermittently used intravenous drugs, but denies that she has used drugs during the last three months, mostly because she can't afford them. She is willing to submit to a urine drug screen. When the results of the screen return the next day, they are negative for drugs of abuse.

SELF-STUDY QUESTION

14. What response, if any, is appropriate for Jennifer's exposure to chickenpox?

    a. No treatment is needed.
    b. Varicella-zoster immune globulin (VZIG) should be given immediately because she is near the end of the 48-hour period within which VZIG is most effective.
    c. VZIG should be given within one week if serology is positive.
    d. VZIG should be given within 96 hours of exposure regardless of serology.

DISCUSSION

Varicella exposure in *susceptible* individuals is a problem both for HIV-infected people and for pregnant women. If the exposure is within the last 96 hours, varicella-zoster immune globulin (VZIG) should be given (1 vial for every 10 kg, with a maximum of 5 vials, injected intramuscularly). If there is some doubt about the patient's varicella susceptibility and serology can be obtained rapidly, the patient can be tested for antibodies and the VZIG given with maximum effectiveness as long as 48 hours have not passed since the exposure. However, if there is doubt about the susceptibility of the patient and serology results cannot be obtained within 48 hours of the exposure, VZIG should be administered. The effectiveness of VZIG as varicella prevention decreases with time, although it will probably have beneficial effects even when given between 48 and 96 hours postexposure.

Varicella exposure is not a concern for people who have already had chicken-pox. Shingles (recurrent varicella disease) emanates from a site of latency in the dorsal root ganglia and has nothing to do with re-exposure. Shingles can be very severe and recurrent in someone with severe immune compromise, but the risk is from previously internalized virus, not a reinfection.

Had Jennifer screened positive for IV drugs, her drug problem would have been difficult to treat. Ideally, Jennifer would have been referred to a specialist in substance abuse. However, treatment programs are often over-subscribed, and in many parts of the United States there may not be treatment programs. If it becomes necessary to supervise her withdrawal, ideally she would stop taking drugs as rapidly as possible. However, this rarely happens, and overly rapid withdrawal may in fact cause medical and psychological problems that lead to continued drug use. A slow withdrawal may maintain the drug dependency for long enough that the addict stays hooked. The answers aren't simple, and consultation with a specialist is indicated if at all possible.

Jennifer is referred to a local obstetrician, and the rest of her pregnancy is uneventful.

C. CASE 3: A NEWBORN CHILD OF AN HIV-POSITIVE MOTHER

HISTORY OF PRESENT ILLNESS

Paul is the 3,000-gram seven-day-old son of Jennifer, the patient described in case 2. He was the product of an uncomplicated labor and delivery, with Apgars of 8 and 9. Height and head circumference were at the 40th percentile. Exam was within normal limits. An HIV ELISA test on the baby was positive.

SELF-STUDY QUESTIONS

15.   On the basis of Paul's ELISA test, you can conclude that

a.   Paul is not infected, since his blood contains circulating maternal antibodies.
b.   Paul is HIV infected.
c.   Paul will develop AIDS.
d.   Paul's mother was infected and he has a 30% chance of being infected.

16.   All of the following conditions would indicate symptomatic HIV infection
       of the infant *except*

       a.   gastroesophageal reflux.
       b.   lymphoid interstitial pneumonitis.
       c.   progressive neurological disease.
       d.   recurrent serious bacterial infections.

DISCUSSION

During the first few months of life, it is very difficult to ascertain whether an
infant is HIV infected or not. As noted earlier, current estimates are that roughly
70% of children born to HIV-infected women will not be infected. The standard
screening test for adult infection, detection of anti-HIV antibodies using an ELISA
test, is of little use in children under a year old. Virtually all children whose
mothers are antibody positive will themselves be antibody positive because of the
transplacental passage of immunoglobulin G molecules. Because of the difficulty
establishing whether children are infected, the CDC included a category of "antibody positive, status unknown" in their classification scheme for pediatric HIV
infection. The classification scheme is summarized in Table 5.1.

TABLE 5.1. CDC Classification Scheme for Pediatric HIV Infection

P-0:	Child ≤ 15 months old who is HIV antibody positive but whose status has yet to be determined
P-1:	Established to be HIV infected and asymptomatic
	P-1A: Asymptomatic and immunologically normal
	P-1B: Asymptomatic and immunologically abnormal
	P-1C: Asymptomatic and immune status not known
P-2:	Established to be HIV infected and symptomatic
	P-2A: Nonspecific symptoms known to be HIV related
	P-2B: Progressive neurological disease
	P-2C: Lymphoid interstitial pneumonitis
	P-2D: Opportunistic infections
	D1: AIDS-defining opportunistic infection
	D2: Recurrent serious bacterial infections
	D3: Other specified infectious conditions
	P-2E: Secondary cancers
	E1: Specific cancers listed as AIDS defining
	E2: Other cancers possibly related to HIV
	P-2F: Other conditions possibly related to HIV

Determining whether a child is HIV infected during the first few months of life is difficult in a general practice setting. Proving the presence of the virus is the only test result with certain meaning. Three tests are currently available to find the virus, while other means of early diagnosis are under exploration. The three tests are:

1. HIV Culture. This technique is generally the most reliable of the three. In a high-quality lab there should be no false positives, but a substantial number of children who are infected may be negative on one or more cultures before they become positive. Nevertheless, its sensitivity is better than antigen testing and is roughly equal to PCR. The most significant problem for HIV culture is its limited availability. The test is difficult and expensive to perform, requires an isolation facility, and can take as long as a month to turn positive. Virus culture methods can also be used to quantitate the amount of virus present in a patient's blood, although the techniques are expensive and only available in research labs.

2. p24 Antigen. Assaying for p24 antigen is the most widely available and least expensive test for detecting the virus. Unfortunately, antigen detection is not as sensitive as culture, although improved techniques are increasing its accuracy. Since false positives are rare, detection of p24 antigen indicates that a patient is infected. P24 is also the best of these three techniques at giving a quantitative measure of virus in a sample. As an example of the usefulness of viral quanti-tation, studies on p24 levels during treatment with zidovudine have shown that the p24 antigen concentrations decrease on therapy. A rapidly rising p24 concen-tration can be a bad prognostic indicator, often preceding an acceleration in the downward clinical course.

3. Polymerase Chain Reaction Test for HIV Genomic Material. The polymer-ase chain reaction test (PCR) is a means of amplifying and then detecting selected gene sequences. If the desired gene is present (for example, one or two pieces of HIV genome), the PCR will detect it in a much more sensitive manner than was possible before the availability of this technique. PCR is approximately equal to culture as a means to detect HIV in the infected host. There are still drawbacks to PCR, however. The test is expensive and technically very difficult. Its availability is limited, although it is becoming more accessible. The sensitivity is so great that false positives can occur because of microscopically small levels of contamination (one copy of a given piece of genomic material may be enough to turn a PCR assay positive). PCR is also not routinely a quantitative assay: the results are expressed as positive or negative.

CASE HISTORY CONTINUED

Paul's HIV culture and antigen were both positive, the latter with 30 ng/mL of p24 antigen. Paul is thus reclassified from CDC class P-0 to P-1.

SELF-STUDY QUESTION

17. Follow-up exams for Paul's positive HIV culture should include all of the following *except*

   a. head circumference.
   b. DPT.
   c. live polio vaccine at two months.
   d. weight measurements.

Since the role of zidovudine in asymptomatic children has yet to be determined, zidovudine was not initiated and Paul was scheduled to return monthly for follow-up. At each visit, close attention is paid to his growth (especially head circumference and weight) and behavioral development. At his two-month visit, Paul is vaccinated with DTP and inactivated polio vaccine. There are no abnormalities until the four-month visit, when bilateral lower extremity hypertonicity and hyperreflexia are noted. A full physical and laboratory assessment are performed.

PHYSICAL EXAM

Small, alert, and mildly fussy infant.

Weight: 5.2 kg (5th to 10th percentile)

Length: 62 cm (25th percentile)

Head Circumference: 40 cm (within 2 SD of normal)

HEENT: Mild to moderate oral thrush.

Lymph Nodes: Mild posterior cervical and axillary adenopathy, with clusters of 5–8 mm nodes.

Lungs: Clear.

Cardiovascular: Normal.

Abdomen: Liver 2 cm below the right costal margin. Spleen not palpable.

No other masses.

Neuro: Alert infant. Follows visual cues. Smiles. Hypertonic lower extremities. Three beats of clonus can be obtained at either ankle or knee.

Skin: Moderate candidal diaper rash.

LABORATORY RESULTS

Complete Blood Count

Hemoglobin: 8.5 g/dL

Hematocrit: 26.0%

White Blood Count: 4,200/mm^3

Differential

Segs:	20%
Lymphs:	60%
Monos:	10%
Eosin:	7%
Baso:	3%

Platelet Count: 140,000/mm^3

Chemistries: Within normal limits.

Urinalysis: Within normal limits.

Lymphocyte Subtyping

CD4: 40%   Absolute CD4 Count: 1,008/mm^3

CD8: 45%   Absolute CD8 Count: 1,323/mm^3

T4/T8 Ratio: 0.89

Immunoglobulins

                        Normal Range

IgG: 980   (300–1,000)

IgA: 75   (3–66)

IgM: 120   (15–150)

Computed Tomography (CT Scan) of the Head: Mild cortical atrophy present.

SELF-STUDY QUESTIONS

18.   Which of the following conclusions *cannot* be drawn from the data about this patient?

    a.   Mild cortical atrophy is a normal finding in infants.
    b.   Paul's elevated IgA titer is a laboratory error.
    c.   Paul is manifesting progressive neurological disease.
    d.   Paul's CD4 count is normal for his age.

19.   Which treatment is indicated?

    a.   Bacterial infections should be treated aggressively with higher-than-normal doses of antibiotics.
    b.   Candidal infection should be treated aggressively with ketoconazole, if necessary.
    c.   Fevers should be treated with acetaminophen and watched.
    d.   Skin tests for anergy should be performed.

20.   Vaccinations for Paul should include all of the following *except*

    a.   DPT at 2, 4, and 6 months.
    b.   follow-up DPT at 18 months.
    c.   MMR at 15 months.
    d.   trivalent oral polio.

DISCUSSION

Paul is already manifesting several signs of HIV. Not only has he rapidly moved from category P-0 to P-1, by the age of four months he can be classified as category P-2 (subtypes A,B, and F). His problems are complicated enough to require sequential discussion.

1. Paul's most significant problem is his rapidly progressive neurological disease, with cortical atrophy on CT scan and hypertonic lower extremities with clonus present. The HIV encephalopathy syndrome in children can have a wide variety of manifestations, especially since the defects can be quite focal. Developmental delay and/or regression is the most typical pattern, sometimes with evidence of cortical atrophy detectable by CT scan or head circumference measurements. Children may also have specific areas of developmental difficulty and generally good overall functioning. Motor function seems to be involved particularly frequently in young children.

2. Paul's CD4 count of 1,008 is quite low for his age. While the normal number of CD4 cells in adults is 800 or greater, in children the numbers are typically much higher, with 3,000 or more CD4 cells present per cubic millimeter in normal five-month-old infants. His ratio of 0.89 is also low. In a patient as

young as Paul, who is less than one year old, using intradermal hypersensitivity tests to evaluate cellular immune function is of little value.

3. Paul's complete blood count shows several hallmarks of HIV infection. He has anemia, neutropenia (his absolute neutrophil count is only 840 PMNs/mm^3), and mild thrombocytopenia. There appear to be several mechanisms at work in the hematological problems suffered by HIV-infected children. First, the virus may have a direct effect on marrow, leading to an inadequate production of blood cells. Second, in some children autoantibodies are produced against the various hematological cell types, probably because of poor B-cell regulation. Treatment for this type of autoimmune disease is still experimental, but attempts have been made using zidovudine (attacking the virus directly), steroids, high-dose intravenous immune globulin (IVIG), erythropoietin, and granulocyte colony stimulating factor (GCSF). The optimal regimen for any one patient, like Paul, is not yet established, although including an antiretroviral drug will generally be an important component.

4. Another immunological problem developing in Paul is hyperimmunoglobulinemia. Children with HIV can be either hypergammaglobulinemic or hypogammaglobulinemic. The latter is less common, but may be associated with false negative HIV antibody tests (both ELISA and Western Blot) and with a poor prognosis. The two immunoglobulin subclasses that are most associated with HIV-induced hyperproduction are IgG and IgA. Paul's IgG concentration is at the high end of normal, but his IgA concentration is already greater than normal. Perhaps because of deficient B-cell regulation, children with HIV are more prone than average to infections with polysaccharide encapsulated bacteria such as *Streptococcus pneumoniae*, *Haemophilus influenzae*, and *Neisseria meningitidis*. In evaluating fevers, blood cultures should be obtained more regularly and antibiotics begun sooner than in normal children. To limit problems related to candidal infections, the antibiotics should be given for as short a time as necessary (e.g., a ten-day course of amoxicillin is not needed if the child's exam is non-focal and the blood cultures are negative).

5. Oral thrush is one of the most common features of HIV infection in children and adults. A multi-step approach to treatment begins with oral nystatin suspension, 1 to 2 cc 3 to 4 times daily. This will usually work for a while, but eventually nystatin loses its efficacy. Another option in older children is clotrimazole troches orally, 10 mg po every 4 hours. When those regimens fail, or in smaller children where troches are not appropriate, ketoconazole can be used. Ketoconazole is sold only as 200-mg tablets, but a skilled pharmacy can prepare a suspension for use in smaller children. The dosage is 5 to 10 mg/kg per day, divided into one or two daily doses. If ketoconazole fails, and it may in patients with severe AIDS, oral fluconazole or intravenous amphotericin B treatments are indicated.

Some children will progress from thrush to candida esophagitis. Treatment with ketoconazole or amphotericin B should be prescribed, depending on how sick the patient appears to be. The diagnosis of candida esophagitis is best confirmed by esophagoscopy and has some significance since candida esophagitis is an AIDS-defining condition and would, in most states, mandate reporting the patient to the state health department and/or CDC.

Vaccination of HIV-infected children basically follows the routine for uninfected children, except that inactivated polio vaccine (IPV) is substituted for the trivalent oral polio vaccine (TOPV). Because of the potential for exposure to wild-type measles, at 15 months the measles-mumps-rubella shot (MMR) is currently recommended, despite the mild risk of the attenuated measles vaccine. To date, the MMR has been safe for HIV-infected children, although some questions remain regarding its efficacy in this population.

D. CASE 4: A 40-YEAR-OLD POSTMAN WITH SKIN LESIONS

CASE HISTORY

Charles is a 40-year-old postman who acknowledges that he is gay, has had many sexual partners, and has never followed safe sex precautions. He has been HIV seropositive for six years, but has not taken antiretroviral therapy. When he was last seen three years ago, his physical exam was normal except for mild lymphadenopathy and his CD4 count was 700 cells/mm^3. He came to the clinic today because he noticed a raised purple lesion on his right calf. He has otherwise been well.

PHYSICAL EXAM

Thin, but well-appearing, 40-year-old male.

Height: 175 cm (5'9")

Weight: 62 kg (137 lb)

Vital Signs: T 37.0° BP 130/78   PR 80   RR 15

Eyes: Several faint white retinal patches, consistent with the necrotic lesions of CMV retinitis. Visual acuity is 20/100 bilaterally.

Mouth: Normal. No thrush or leukoplakia.

Lymphatics: Posterior cervical nodes—multiple 15 × 10 mm nodes bilaterally.

Axillary Nodes: 25 × 25 mm node clusters bilaterally.

Inguinal Nodes: Multiple 15 × 10 mm nodes bilaterally.

Lungs and Cardiovascular: Normal.

Abdomen: Liver not palpable. Spleen 2 cm below the left costal margin.

Genitalia: Normal.

Skin: Two raised purple lesions. The one on the right calf is 2.5 × 2 cm. There is a second lesion, 3 × 1.5 cm, on the left buttock.

Neurological Exam: Within normal limits.

LABORATORY RESULTS

Complete Blood Count

Hemoglobin: 12.5 g/dL

Hematocrit: 38.0%

Mean Corpuscular Volume (MCV): 78 fl

White Blood Count: 6,700/mm^3

Differential

Segs:	70%
Lymphs:	20%
Monos:	7%
Eosin:	3%

Platelet Count: 300,000/mm^3

Chemistries: Within normal limits.

Urinalysis: Within normal limits.

Lymphocyte Subtyping

CD4: 12%   Absolute CD4 Count: 161/mm^3

CD8: 70%   Absolute CD8 Count: 938/mm^3

T4/T8 Ratio: 0.17

Chest X-Ray: Moderate bilateral hilar adenopathy. Clear lung fields.

SELF-STUDY QUESTIONS

21. Differential diagnosis of Charles's physical findings includes all of the following *except*

   a. cytomegalovirus retinitis.
   b. Kaposi's sarcoma.
   c. *Pneumocystis carinii* pneumonia.
   d. toxoplasma retinitis.

22. Treatment options that you should offer Charles include all of the following *except*

   a. aerosolized pentamidine.
   b. dextran sulfate.
   c. interferon.
   d. zidovudine.

23. Appropriate response to Charles's optic symptoms is

   a. change eyeglass prescription.
   b. ganciclovir or foscarnet.
   c. no treatment for three months, then reevaluate.
   d. steroid eye drops.

DISCUSSION

Charles appears to have two problems developing. He has Kaposi's sarcoma, and thus now meets the criteria for AIDS. Of the various categories of AIDS in adults, Kaposi's sarcoma generally has the best prognosis. However, therapy is still indicated, and Charles is started on zidovudine 200 mg q4h 5 times a day. Some studies have suggested that the addition of alpha interferon to zidovudine might improve the therapeutic outcome in Kaposi's, but the side effects of interferon are quite substantial (fevers, myalgias, headaches), so Charles opted to take zidovudine alone.

   Charles's second problem is his eye lesions. The areas of white necrosis, often associated with patches of intra-retinal hemorrhage, are characteristic of cytomegalovirus retinitis, and herald more serious ophthalmologic disease in the future. There are two effective therapies for CMV retinitis, ganciclovir and foscarnet. Unfortunately, each has significant side effects and both must be given intravenously. Ganciclovir is a potent suppressor of hematopoiesis, especially when used in combination with zidovudine. Foscarnet can produce severe renal dysfunction. A recent study indicated that survival in adults with CMV retinitis was better with foscarnet than with ganciclovir, perhaps because of foscarnet's antiretroviral effects, but foscarnet was associated with more side effects and was more difficult to administer. Because Charles has not noticed a change in his vision, he opts not to begin anti-cytomegalovirus treatment, despite your firm advice to the contrary.

With a CD4 lymphocyte count below 200, Charles should be on pneumocystis prophylaxis, as discussed in case 1. He chooses to take aerosolized pentamidine on a monthly basis at an evening clinic supported by the local gay health co-operative.

FURTHER HISTORY

Charles returns to your office four months later, having missed several scheduled appointments because of "pressure at work." He has lost five pounds in the interim. He complains that his vision is worse, and is particularly bothered by headaches and daily fevers. He has many more Kaposi's lesions. He is also worried that he has been confused several times while trying to perform his mail route.

PHYSICAL EXAM

Charles has lost weight. He looks mild to moderately ill, and is easily confused by your questions, in contrast to his previously precise nature.

Weight: 57 kg (125.4 lb)

Vital Signs: T 38.0°   BP 120/80   PR 90   RR 17

Eyes: Fundoscopic exam shows marked progression of the previously noted CMV retinitis. In addition, the fundus demonstrates severe papilledema. The visual acuity is 20/150.

Mouth: Mild thrush present.

Lymphatics: Posterior cervical nodes—multiple 10 × 5 mm nodes bilaterally.

Axillary Nodes: 15 × 15 mm node clusters bilaterally.

Inguinal Nodes: Multiple 10 × 5 mm nodes bilaterally.

Lungs and Cardiovascular: Normal.

Abdomen: Liver palpable 1 cm below the right costal margin. Spleen tip barely palpable.

Skin: 23 raised, purple, 2–4 cm lesions are scattered on the extremities, face, and trunk.

NEUROLOGICAL EXAM

Mental Status: Cooperative but easily befuddled. Attention span is short. During performance of serial 7s the patient often forgets his place. Short-term memory appears to be more severely affected than long-term.

Cranial Nerves: Grossly intact, although the pupillary response to light is slow.

Motor: Generalized muscle atrophy and mild weakness. Stamina is decreased from normal.

Sensory: Normal.

Reflexes: Within normal limits.

LABORATORY RESULTS

Complete Blood Count

Hemoglobin: 10.5 g/dL

Hematocrit: 31.0%

Mean Corpuscular Volume (MCV): 80 fl

White Blood Count: 3,900/mm^3

Differential

Segs:	83%
Lymphs:	12%
Monos:	2%
Eosin:	3%

Platelet Count: 240,000/mm^3

Chemistries

Total Bilirubin: 1.0 mg/dL

AST (SGOT): 100 U/L

ALT (SGPT): 75 U/L

Alk Phos: 90 U/L

Urinalysis: Within normal limits.

Lymphocyte Subtyping

CD4: 9%   Absolute CD4 Count: $42/mm^3$

CD8: 75%   Absolute CD8 Count: $351/mm^3$

T4/T8 Ratio: 0.12

Chest X-Ray: Moderate bilateral hilar adenopathy. Focal 3–4 cm lesions in both lung fields.

SELF-STUDY QUESTIONS

24.   What is the most probable explanation why Charles's MCV has not changed on zidovudine treatment?

   a.   folate deficiency.
   b.   noncompliance.
   c.   worsening HIV infection.
   d.   zidovudine treatment failure.

25.   Differential diagnosis of Charles's encephalopathy includes all of the following *except*

   a.   Epstein-Barr virus.
   b.   fungal abscess.
   c.   multifocal bacterial abscess.
   d.   *Toxoplasma gondii* encephalitis.

26.   Which test would be sufficient to confirm diagnosis of *Toxoplasma gondii* encephalitis?

   a.   blood culture positive for toxoplasma.
   b.   brain biopsy.
   c.   positive IgG titer to toxoplasma.
   d.   positive IgM antibodies to toxoplasma.

ADDITIONAL HISTORY

When you note that his MCV has not increased, despite four months of zidovudine, Charles admits that he stopped taking the medicine after two weeks because his friends told him, "It won't do any good." Instead, they suggested that he try a vitamin-enriched diet. He has continued to go into the clinic for his pentamidine treatments.

DISCUSSION

Charles's AIDS has advanced rapidly during the last four months. His Kaposi's sarcoma has continued to disseminate, probably to his lungs; his CMV retinitis is worse; and his papilledema and confusion raise the possibility that he may have an invasive central nervous system process. Had Charles taken his zido-vudine, it might have slowed the progress of his disease.

In most patients, zidovudine produces an increase in the size of red blood cells (MCV) within four to six weeks. This change is reliable enough that the absence of an increasing MCV can be considered a marker of noncompliance.

Because of his deteriorating mental status, a lumbar puncture and head CT scan are performed.

Lumbar Puncture

Opening Pressure: 250 mm H_2O

Glucose: 60 mg/dL (Systemic: 100 mg/dL)

Protein: 150 mg/dL

Cell Count

RBC: 3 cells/mm^3
WBC: 20 cells/mm^3

Differential

Segs: 40%
Lymphs: 10%
Monos: 50%

India Ink: Negative (fungal culture eventually negative)

Cryptococcal Antigen: Negative

Gram's Stain: Negative (culture eventually negative)

Stain for AFB: Negative (culture eventually negative)

CT Scan: Five 2–3 cm circular, ring enhancing lesions are seen in the cortical white matter and basal ganglia. Mild cortical atrophy is present. Several small areas of calcification in the basal ganglia are seen.

Serum Toxoplasma Antibodies

IgG: 1,024
IgM: Negative

DISCUSSION

Charles's central nervous system disease is consistent with *Toxoplasma gondii* encephalitis, although multifocal bacterial or fungal abscesses cannot be excluded. A brain biopsy is necessary to make a confirmed diagnosis. A positive IgG titer against *Toxoplasma gondii* means that toxoplasma is possible, although antibody assays cannot establish whether acute disease is present. IgM antibodies against toxoplasma are usually not found during an episode of encephalitis, perhaps because the disease is a reactivation of a previously latent infection. A negative IgG titer against *Toxoplasma gondii* would largely exclude toxoplasmosis as an etiologic possibility.

The treatment regimen for toxoplasma encephalitis in an AIDS patient consists of pyrimethamine (200 mg po, then 50 to 100 mg daily) and sulfadiazine (100 mg/kg per day, up to 8 g per day, divided q12h). Many physicians add folinic acid (10 mg per day), although this may decrease the anti-toxoplasma therapeutic effect by an uncertain degree.

Confronted with the possibility that he would have to take zidovudine, ganciclovir, pyrimethamine, sulfadiazine, and folinic acid, and that his hematological values would need very careful monitoring, Charles opted for no treatment. His parents participated in the discussion and agreed that Charles was still able to reason soundly enough that he could make a rational decision. Therapy was terminated and Charles died of toxoplasma encephalitis eight weeks later.

SUMMARY

Therapy for HIV infection is improving slowly as basic and applied research increases our understanding and provides new treatments. There are now some long-term survivors with AIDS. However, treatment of patients with HIV infection remains a complex and emotionally exhausting field. Physicians need to find means to encourage themselves and their patients in the short term, while research continues that will ultimately provide long-term improvement in prognosis.

REFERENCES

1. Centers for Disease Control. Update: acquired immunodeficiency syndrome and human immunodeficiency virus infection among health-care workers. *MMWR*. April 22, 1988;37(15):229–234.

RECOMMENDED FOLLOW-UP

In addition to the article in the reference section, the reader may wish to consult the following sources:

Falloon J, Eddy J, Wiener L, et al. Human immunodeficiency virus infection in children. *J Pediatr*. 1989;114:1–30.

McKinney RE. Antiviral therapy for human immunodeficiency virus infection in children. *Pediatr Clin North Am*. 1991;38:133–151.

CONTINUING MEDICAL EDUCATION POSTTEST

DIRECTIONS. To receive CME credit for this program, carefully follow the instructions on the Continuing Medical Education Posttest Answer Sheet at the end of this chapter.

1. Which of the following is *not* a documented method of transmission for the virus that causes AIDS?

    a. contamination of food products
    b. cross-placental infection from mother to fetus
    c. heterosexual intercourse
    d. transfusion of infected blood products

2. The cell that suffers the most damage in HIV infection is the

    a. B cell.
    b. macrophage.
    c. T helper/inducer cell.
    d. T suppressor cell.

3. The major function of the immune system that suffers damage in AIDS is the ability to

    a. attach antibodies to antigens.
    b. distinguish "self" from foreign protein.
    c. initiate a cell-mediated immune response.
    d. remove cellular debris.

4. The major action of the cellular immune system is the activation of

    a. B lymphocytes.
    b. plasma cells.
    c. stem cells.
    d. T lymphocytes.

5. The major function of B lymphocytes is the production of

    a. antigens.
    b. antibodies.
    c. lymphokines.
    d. plasma cells.

6.   Which of the following is *not* a result of HIV infection of a host cell?

   a.   It can cause the functional impairment of CD4 lymphocytes.
   b.   It can form buds that break off from the host cell.
   c.   It kills the host cell and infects new cells.
   d.   It reproduces new virus cells by mitotic division.

7.   Cells that express CD4 antigen on their cell surface

   a.   are immune to infection by HIV.
   b.   are present only during active HIV infection.
   c.   include T cells, monocytes, and macrophages.
   d.   selectively kill the AIDS virus.

8.   Monoclonal antibodies are

   a.   a sign of a failing immune system.
   b.   less efficient than polyclonal antibodies at combining with their specific antigen.
   c.   produced in response to a single epitope.
   d.   the most common antibodies produced in HIV infection.

9.   All of the following are common side effects of zidovudine *except*

   a.   anemia.
   b.   granulocytopenia.
   c.   macrocytosis.
   d.   thrombocytopenia.

10.   What is the main advantage of didanosine over zidovudine that we have seen to date?

   a.   Didanosine causes less peripheral neuropathy than zidovudine.
   b.   Didanosine has been shown to attack the HIV virus *in vitro*.
   c.   Didanosine has not caused the hematologic toxicities that have been seen with zidovudine.
   d.   Didanosine will probably be much less expensive than zidovudine.

11.   A patient's risk of developing clinical AIDS

   a.   increases as CD4 cell count decreases.
   b.   increases as CD4 cell count increases.
   c.   increases only when CD4 cell count drops below 200.
   d.   is unrelated to CD4 cell count.

12.   The FDA has approved zidovudine for

       a.   patients with AIDS.
       b.   patients with AIDS and advanced AIDS-related complex.
       c.   HIV-positive patients who have CD4 counts of 500 cells/mm^3 or less.
       d.   any patient with a CD4 count of 500 cells/mm^3 or less.

13.   The toxicities of didanosine include all of the following *except*

       a.   hepatitis.
       b.   peripheral neuropathy.
       c.   pancreatitis.
       d.   thrombocytopenia.

14.   Experimental therapies being investigated for the treatment of HIV infection include

       a.   reverse transcriptase inhibitors.
       b.   inhibitors of other elements in the virus life cycle such as HIV protease.
       c.   immune-based therapies.
       d.   all of the above.

15.   *Pneumocystis carinii* pneumonia

       a.   is caused by a virulent form of bacteria.
       b.   is usually fatal.
       c.   may initially present with mild cough and malaise.
       d.   rarely occurs in conjunction with other infections.

16.   A patient who is seropositive for HIV and presents with retinitis is most probably suffering from

       a.   cytomegalovirus infection.
       b.   diabetic retinopathy.
       c.   toxoplasmosis.
       d.   zidovudine toxicity.

17.   Defining AIDS as a legal handicap implies that

       a.   AIDS-affected employees can be considered handicapped in their ability to perform their jobs.
       b.   AIDS-affected employees may not be fired because of their disease.
       c.   medical care must be given under certain circumstances.
       d.   workers with AIDS must be given a medical leave of absence.

18. Which of the following statements about informed consent is true?

   a. It assumes that the patient has received adequate teaching about the procedure and its possible consequences.
   b. It can be obtained after the test has been performed, but before the results are known.
   c. It implies that the patient gives medical staff permission to disclose results to family members.
   d. It must always be obtained before performing a test for HIV antibodies.

19. Which of the following groups is usually *not* subject to involuntary testing?

   a. applicants for immigration
   b. health care professionals
   c. prison inmates
   d. prostitutes

20. An employer who determines that a health care worker is HIV positive

   a. may terminate employment based on anticipated disability.
   b. must base decisions about transfer on actual risk of HIV transmission.
   c. must transfer other workers away from that worker if they request transfer.
   d. must transfer that worker away from direct patient care.

21. What percentage of infants born to HIV-infected women will become infected?

   a. 5% to 10%
   b. 20% to 30%
   c. 75%
   d. 100%

22. What is the best therapeutic agent available for CMV retinitis?

   a. acyclovir
   b. ganciclovir
   c. interferon
   d. zidovudine

23. Zidovudine doses must sometimes be reduced to avoid

   a. hair growth.
   b. hepatitis.
   c. hematologic toxicity.
   d. renal failure secondary to crystalluria.

24.   Why isn't a positive HIV ELISA antibody test diagnostic for HIV infection in children less than 15 months?

a.   Children often have false positive cross-reactions.
b.   It is diagnostic.
c.   Maternal antibody against HIV may be present even though the virus is not.
d.   The virus may complex the antibodies and affect test results.

25.   The options for pneumocystis prophylaxis include all of the following *except*

a.   aerosolized pentamidine.
b.   aerosolized ribavirin.
c.   dapsone.
d.   trimethoprim/sulfamethoxazole.

26.   The initial evaluation of a patient newly diagnosed with HIV infection should include a skin test for tuberculosis.

a.   true
b.   false

27.   Which of the following is *not* a reason for giving pneumocystis prophylaxis to an HIV-positive patient?

a.   Oral candidiasis is present.
b.   The absolute CD4 count is less than 200.
c.   The patient has any AIDS-defining condition.
d.   The absolute CD4 count is less than 1,000.

Case Study 1. J.G. is a 24-year-old black female with a brief history of intravenous drug abuse. She is in her second trimester of pregnancy and found to be HIV positive. Her absolute CD4 count is 460.

28.   Pregnancy in an HIV-positive patient

a.   accelerates the prognosis of HIV symptomatology.
b.   has no effect on the natural history of progression to AIDS.
c.   should be terminated.
d.   will only rarely result in an HIV-infected newborn.

29. In an HIV-positive pregnant patient who requires pneumocystis pro-phylaxis,

   a. aerosolized pentamidine is preferred because of minimal systemic absorption.
   b. no therapeutic option is available because of danger to the fetus.
   c. sulfa drugs should be avoided during the late stages because they may contribute to kernicterus in the newborn.
   d. a and c are correct.

30. Once J.G. has delivered, determining whether her infant is HIV-infected is best done by

   a. HIV culture of the newborn.
   b. HIV ELISA test on the newborn.
   c. p24 antigen assay on the mother.
   d. Western Blot Test on the mother.

Case Study 2. P.R. is a 6-year-old hemophiliac who has been HIV seropositive for one year. Recently, his mother has noticed creamy white patches of exudate on his buccal mucosa.

31. Treatment for this condition usually starts with

   a. intravenous amphotericin B.
   b. oral nystatin suspension, 1 to 2 cc 3 to 4 times daily.
   c. saline gargles.
   d. zidovudine.

32. Oral candidiasis is a common feature of HIV infections in children but not in adults.

   a. true
   b. false

33. P.R. develops the symptoms of candidal esophagitis; this is confirmed by esophagoscopy. Which of the following statements is now true?

   a. Because of its toxicity, amphotericin B is contraindicated regardless of the patient's condition.
   b. Candidal esophagitis is not an AIDS-defining condition.
   c. It is mandatory in all states to report the patient to the state health department.
   d. Treatment may consist of ketoconazole or amphotericin B.

34.   Immune thrombocytopenia in HIV-seropositive patients may be treated with

    a. zidovudine.
    b. IVIg.
    c. steroids.
    d. all of the above.

35.   Hypergammaglobulinemia in children with HIV

    a. is less common than hypogammaglobulinemia.
    b. is typically due to hyperproduction of IgM and IgG.
    c. may be associated with false negative HIV antibody tests.
    d. predisposes them to infections with polysaccharide encapsulated bacteria.

CONTINUING MEDICAL EDUCATION
POSTTEST ANSWER SHEET

Care and Management of Patients with HIV Infection
AMA Category 1 CME, 0.7 CEU (7 Hours)

To obtain AMA Category 1 CME credit for your participation in this independent-study program, complete this Continuing Medical Education Posttest Answer Sheet and attach payment in the amount of $20.00 payable to Duke University Medical Center and mail to:

> Office of Continuing Medical Education
> Box 3108
> Duke University Medical Center
> Durham, NC 27710

SOCIAL SECURITY NO. ☐☐☐ – ☐☐ – ☐☐☐☐

Name ☐☐☐☐☐☐☐☐☐☐☐☐☐ ☐ ☐☐☐☐☐☐☐☐☐☐☐☐☐
First   M.I.   Last

Home Address ☐☐☐☐☐☐☐☐☐☐☐☐☐☐☐☐☐☐☐☐☐☐☐☐☐☐☐☐☐☐☐

☐☐☐☐☐☐☐☐☐☐☐☐☐☐ ☐☐ ☐☐☐☐☐ – ☐☐☐☐
City   State   Zip Code

Home Phone ( ) – ☐☐☐ – ☐☐☐☐   **Bus. Phone** ( ) – ☐☐☐☐☐☐☐

AMA Category 1 CME credit for successful completion of this program will be awarded up to December 31, 1994 (renewal and extension is expected).

For each question, decide on the best answer, and place an X through that letter. If you change an answer, be sure to erase completely. Mark only **one** answer for each question. To receive credit, your score must be 80% or greater. Please allow 3 to 4 weeks for test processing. Test results will be mailed to participants only.

1.	A	B	C	D	**13.**	A	B	C	D	**25.**	A	B	C	D
2.	A	B	C	D	**14.**	A	B	C	D	**26.**	A	B	C	D
3.	A	B	C	D	**15.**	A	B	C	D	**27.**	A	B	C	D
4.	A	B	C	D	**16.**	A	B	C	D	**28.**	A	B	C	D
5.	A	B	C	D	**17.**	A	B	C	D	**29.**	A	B	C	D
6.	A	B	C	D	**18.**	A	B	C	D	**30.**	A	B	C	D
7.	A	B	C	D	**19.**	A	B	C	D	**31.**	A	B	C	D
8.	A	B	C	D	**20.**	A	B	C	D	**32.**	A	B	C	D
9.	A	B	C	D	**21.**	A	B	C	D	**33.**	A	B	C	D
10.	A	B	C	D	**22.**	A	B	C	D	**34.**	A	B	C	D
11.	A	B	C	D	**23.**	A	B	C	D	**35.**	A	B	C	D
12.	A	B	C	D	**24.**	A	B	C	D					

SURVEY QUESTIONS

1. How long ago did you complete your last degree: (Check one.)

   Less than 1 yr   1–5 yrs   6–10 yrs   11–20 yrs   21–30 yrs   More than 30 yrs

2. I found the activity: (Circle the appropriate number/level.)

Not Practical	1	2	3	4	5	Very Practical
Poorly Written	1	2	3	4	5	Expertly Written
Difficult to Understand	1	2	3	4	5	Easily Understood

3. The posttest was: (Circle the appropriate number/level.)

Too Short	1	2	3	4	5	Too Long
Too Difficult	1	2	3	4	5	Too Easy
Poorly Written	1	2	3	4	5	Clearly Written

4. Please list other topics that you feel would be of interest for future CE activities.

   _____

   _____

   _____

   _____

   _____

   _____

   _____

   _____

CARE AND MANAGEMENT OF PATIENTS WITH HIV INFECTION

Chapter 6: The Role of the Pharmacist in the Care of Patients with HIV Infection

Kenneth W. Shipp, BS Pharm
Clinical Pharmacist
AIDS Treatment Evaluation Unit
Duke University Medical Center

Karen L. Nabors, PharmD
Pharmacy Resident, Department of Pharmacy
Duke University Medical Center

CONTENTS

Introduction 229
Objectives 229
Recommended Preparation 230
   I.   The Role of the Pharmacist in Caring for Patients with HIV
       Infection 231
  II.   The Drug Development Process 233
Review Questions (I & II) 235
  III.   Drug Therapy for HIV-infected Patients 236
      A. Antiretroviral Drugs Approved for Treatment of HIV
         Infection 236
      B. Drugs Approved and Indicated for Treatment or Prophylaxis
         of Opportunistic Infections 248
      C. Drugs Licensed and Being Used for Treatment or Prophylaxis
         of Opportunistic Infections Outside Indication 279
      D. Drugs in Development 289
Summary 293
Answers to Review Questions 294
References 295
Pharmacy Continuing Education Posttest 298
Test Grading Options 305
Facsimile Grading Posttest Answer Sheet 307
Mail-in Grading Scannable Form . . . . end of book

INTRODUCTION

This chapter of *Care and Management of Patients with HIV Infection* is recommended for pharmacists who desire an overview of the role of pharmacists in the treatment of AIDS. AIDS and its attendant opportunistic infections force patients to manage a complicated array of medications that often have side effects and interactions. This chapter is designed to facilitate your involvement with such patients.

The investigational drug process is presented, since pharmacists are frequently asked by their patients why it takes so long to get new drugs on the market. This chapter also reviews current drug therapy for HIV-infected patients, including antiretroviral agents as well as drugs used to combat opportunistic infections.

OBJECTIVES

Objectives presented here are intended to focus the reader's attention on expected learning outcomes.

On completion of this chapter, the reader should be able to:

1. Describe the pharmacist's role in caring for patients with HIV infection.

2. Explain the process of development and approval of drugs used to treat HIV infection and HIV-related opportunistic infections.

3. Identify the indications for zidovudine, zalcitabine, and didanosine.

4. Describe the side effects of zidovudine, zalcitabine, and didanosine.

5. Compare the therapeutic effects of particular drugs used to treat opportunistic infections.

6. Describe the side effects of drugs used to treat opportunistic infections.

7. Recognize monitoring parameters used for antiretroviral drugs and drugs used to treat opportunistic infections.

RECOMMENDED PREPARATION

Since this chapter contains a continuing education posttest that is comprehensive of chapters 1 through 4 as well as chapter 6, the reader is encouraged to review the first four chapters, which cover the pathophysiology, diagnosis, and treatment of acquired immunodeficiency syndrome and its associated infections.

I. THE ROLE OF THE PHARMACIST IN CARING FOR PATIENTS WITH HIV INFECTION

As pharmacists, our role in caring for patients with HIV disease is, for the most part, no different from our role in caring for any other patient. We dispense medications, counsel patients on the proper use of the medications, and, when appropriate, stress the importance of patients' keeping follow-up appointments for toxicity monitoring with their physicians. Patients with HIV disease do, however, present several interesting challenges and problems for pharmacists.

Patients in the late stages of their disease may be taking multiple medications: medications for their primary infection, for opportunistic infections, for pain, for depression, etc. Pharmacists can contribute to patient care by monitoring each patient's drug profile for possible drug interactions, especially for the possibility of additive toxicities. Several of the drugs used to treat opportunistic infections have toxicities similar to those of antiretroviral drugs. Antiretroviral drugs may have to be stopped until treatment for the opportunistic infection has been completed, or the dose of one or both of the drugs may have to be reduced. The drug monographs that follow contain specific information on drug interactions, toxicities, and dose modifications.

Pharmacists also have a role in providing information to patients about new therapies. Many patients with HIV disease are keenly interested in the ongoing research of the disease. They read the medical literature and newsletters published by governmental health agencies and AIDS activist groups; they read computer bulletin boards and on-line computer databases that focus on HIV disease; they hear about new experimental therapies from their friends at support group meetings. They often question pharmacists about these potential new therapies. This challenges pharmacists to keep abreast of the current literature so they can answer the patient's questions accurately and steer the patient in the right direction: towards proven treatments and complementary therapies and away from quackery.

Protecting the confidentiality of HIV-infected patients is an especially important role of the pharmacist. Many patients have a legitimate concern that they may lose their jobs and that they may be ostracized by friends, neighbors, and family members if knowledge of their HIV infection gets out in the community. Pharmacists have an ethical and legal responsibility to protect their patients' confidentiality. Chapter 4 discusses the legal duty of health care providers in protecting patients' confidentiality.

Pharmacists are in a good position to counsel HIV-infected patients and other patients on the proper selection and use of condoms. Important points to stress are listed below.

The condom user should be aware of the following recommendations:

1. Use condoms made of latex. Latex is an effective barrier to the virus. Lambskin or natural membrane condoms are too porous and are not effective barriers to HIV.

2. A condom with a spermicide may provide additional protection: the spermicide nonoxynol-9 has been shown to kill the virus *in vitro*. Place the spermicide in the tip and on the outside of the condom.

3. It is safer to use a condom with a lubricant, but use water-based instead of petroleum-based lubricants; petroleum-based lubricants weaken condoms, causing them to tear.

Pharmacists also have a role in providing information to the community at large about the risks of contracting HIV disease, about how people can protect themselves from the virus, and about the progress being made in HIV research. They can speak on these topics at civic club meetings and other community gatherings. They can also openly discuss these issues with their other patients (not infected with HIV) who have questions or express concerns. People are still very much afraid of contracting HIV infection, and all health care providers can help alleviate fears by stressing that HIV infection is not transmitted by casual contact. The routes of transmission remain intimate sexual contact, bloodstream exposure to contaminated blood, and transmission from an infected mother to her unborn child, either *in utero* or during delivery.

Hospital pharmacists have an additional role in helping to design and carry out investigational drug studies. Pharmacists working in home health care agencies have a role in preparing approved and investigational drugs for HIV-infected patients and assuring that the drugs are administered properly.

II. THE DRUG DEVELOPMENT PROCESS

Before investigators can begin clinical trials, they must complete an extensive evaluation of a drug's pharmacokinetic, pharmacodynamic, and toxic properties *in vitro* and in several species of animals. They give the animals increasing doses of the drug and watch for toxicity. Based on these studies, they decide whether or not the drug is safe for testing in humans. The investigators must submit these findings to the Food and Drug Administration (FDA) in the form of an application for an investigational new drug (IND). When the FDA has approved the IND, the investigators may begin clinical testing. It normally requires about eight years to complete these clinical tests.

Clinical tests are performed in phases. Three phases must be completed before a new drug application can be submitted.[1] Phase I trials are usually conducted using a small number of volunteers. They are designed to determine the biological effects, the metabolism, and the safe dosage range of the drug in humans.

Early phase II trials are usually conducted in a small number of selected patients and are designed to determine the potential usefulness of the drug and to refine the therapeutic dosage range. Later phase II studies are conducted using a larger number of selected patients who receive drug for a longer period of time. These studies continue to evaluate the drug's effectiveness, and are designed to determine the final dosage range and collect more data on drug elimination, especially by metabolism. Phase I and II trials usually take about four years to complete.

Phase III trials are broad clinical trials using a large number (usually 500 to 3,000) of selected patients. They are designed to collect longer-term safety and efficacy data on the drug. Phase III trials usually take about two years to complete. After these clinical trials have been completed and the drug has been shown to be safe and effective, investigators can submit a new drug application (NDA). In approving the NDA, the FDA approves the drug for marketing.

It should be noted that when investigators determine a drug to be safe, they mean that it is *relatively* safe, based on the severity of the disease or condition that it is used to treat. No drug is completely safe, and investigators and the FDA are willing to accept more severe side effects from a drug used to treat a life-threatening disease, such as HIV infection, than from a drug used to treat a head cold. Antiretroviral drugs have severe side effects, but these drugs can be safely used to treat HIV infection if the patient is carefully followed by a physician experienced in their use.

In 1987, the FDA created a new treatment category designed to expedite the evaluation of promising new treatments for such serious illnesses or life-threatening diseases as AIDS or HIV infection. This category, called "treatment

IND," allows for wider distribution of a drug that has been shown to be safe and possibly effective before efficacy studies have been completed or a new drug application approved. Also if a drug shows sufficient promise in phase I trials, the FDA may agree to combine phase II and III studies to reduce the development time by two to three years. This streamlined process is called "expedited review" and is restricted to drugs that are targeted to serious and life-threatening conditions such as AIDS and cancer.

A complete protocol must be written for each investigational drug study and must include the information about the drug to date, a detailed plan of the study, descriptions of how toxicities will be managed, study endpoints, and how the data will be analyzed. The protocol and a patient consent form that describes the study and its possible risks to the patient must be approved by the FDA and by the Institutional Review Board (IRB) of each center that participates in the study. Each patient who participates in the study must read and sign a copy of the consent form before they receive the first dose of medication under study. Each protocol has a very specific set of inclusion and exclusion criteria for trial subjects. These criteria are established for the purpose of selecting patients who are in similar condition, thereby eliminating as many variables as possible.

It is important that all new drugs pass through this investigative process. The only way that investigators can know that new drugs are relatively safe and effective is through the analysis of solid, objective data obtained from these trials.

REVIEW QUESTIONS (I & II)

DIRECTIONS. Circle the letter corresponding to the correct response in each of the following.

1. A pharmacist counseling a patient who is taking both zidovudine and therapy for opportunistic infections should be particularly concerned about

    a. additive hematologic toxicity.
    b. competitive inhibition of zidovudine.
    c. depression.
    d. masking of opportunistic infection.

2. Which of the following statements about condoms is true?

    a. Clinical studies support the use of nonoxynol-9 to kill the HIV virus.
    b. Condom users should avoid using lubricants.
    c. Natural membrane condoms are designed specifically to block passage of the HIV virus.
    d. Spermicide should be applied both inside and outside the condom.

3. Methods of transmission for the HIV virus have been established for all of the following forms of contact *except*

    a. "deep" kissing with exchange of saliva.
    b. delivery of a child by an HIV-infected mother.
    c. sharing needles for IV drug use.
    d. unprotected sexual intercourse.

4. An NDA is issued

    a. at the beginning of the drug development process.
    b. at the completion of phase II trials.
    c. based on phase III data for safety and efficacy.
    d. when a drug has been shown to lack serious side effects.

5. A treatment IND has all of the following characteristics *except*

    a. it expedites the drug development process.
    b. it is a response to community pressure for new drugs.
    c. it may lead to an NDA based on data from an expanded phase II trial.
    d. it restricts distribution of a drug with serious side effects.

Check your responses on page 294.

III. DRUG THERAPY FOR HIV-INFECTED PATIENTS

Drug therapy for HIV infection and its consequent opportunistic infections is a complex and rapidly changing field. This section provides comprehensive descriptions of drugs that are being given to HIV-infected patients. These summaries will serve as a review for you and as source material to guide your consultation with patients. Unreferenced material is compiled from the *AHFS Drug Information 92*,[2] *USP DI (v2)*,[3] *Drug Facts and Comparisons*,[4] and *The Sanford Guide to HIV/AIDS Therapy 1992*.[5]

A. ANTIRETROVIRAL DRUGS APPROVED FOR TREATMENT OF HIV INFECTION

Three antiretroviral agents have been approved by the FDA for the treatment of HIV infection (see Table 6.1). Zidovudine (AZT, Retrovir®) remains the initial drug of choice due to accumulated experience with its use, and it continues to be the only antiretroviral agent that has shown survival or natural history benefit. Two new drugs, didanosine (dideoxyinosine, ddI, Videx®) and zalcitabine (dideoxycytidine, ddC, Hivid®) have recently been approved by the FDA for patients who become intolerant of zidovudine or who show signs of rapid disease progression while on zidovudine. The FDA approval of these two agents was based upon evidence of "clinical activity" (suppression of HIV and transient rise in CD4 counts), and not "clinical efficacy" (survival or natural history benefit). These approvals were unprecedented on the basis of such preliminary data and reflect the FDA's commitment to the expedited review process.

TABLE 6.1. Antiretroviral Agents Used for Treatment of HIV-Infected Patients

Generic Name	Brand Name	Manufacturer
Zidovudine	Retrovir®	Burroughs Wellcome
Didanosine	Videx®	Bristol-Myers Squibb
Zalcitabine	Hivid®	Roche

Most AIDS experts begin zidovudine therapy when a patient's CD4 cell count falls below 500 per mm³. There is currently no evidence to show that antiretroviral therapy is of benefit to patients with CD4 cell counts greater than 500 per mm³, but a placebo-controlled trial is ongoing.

Physicians will switch to didanosine once the patient can no longer tolerate zidovudine. If the patient is showing signs of rapid disease progression while on zidovudine therapy, physicians will either switch to didanosine or add didanosine or zalcitabine to the patient's zidovudine regimen. If they add didanosine or zalcitabine, they generally prescribe both drugs (zidovudine and didanosine or zalcitabine) at full dose: this is possible because the side effects of didanosine and zalcitabine are different from those of zidovudine.

Most experts prefer not to use zalcitabine alone. The results of the AIDS Clinical Trials Group (ACTG) protocol 114 suggest that zalcitabine monotherapy is less effective than zidovudine monotherapy. This study was a randomized, double-blind trial comparing zidovudine and zalcitabine in 635 AIDS and advanced ARC patients with CD4 counts below 200 who had received less than three months of previous zidovudine therapy. The study was halted early after a one-year interim analysis showed a significantly higher survival rate among patients receiving zidovudine compared with those receiving zalcitabine (89% versus 82%).[6]

This section presents drug profiles on zidovudine, didanosine, and zalcitabine. We refer the reader back to chapter 3 for a discussion of experimental therapies.

1.   ZIDOVUDINE (AZT, Retrovir®)

Pharmacology

Antiviral; appears to interfere with viral replication by inhibiting the reverse transcriptase of the human immunodeficiency virus and causing DNA chain termination.

Pharmacokinetics

Absorption: rapidly absorbed from gastrointestinal tract with peak serum levels occurring within 0.5 to 1.5 hours. Zidovudine appears to undergo first-pass metabolism. About 65% of an oral dose reaches systemic circulation as unchanged drug. Preliminary studies indicated that food and/or milk did not appear to substantially affect GI absorption. However, further study is needed, since results of one study indicate that the rate of absorption and peak plasma concentrations of zidovudine may be decreased substantially if the drug is taken with a high-fat meal.[7]

Distribution: appears to be widely distributed; the apparent volume of distribution is 1.4 to 1.6 L/kg in adults and 22 to 64 L/m^2 in children. The
  drug is 34% to 38% protein bound. Zidovudine is distributed into CSF
  following oral and IV administration. The ratio of CSF/plasma concentrations ranges from 0.15 to 0.98.

Elimination: metabolized hepatically and eliminated renally; half-life is 1
  hour.

Uses

Antiviral therapy against HIV.

Adverse Reactions

Granulocytopenia, anemia, headache, malaise, somnolence, nausea, vomiting,
  taste disturbances, increase in liver function test values, myalgia, pigmentation of fingernails and toenails, paresthesia, dizziness, confusion,
  agitation, diarrhea, fever, rash.

Contraindications

Hypersensitivity.

Precautions

Check CBC: may need to adjust dosage; blood transfusions are sometimes
  necessary.

Drug Interactions

Drugs that may increase bone marrow toxicity—e.g., amphotericin B, dapsone. Monitor CBC frequently.

Ganciclovir: increased bone marrow toxicity (neutropenia). Zidovudine
  should be held during induction therapy with ganciclovir and can be
  reinstituted with caution during maintenance therapy. Hematopoietic
  growth factors may be necessary to treat neutropenia.

Methadone: decreased zidovudine metabolism. Monitor for zidovudine toxicity when methadone is started or methadone dose is increased.

Phenytoin: increased or decreased phenytoin levels. Monitor phenytoin levels.

Sulfadiazine/pyrimethamine: decreased zidovudine clearance, increased bone
  marrow toxicity. Zidovudine's half-life may double in patients receiving
  both agents. Clinical significance is unknown. Consider holding zidovu-

dine during induction therapy and reinstituting it when maintenance therapy begins. Give folinic acid with pyrimethamine.

TMP/SMX: possible increased anemia, neutropenia. Anemia and neutropenia are more common when zidovudine and high-dose TMP/SMX are combined. Consider holding zidovudine during acute therapy for PCP with high-dose TMP/SMX. Zidovudine may be taken with low-dose TMP/SMX for PCP prophylaxis.

Usual Dosage

Adults (oral):

Symptomatic HIV infection: initial dose of 200 mg q4h around the clock. After 1 month the dose may be reduced to 100 mg q4h. The effectiveness of this lower dose in improving neurologic dysfunction associated with HIV infection, however, is not known.[8,9]

Asymptomatic HIV infection in patients with CD4 counts less than or equal to 500 cells per mm^3: 100 mg q4h while awake (500 mg per day).[10]

Many physicians are now using a regimen of 200 mg q8h or 3 times a day. This regimen is easier for the patient to schedule and encourages compliance. Patients on combination therapy with zidovudine and zalcitabine can take both drugs on the same schedule. New clinical trials comparing zidovudine with other antiretroviral drugs are also using this regimen. Note, however, that this regimen is not approved by the FDA.

Children ages 3 months to 12 years: 180 mg/m^2 q6h, not to exceed 200 mg q6h.[11]

IV: 1 to 2 mg/kg infused over 1 hour q4h around the clock.[11]

Patient Instructions

(1) If this medication upsets your stomach, you can take it with light food. Do not take this medication with a high-fat meal.

(2) Long-term adverse reactions are unknown at this time.

(3) This medication has not been shown to reduce the risk of transmission of the AIDS virus to others through sexual contact.

2.   DIDANOSINE (ddI, dideoxyinosine, Videx®)

Pharmacology

Antiviral; appears to interfere with viral replication by inhibiting the reverse
   transcriptase of the human immunodeficiency virus and causing DNA
   chain termination.

Pharmacokinetics

Absorption: rapidly degraded at acid pH, therefore, all oral formulations contain buffering agents. Patients must take 2 tablets per dose to achieve
   needed level of buffer. All doses must be taken on an empty stomach.
   C_{max} and AUC increase in proportion to dose. Bioavailability varies widely but is in the neighborhood of 35%.

Distribution: average Vd = 54 L (range 22 to 103). The drug does cross the
   blood-brain barrier. CSF concentration 21% of plasma concentration.

Elimination: half-life is 1.6 hours. Renal clearance equals about half of total
   body clearance. There is no evidence of accumulation after IV or po dosing.

Uses

Didanosine is indicated for the treatment of adult and pediatric patients
(greater than 6 months of age) with advanced HIV infection who are intolerant of zidovudine therapy or who have demonstrated significant clinical or
immunologic deterioration during zidovudine therapy.

   ACTG protocol 116B/117 (a randomized, double-blind study comparing
zidovudine with 2 doses of didanosine) has shown that didanosine is more
effective than zidovudine in preventing the onset of opportunistic infections
in patients who have previously received more than 16 weeks of zidovudine
therapy. This benefit was not seen in patients who entered the study with
AIDS, but only those who entered with asymptomatic HIV infection or ARC.
There were no differences in survival between the patients on zidovudine and
those on didanosine.[12]

   Despite these encouraging preliminary results, clinical practice is not yet
ready to automatically switch patients who have been on zidovudine therapy
for more than 16 weeks to didanosine. Most physicians prefer to wait until
patients show either signs of zidovudine intolerance or signs of clinical or
immunologic deterioration.

Adverse Reactions

Major toxicities are pancreatitis (1% to 9%) and peripheral neuropathy (7% to 34%). Therapy should be discontinued in patients who show signs of pancreatitis (nausea, vomiting, abdominal pain, or elevated amylase levels). Patients should be instructed to discontinue the drug and call their physicians at the first signs of peripheral neuropathy (numbness, tingling, or pain in the feet or hands).

Other toxicities are headache, diarrhea, asthenia, insomnia, nausea, vomiting, rash, pruritus, abdominal pain, hepatitis, hypertriglyceridemia, CNS depression, constipation, stomatitis, myalgia, arthritis, taste loss, taste perversion, pain, dry mouth, alopecia, and dizziness.

Contraindications

Hypersensitivity.

History of pancreatitis.

Peripheral neuropathy.

Precautions

Didanosine tablets contain phenylalanine and may cause phenylketonuria.

Use didanosine with caution in patients on sodium-restricted diets: each didanosine tablet contains 264.5 mg sodium, and each didanosine packet contains 1,380 mg of sodium.

Didanosine has been associated with hyperuricemia; consider suspending treatment if clinical measures aimed at reducing uric acid levels fail.

Didanosine causes diarrhea in approximately 34% of patients.

Drug Interactions

The buffers in didanosine interfere with the absorption of drugs that require an acidic pH for absorption (e.g., ketoconazole, dapsone). Administer such drugs at least 2 hours away from didanosine.

IV pentamidine: increased risk of pancreatitis. Hold didanosine therapy while patient is receiving IV pentamidine for treatment of PCP.

Ganciclovir: possible increased risk of pancreatitis. Use these drugs together with caution.

Coadministration of didanosine with other drugs known to cause peripheral neuropathy may increase the chance of developing this side effect. Closely monitor patients who are on such combinations. Drugs that have been associated with peripheral neuropathy are chloramphenicol, cisplatin, dapsone, disulfiram, ethionamide, glutethimide, gold, hydralazine, iodoquinol, isoniazid, metronidazole, nitrofurantoin, phenytoin, ribavirin, vincristine. Concomitant use of zalcitabine and didanosine is not recommended.

Tetracyclines: the aluminum and magnesium in didanosine tablets and packets will chelate tetracycline. Do not give tetracycline at the same time as didanosine.

Quinolones: plasma concentrations of some quinolones are decreased when they are administered with products containing aluminum or magnesium. Administer quinolones at least 2 hours away from didanosine.

Antacids: coadministration of antacids with didanosine may potentiate the side effects of the antacids. Of particular concern are the possible changes in fluid and electrolyte balance that may occur.

Food: administration of didanosine with food reduces the absorption of didanosine by 50%. Give didanosine on an empty stomach.

Usual Dosage

Use a 12-hour dosing interval. Administer each dose on an empty stomach, at least ½ hour before or 2 hours after meals.

Adults: take 2 tablets at each dose. This is necessary to provide the proper amount of buffer.

Patient Weight (kg)	Tablets	Powder Packets
≥ 75	300 mg b.i.d.	375 mg b.i.d.
50–74	200 mg b.i.d.	250 mg b.i.d.
35–49	125 mg b.i.d.	167 mg b.i.d.

Children: to prevent gastric acid degradation, children greater than 1 year old should receive 2 tablets, children less than 1 year old should receive 1 tablet.

Body Surface Area (m^2)	Tablets	Powder	(Vol/10 mg/mL) Admixture
1.1–1.4	100 mg b.i.d.	125 mg b.i.d.	(12.5 mL b.i.d.)
0.8–1.0	75 mg b.i.d.	94 mg b.i.d.	(9.5 mL b.i.d.)
0.5–0.7	50 mg b.i.d.	62 mg b.i.d.	(6.0 mL b.i.d.)
< 0.4	25 mg b.i.d.	31 mg b.i.d.	(3.0 mL b.i.d.)

Method of Preparation:

Tablets:

1. Do not take tablets whole.

2. Thoroughly chew, crush, or disperse tablets.

3. To disperse, add tablets to at least 1 ounce of water and stir until tablets are thoroughly dispersed; drink entire dispersion immediately.

Buffered powder for oral solution:

1. Open packet carefully and pour contents into approximately 4 ounces of water. Do not mix with fruit juice or other acid-containing liquid.

2. Stir until the powder completely dissolves (approximately 2 to 3 minutes).

3. Drink the entire solution immediately.

Pediatric powder for oral solution:

1. Constitute the powder to 20 mg/mL by adding 100 mL or 200 mL of Purified Water, USP to the 2- or 4-g bottle of powder, respectively.

2. Immediately mix 1 part of the 20-mg/mL initial solution with 1 part of either Mylanta Double Strength Liquid or Maalox TC Suspension for a final concentration of 10 mg/mL. This admixture is stable for 30 days under refrigeration.

3. Instruct the patient to shake the admixture thoroughly prior to use and to store the tightly closed container in the refrigerator for up to 30 days.

Patient Instructions

(1) Take this medication on an empty stomach, at least 30 minutes before or 2 hours after eating.

(2) See Method of Preparation above for instructions on mixing, taking, and storing the various preparations.

(3) Check with your physician if you experience nausea, vomiting, or abdominal pain or notice any numbness, tingling, burning, or pain in your hands or feet.

(4) Didanosine is not a cure for HIV infection and has not been shown to reduce the risk of transmission of the AIDS virus to others through sexual contact.

3.   ZALCITABINE (ddC, dideoxycytidine, Hivid®)[4]

Pharmacology

Antiviral; appears to interfere with viral replication by inhibiting the reverse transcriptase of the human immunodeficiency virus and causing DNA chain termination.

Pharmacokinetics

Absorption: following oral administration, bioavailability is greater than 80%. The absorption rate and the maximum plasma concentration (C_{max}) are decreased when zalcitabine is administered with food. This results in a 39% decrease in C_{max} and a twofold increase in time to achieve C_{max} (from 0.8 hours under fasting conditions to 1.6 hours when the drug is given with food). The extent of absorption is increased by 14% when the drug is given with food.

Distribution: Vd = 0.534 L/kg. Zalcitabine does penetrate through the blood-brain barrier. The CSF/plasma concentration ratio ranges from 9% to 37% (mean, 20%).

Elimination: not significantly metabolized by the liver, eliminated renally; half-life is 2 hours.

Uses

Zalcitabine is indicated for use in combination with zidovudine in adult patients with advanced HIV infection (CD4 counts less than or equal to 300 cells per mm^3) who have demonstrated significant clinical or immunologic deterioration. As stated earlier in this section, ACTG protocol 114 showed that zalcitabine is inferior to zidovudine as single-agent therapy. The indication for combination therapy is based on the results of two small studies in zidovudine-naive patients with advanced disease. They showed that zalcitabine in combination with zidovudine produced a greater and more prolonged increase in CD4 cell counts than zidovudine alone. There have been no studies to show that zalcitabine in combination with zidovudine has any effect on clinical outcome (survival or a decrease in the number of opportunistic infections).[13]

The first study (N3447/ACTG 106) tested zalcitabine in combination with zidovudine in 56 patients with CD4 counts below 200. Patients on combination therapy had a mean peak CD4 cell count increase of 97/mm^3. This study has been criticized because the zidovudine single-agent control arm used a dose of 150 mg per day: a dose much lower than the recommended dose of 500 to 600 mg per day.[13]

The second study (BW 34,225-02) randomized 92 patients to receive either zidovudine in combination with zalcitabine or zidovudine alone. The patients in the zidovudine/zalcitabine combination arm had a higher increase in CD4 cell counts (94/mm^3 compared with an increase of 53/mm^3 for patients receiving zidovudine 200 mg q8h).[13]

Adverse Reactions

Major toxicities are peripheral neuropathy and rarely pancreatitis. The incidence of peripheral neuropathy in patients taking combination therapy is unknown, but the incidence of moderate to severe neuropathy in patients taking zalcitabine alone is 17% to 31%. Neuropathy may be reversed if zalcitabine is stopped early enough, therefore, patients should be encouraged to report immediately any early signs of peripheral neuropathy (such as numbness and burning dysesthesia in the feet and legs). Pancreatitis has occurred in less than 1% of patients taking zalcitabine alone; however, fatal cases of pancreatitis have occurred both in patients taking zalcitabine alone as well as in combination with zidovudine. Zalcitabine should be stopped if symptoms of pancreatitis, such as nausea, vomiting, or abdominal pain, occur.

Other toxicities include oral ulcers, nausea, dysphagia, anorexia, abdominal pain, vomiting, constipation, diarrhea, rash, pruritus, headache, dizziness, myalgias, arthralgias, fatigue, pharyngitis, fever, rigors, chest pain, and weight loss.

Contraindications

Hypersensitivity.

Preexisting neuropathy.

Precautions

Check CBC and clinical chemistries before initiating therapy and at regular intervals thereafter.

Check baseline serum amylase and triglyceride levels in patients with a prior history of pancreatitis, elevated amylase levels, or ethanol abuse, as well as in patients on parenteral nutrition.

Drug Interactions

IV pentamidine: increased risk of pancreatitis. Hold zalcitabine therapy while patient is receiving IV pentamidine for treatment of PCP.

Coadministration of zalcitabine with other drugs known to cause peripheral neuropathy may increase the chance of developing this side effect. Closely monitor patients who are on such combinations. Drugs that have been associated with peripheral neuropathy are chloramphenicol, cis-platin, dapsone, disulfiram, ethionamide, glutethimide, gold, hydralazine, iodoquinol, isoniazid, metronidazole, nitrofurantoin, phenytoin, ribavirin, vincristine. Concomitant use of zalcitabine and didanosine is not recommended.

Food: absorption of zalcitabine is decreased when taken with food.

Usual Dosage

0.75 mg plus 200 mg zidovudine q8h for patients weighing ≥ 30 kg.

Patient Instructions

(1) Check with your physician if you experience nausea, vomiting, or abdominal pain or notice any numbness, tingling, burning, or pain in your hands or feet.

(2) Zalcitabine is not a cure for HIV infection and has not been shown to reduce the risk of transmission of the AIDS virus to others through sexual contact.

In addition to the three antiretroviral agents used to treat HIV infection, pharmacists must stay abreast of numerous agents used to treat a variety of opportunistic infections that frequently occur in AIDS patients. Because of their compromised immune systems, AIDS patients are susceptible to multiple infections, often with organisms that until recently had not posed a sufficient threat to community health to necessitate active investigation of new agents. Treatment will often involve a combination of drugs with potentially serious side effects and interactions, and may include simultaneous use of standard and investigational drugs. Table 6.2 lists a number of drugs indicated for various opportunistic infections, as well as those agents that are being used outside of their labeling and those that are in development.

TABLE 6.2. Drugs Used to Treat Opportunistic Infections

Indication	FDA-Approved Drugs Labeled for Indication	FDA-Approved Drugs *Not* Labeled for Indication	Drugs in Development
Pneumocystis carinii pneumonia	atovaquone pentamidine trimethoprim/ sulfamethoxazole (TMP/SMX)	clindamycin dapsone primaquine	eflornithine trimetrexate
Fungal infections	amphotericin B clotrimazole troches fluconazole flucytosine ketoconazole nystatin		
Mycobacterial infections	aminoglycosides (amikacin, streptomycin) ethambutol isoniazid pyrazinamide rifabutin rifampin	azithromycin ciprofloxacin clarithromycin clofazimine	
Cytomegalovirus infections	foscarnet ganciclovir		
Toxoplasma gondii infections	pyrimethamine sulfadiazine	clindamycin	
Herpes virus infections	acyclovir	foscarnet	

The following sections present profiles of the drugs used to treat opportunistic infections. Chapter 3, on diagnosis and treatment, discussed the treatment of opportunistic infections, and we refer the reader back to that chapter for a complete discussion of each drug's place in therapy.

B. DRUGS APPROVED AND INDICATED FOR TREATMENT OR PROPHYLAXIS OF OPPORTUNISTIC INFECTIONS

DRUG THERAPY FOR *PNEUMOCYSTIS CARINII* PNEUMONIA

Trimethoprim/sulfamethoxazole (TMP/SMX) is the drug of choice for treatment of *Pneumocystis carinii* pneumonia (PCP). Alternate therapies for patients with mild PCP include atovaquone and aerosolized pentamidine. Alternative therapies for acutely ill patients include IV TMP/SMX and pentamidine. Duration of therapy is at least 21 days.

Steroid therapy has been shown to decrease the incidence of respiratory failure in patients with a PO_2 value less than 70 mm Hg. The regimen is prednisone (or its equivalent) 40 mg po b.i.d. for 5 days, then 40 mg po q.d. for 5 days, then 20 mg po q.d. for the remainder of anti-PCP treatment (11 days). The first dose of prednisone should be given a few minutes before the first dose of anti-PCP drug.[14]

Physicians begin primary prophylactic treatment against PCP when patients' CD4 cell counts drop below $200/mm^3$ or the percentage of CD4 cells drops below 20%. TMP/SMX and aerosolized pentamidine are being used for prophylaxis. Studies are under way to determine which drug is most effective.

Following their first episode of PCP, patients should be treated with drugs for secondary prophylaxis, regardless of their CD4 cell counts. The drugs used for secondary prophylaxis are the same drugs used for primary prophylaxis.

1.   ATOVAQUONE[15]

Pharmacokinetics

Absorption: poorly absorbed without fat; absorption increased 3- to 6-fold when taken with fatty foods. The drug enters the enterohepatic circulation, and most patients exhibit a double peak plasma profile.

Elimination: half-life is 75 hours (but drug is given t.i.d.).

Uses

Pneumocystis carinii pneumonia.

Potentially toxoplasma encephalitis.

Adverse Reactions

Toxicity low (12%).

Rash, fever.

Usual Dosage

750 mg po t.i.d. with food for 21 days.

2.   PENTAMIDINE (Pentam®)

Pharmacology

Antiprotozoal; may inhibit the organism's glucose metabolism, protein and
    RNA synthesis, and intracellular amino acid transport.

Pharmacokinetics

Absorption: not absorbed orally; inhalation—small amounts available in
    systemic circulation, but no accumulation occurs.

Distribution: appears to be extensively distributed and/or bound to tissues;
    69% protein bound.

Elimination: little is known; drug appears to be eliminated very slowly from
    tissues in which drug principally accumulates (liver, lungs); renal excre-
    tion is 5% or less.

Uses

Treatment and prophylaxis of *Pneumocystis carinii* pneumonia.

Adverse Reactions

IV: nephrotoxicity, hypotension, cardiac arrhythmias, facial flushing, pain and erythema at injection site, phlebitis, pruritus, rash, hypoglycemia, hyperglycemia, leukopenia, thrombocytopenia, increase in liver function test values, nausea, vomiting, diarrhea, unpleasant taste, hypocalcemia, fever, acute pancreatitis, confusion.

Inhaled: bronchospasm, cough, unpleasant taste.

Contraindications

IV: hypersensitivity.

Inhaled: severe asthma, known extrapulmonary pneumocystis infection, severe *Pneumocystis carinii* pneumonia.

Precautions

Check CBC, platelet count, LFTs, blood glucose, renal function, and serum calcium closely while on therapy.

Check blood pressure closely when administering IV—medication should be given over at least 60 minutes.

Usual Dosage

IV: 4 mg/kg IV q.d. for 14 to 21 days; renal impairment—unclear; need to decrease dosage must be based on clinical status of patient and potential risks and benefits.

Inhaled: prophylaxis—300 mg once every 4 weeks in 6 mL sterile water via Respirgard® II nebulizer.[16]

Patient Instructions

(1) IV:

    a)   This medication should be given over at least 60 minutes to minimize severe low blood pressure. Lie down while receiving the medication to avoid this complication.

    b)   This medication may cause a rash. Contact your physician if this occurs.

   c) This medication may cause hypoglycemia (irritability, shakiness, sweating, increased heart rate, confusion) or hyperglycemia (increased thirst, increased urination). Contact your physician if you notice these symptoms.

(2) Inhaled: a bronchodilator may be administered by inhaler before the aerosolized treatment to minimize tightening of the airways and cough that may occur with this medication.[16]

3. TRIMETHOPRIM/SULFAMETHOXAZOLE (various)

Pharmacology

Antibacterial. Sulfamethoxazole: inhibits the formation of dihydrofolic acid from PABA by inhibiting dihydrofolate reductase. Trimethoprim: inhibits formation of tetrahydrofolic acid from dihydrofolic acid.

Pharmacokinetics

Absorption: well absorbed from the gastrointestinal tract; peak concentration in 1 to 4 hours.

Distribution: widely distributed into tissues and body fluids; sulfamethoxazole—70% protein bound; trimethoprim—44% protein bound.

Elimination: metabolized hepatically, then excreted in the urine. Half-life: sulfamethoxazole—10 to 13 hours; trimethoprim—8 to 11 hours.

Uses

Treatment and prophylaxis of *Pneumocystis carinii* pneumonia.

Adverse Reactions

Rash, fever, urinary retention, nausea, vomiting, hepatitis, bone marrow suppression, thrombocytopenia, headache, insomnia, fatigue, nervousness, tinnitus, peripheral neuritis, depression, renal dysfunction.

Contraindications

Hypersensitivity.

Patients with documented megaloblastic anemia secondary to folate deficiency.

Patients with creatinine clearance less than 15 mL/min (some clinicians disagree).

Precautions

Carefully follow for rash or other signs of hypersensitivity.

Use with caution in patients with impaired renal or hepatic function, severe allergy, bronchial asthma, or a possible folate or G6PD deficiency.

Injectable form contains a sulfite that can cause allergic reactions in susceptible individuals.

Drug Interactions

Warfarin: may prolong PT by inhibiting the clearance of warfarin.

Usual Dosage

Treatment: oral—2 double-strength tablets 4 times per day (total of 15 to 20 mg/kg per day trimethoprim component) for 21 days; IV—20 mg/kg of trimethoprim divided q6h or q8h for 21 days; renal impairment—creatinine clearance 15 to 30 mL/min—half normal dose; creatinine clearance < 15 mL/min—contraindicated (some recommend decreasing dose further).

Prophylaxis: 1 double-strength tablet q.d. or 3 times per week.[17]

Patient Instructions

(1) If you develop a severe rash, stop medication and contact your physician immediately.

(2) If you miss a dose of this medication, take it as soon as possible. If it is almost time for your next dose and your dosing schedule is twice a day, space the missed dose and the next dose 5 to 6 hours apart. If it is almost time for your next dose and your dosing schedule is 3 or more doses per day, space the missed dose and the next dose 2 to 4 hours apart or double your next dose and get back on your regular dosing schedule.

(3) Increase water intake (8 ounces per dose) while on medication to help clear the drug out of the kidneys.

(4) Do not take this medication with high doses of vitamin C.

(5) Contact your physician if you notice any blood in your urine, stools, or vomitus.

(6) This medication may increase your sensitivity to sunlight. Avoid overexposure to sunlight until you know how you will react.

DRUG THERAPY FOR FUNGAL INFECTIONS

Fluconazole, ketoconazole, clotrimazole, and nystatin are all approved drugs for the treatment of candidiasis. Fluconazole is recommended for maintenance therapy of cryptococcal meningitis and for acute therapy of mild to moderate cryptococcal meningitis. Amphotericin B, with or without flucytosine, is the drug of choice for high-risk cryptococcal meningitis.

4. AMPHOTERICIN B (Fungizone®)

Pharmacology

Antifungal; binds to sterols in fungal cell membranes, which increases the permeability of the cell.

Pharmacokinetics

Absorption: poorly absorbed orally.

Distribution: apparently multicompartmental and widely distributed; 90% to 95% protein bound.

Elimination: unknown; 3% is excreted in the urine unchanged; drug can be detected in blood up to 4 weeks after discontinuing therapy.

Uses

Disseminated fungal infections—aspergillosis, blastomycosis, candidiasis, coccidioidomycosis, cryptococcosis, histoplasmosis.

Adverse Reactions

During administration: headache, chills, fever, malaise, muscle and joint pain, anorexia, cramping, nausea, vomiting, phlebitis.

Systemic: nephrotoxicity, hypokalemia, hypomagnesemia, systemic acidosis, anemia, bone marrow suppression, cardiac toxicity, hepatotoxicity.

Contraindications

Hypersensitivity.

Precautions

Other nephrotoxic drugs should be avoided, if possible, to prevent renal toxicity.

Check renal function, serum potassium, and serum magnesium closely while on therapy.

Check LFTs: acute hepatic failure has been reported.

Drug Interactions

Nephrotoxic drugs: additive effect.

Corticosteroids: may enhance potassium depletion.

Usual Dosage

Treatment: 0.3 to 0.8 mg/kg IV q.d.

Patient Instructions

(1) This medication may cause bleeding problems. Be careful when using toothbrushes, dental floss, and toothpicks.

(2) You may be prescribed Tylenol® (acetaminophen) and Benadryl® (diphenhydramine) to be given before your infusion to decrease side effects of administration. You should take these 30 minutes before starting the infusion.

5.   CLOTRIMAZOLE TROCHES (Mycelex® Troches)

Pharmacology

Antifungal; alters cell membrane permeability, apparently by binding with phospholipids in the fungal cell membrane.

Pharmacokinetics

Topical preparation—concentrations in saliva sufficient to inhibit *Candida* species present for 3 hours.

Uses

Oral candidiasis.

Adverse Reactions

Nausea, vomiting, abnormal liver function test values.

Contraindications

Hypersensitivity.

Precautions

LFTs should be conducted periodically, especially in patients with existing hepatic impairment.

Usual Dosage

10 mg po 5 times per day.

Patient Instructions

(1) Allow the troche to dissolve slowly and swish the dissolved material around in the mouth and then swallow. Effectiveness is improved with a longer contact time.

(2) If you miss a dose of this medication, take it as soon as possible; if it is almost time for your next dose, skip the missed dose and get back on your regular dosing schedule.

6.   FLUCONAZOLE **(Diflucan®)**[18]

Pharmacology

Antifungal; inhibits ergosterol biosynthesis; may also exhibit primary attack on membrane phospholipids and cause an increase in intracellular peroxide generation.

Pharmacokinetics

Absorption: well absorbed from the gastrointestinal tract; peak concentration in 1 to 4 hours.

Distribution: well distributed in body tissues and fluids (> 60% in CNS); approximates total body water; 11% is protein bound.

Elimination: 64% excreted in the urine; half-life is 22 hours.

Uses

Oral and/or esophageal candidiasis.

Initial treatment of mild to moderate cryptococcal meningitis.

Maintenance therapy of cryptococcal meningitis.

Adverse Reactions

Nausea, vomiting, abdominal pain, headache, rash, diarrhea, abnormal liver function test values.

Contraindications

Hypersensitivity.

Precautions

Check LFTs closely for evidence of toxicity.

Drug Interactions

Weak inhibitor of cytochrome P-450 enzymes; may affect serum concentrations of drugs metabolized by this route.

Warfarin: may cause increase in PT.

Usual Dosage[19]

Acute therapy of cryptococcal meningitis in AIDS patients: 400 mg per day for 12 weeks. High-risk patients require initial treatment with amphotericin B until stable, then may be switched to fluconazole to complete 12 weeks of therapy.

Maintenance therapy of cryptococcal meningitis in AIDS patients: 200 mg daily.

Oral and esophageal candidiasis: 100 to 200 mg po daily for 14 to 21 days.

Patient Instructions

(1) This medication may cause a rash or diarrhea. If this occurs, contact your physician.

(2) This medication may cause stomach upset. If this occurs, try taking the medication with food.

7. FLUCYTOSINE (Ancobon®)

Pharmacology

Antifungal; appears to penetrate fungal cells where it is deaminated to fluorouracil by cytosine deaminase, leading to cell death.

Pharmacokinetics

Absorption: well absorbed from the gastrointestinal tract; peak concentration in 6 hours, decreased with increased use.

Distribution: widely distributed into body tissues and fluids; 2% to 4% protein bound.

Elimination: excreted in the urine; half-life is 2.5 to 6 hours.

Uses

Disseminated fungal infections in conjunction with amphotericin B (candidiasis, cryptococcosis).

Adverse Reactions

Bone marrow suppression, eosinophilia, nausea, vomiting, anorexia, abdominal bloating, diarrhea, liver toxicity, rash, confusion, hallucinations, headache, sedation, vertigo.

Contraindications

Hypersensitivity.

Precautions

Check CBC, LFTs, and renal function tests closely while on therapy.

Use with caution in patients with suppressed bone marrow or impaired renal function.

Flucytosine levels should be checked and should be in the range of 25 to 100 mcg/mL.

Usual Dosage

50 to 150 mg/kg per day po divided q6h.

Renal impairment: creatinine clearance 20 to 40 mL/min—12.5 to 37.5 mg/kg q12h; creatinine clearance 10 to 20 mL/min—12.5 to 37.5 mg/kg q24h; creatinine clearance < 10 mL/min—12.5 to 37.5 mg/kg q24–48h.

Patient Instructions

(1) This medication may cause nausea and vomiting. If you are taking more than 1 capsule for each dose, you may space them out over 15 minutes to help lessen this side effect.

(2) If you miss a dose of this medication, take it as soon as possible; if it is almost time for your next dose, skip the missed dose and go back to your regular dosing schedule. DO NOT DOUBLE DOSE.

(3) This medication may cause bleeding problems. Be careful when using toothbrushes, dental floss, and toothpicks.

(4) This medication may cause dizziness or light-headedness. Be careful when driving or operating heavy machinery.

8. KETOCONAZOLE (Nizoral®)

Pharmacology

Antifungal; presumably alters cell membranes, resulting in increased permeability, secondary metabolic effects, and growth inhibition.

Pharmacokinetics

Absorption: absorption depends on pH of stomach (increased pH decreases absorption of the drug); peak concentration in 1 to 4 hours.

Distribution: has been detected in urine, bile, saliva, sebum, cerumen, synovial fluid, and CSF (unpredictable) in adults; 84% to 99% protein bound.

Elimination: metabolized hepatically and excreted in the feces via the bile; half-life is 8 hours.

Uses

Candidiasis.

Adverse Reactions

Nausea, vomiting, anorexia, rash, lethargy, hepatotoxicity, diarrhea, dizziness, increased sensitivity of eyes to light, insomnia, gynecomastia, arthralgia, tinnitus, bone marrow suppression (rare).

Contraindications

Hypersensitivity.

Precautions

Check LFTs closely to watch for hepatotoxicity.

Drug Interactions

Antacids, H_2-antagonists, and antimuscarinics decrease absorption of ketoconazole.

Other hepatotoxic medications have an additive effect.

Rifampin: decreased serum levels of ketoconazole.

Warfarin: may increase PT.

Cyclosporine: increased plasma levels of cyclosporine and serum creatinine.

Phenytoin: may alter metabolism of one or both of the drugs.

Theophylline: decreases theophylline concentrations in a limited number of patients.

Terfenadine: inhibited terfenadine metabolism, which may lead to symptomatic life-threatening ventricular arrhythmias.

Usual Dosage

200 to 400 mg once daily.

Patient Instructions

(1) If you miss a dose of this medication, take it as soon as possible. If it is almost time for your next dose, space the missed dose and the next dose 10 to 12 hours apart, then go back to your regular dosing schedule.

(2) Take this medication on an empty stomach.

(3) Antacids and medications used to treat ulcers will decrease the effectiveness of the medication. Take them 2 hours before or after the ketoconazole.

(4) Avoid excessive alcohol with this medication, since it can increase liver problems.

(5) This medication may cause your eyes to become more sensitive to sunlight. Wear sunglasses and avoid bright lights to prevent discomfort if this is a problem.

(6) This medication may cause dizziness and drowsiness. Be careful when driving or operating heavy machinery.

9. NYSTATIN (various)

Pharmacology

Antifungal; binds to sterols in the fungal cell membrane, which increases permeability of the cell.

Pharmacokinetics

Topical preparation: salivary levels sufficient to inhibit *Candida* species persist for 2 hours.

Uses

Oral candidiasis.

Adverse Reactions

High doses: diarrhea, nausea, vomiting, stomach pain.

Contraindications

Hypersensitivity.

Usual Dosage

500,000 to 1,000,000 units as "swish and swallow" 3 to 5 times per day for 14 days.

Patient Instructions

(1) Take this medication by placing half of the dose on each side of your mouth. Hold the medication in your mouth or swish it around in your mouth for as long as possible; gargle and swallow.

(2) If you miss a dose of this medication, take it as soon as possible; if it is almost time for your next dose, skip the missed dose and go back to your regular dosing schedule. DO NOT DOUBLE DOSE.

(3) Keep the oral liquid form of this medication from freezing.

DRUG THERAPY FOR MYCOBACTERIAL INFECTIONS

Most physicians are treating drug-sensitive cases of tuberculosis with a combination of isoniazid, rifampin, and pyrazinamide, with or without the addition of ethambutol. The most effective therapy for multidrug-resistant TB is not known. Suggested regimens include 4 to 5 drugs; amikacin is often used in these regimens.

The optimal regimen for treating *Mycobacterium avium-intracellulare* (MAI) has not been established, and several studies are under way to evaluate the effectiveness of primary prophylactic regimens against MAI infection.

10. AMINOGLYCOSIDES—Amikacin (Amikin®), Streptomycin

Pharmacology

Antibacterial, antimycobacterial; appear to inhibit protein synthesis in susceptible organisms by irreversibly binding to 30S ribosomal subunits.

Pharmacokinetics

Absorption: poorly absorbed from the gastrointestinal tract.

Distribution: widely distributed into body fluids, primarily in the extracellular fluid volume. Streptomycin: 35% protein bound; amikacin: minimally bound.

Elimination: excreted in the urine; half-life is 2 to 4 hours.

Uses (both drugs)

Mycobacterium tuberculosis and *Mycobacterium avium-intracellulare* infections.

Adverse Reactions

Ototoxicity, nephrotoxicity, varying degrees of neuromuscular blockade, hypersensitivity reactions, peripheral neuropathy, nausea, vomiting, bone marrow suppression, increases in liver function tests.

Contraindications

Hypersensitivity.

Precautions

Some preparations contain sulfites that can induce allergic reactions in susceptible individuals.

Patients with preexisting tinnitus, vertigo, subclinical hearing loss, and renal impairment are highly susceptible to ototoxicity.

Check serum levels of amikacin to avoid adverse reactions: peak is 25 to 30 mcg/mL; trough is 5 to 10 mcg/mL.

Check auditory and renal function closely.

If possible, discontinue medication if urine output decreases or azotemia occurs.

Use with caution in patients with neuromuscular disorders; may aggravate muscle weakness.

Drug Interactions

Other neurotoxic, ototoxic, or nephrotoxic drugs: toxicity may be additive.

General anesthetics and neuromuscular blocking drugs: may potentiate neuromuscular blockade.

Usual Dosage

Amikacin: 15 mg/kg IV daily, given every 8 to 12 hours—adjust dosage based on serum levels; renal impairment: load with 5 to 7.5 mg/kg, then base maintenance dose on patient's creatinine clearance.

Streptomycin: 15 mg/kg IM q.d.; renal impairment: creatinine clearance 50 to 80 mL/min—7.5 mg/kg q24h; creatinine clearance 10 to 50 mL/min—7.5 mg/kg q24–72h; creatinine clearance < 10 mL/min—7.5 mg/kg q72–96h.

11. ETHAMBUTOL (Myambutol®)

Pharmacology

Antimycobacterial; appears to inhibit the synthesis of one or more metabolites in susceptible organisms, resulting in impairment of cellular metabolism, arrest of multiplication, and cell death.

Pharmacokinetics

Absorption: well absorbed from gastrointestinal tract; peak concentration in 2 to 4 hours.

Distribution: widely distributed into most body tissues and fluids; 22% protein bound.

Elimination: partially metabolized hepatically; 50% excreted unchanged in urine; unabsorbed drug excreted in the feces; half-life is 3.3 hours.

Uses

Mycobacterium tuberculosis and *Mycobacterium avium-intracellulare* infections.

Adverse Reactions

Optic neuritis, dermatitis, pruritus, headache, malaise, dizziness, fever, disorientation, joint pain, nausea, vomiting, abdominal pain, peripheral neuritis.

Contraindications

Patients with optic neuritis.

Hypersensitivity.

Precautions

Check visual function, renal function, LFTs, and CBC closely.

Use with caution in patients with renal dysfunction and ocular defects.

Usual Dosage

15 mg/kg po q.d.; renal impairment: creatinine clearance 10 to 50 mL/min—q24–36h; creatinine clearance < 10 mL/min—q48h.

Patient Instructions

(1) This medication may be taken with food if it upsets your stomach.

(2) If you miss a dose of this medication, take it as soon as possible. If it is almost time for your next dose, skip the missed dose and get back on your regular dosing schedule. DO NOT DOUBLE DOSE.

(3) If you notice any blurred vision, eye pain, red-green color blindness, or loss of vision, contact your physician.

(4) This medication may cause dizziness. Be careful when driving or operating heavy machinery.

12. ISONIAZID (various)

Pharmacology

Antimycobacterial; appears to inhibit mycolic acid synthesis, which leads to loss of acid fastness and disruption of bacterial cell wall.

Pharmacokinetics

Absorption: well absorbed from the gastrointestinal tract; peak concentration in 1 to 2 hours.

Distribution: widely distributed to body tissues and fluids; not substantially bound to protein.

Elimination: metabolized hepatically and excreted in the urine.

Uses

Mycobacterium tuberculosis infections.

Adverse Reactions

Hepatotoxicity, coordination difficulties, dark urine, anorexia, nausea, vomiting, neuropathy, fatigue, weakness, dizziness, CNS disturbances, fever, rash, bone marrow suppression, pyridoxine deficiency, hyperglycemia, urinary retention.

Contraindications

Hypersensitivity.

Acute liver disease or history of previous isoniazid-associated hepatic injury.

Precautions

Check LFTs and signs and symptoms closely. Some authorities recommend stopping medication if LFTs > 3 times normal (more likely to occur in patients > 35 years old).

Use with caution in patients that use alcohol every day, have chronic liver disease, or have severe renal impairment.

Periodic ophthalmologic exams should be performed in patients that develop visual symptoms.

In patients that are malnourished or predisposed to neuropathy, pyridoxine should be given concomitantly.

Drug Interactions

Phenytoin: increases phenytoin levels by inhibition of hepatic metabolism.

Aluminum hydroxide gel: decreases GI absorption of isoniazid.

Disulfiram: coordination difficulties and psychotic episodes have occurred, probably due to changes in dopamine metabolism.

Usual Dosage

5 mg/kg per day (maximum 300 mg) po as a single daily dose.

Patient Instructions

(1) This medication may be taken with food.

(2) Avoid antacids containing aluminum within 1 hour of taking isoniazid.

(3) Pyridoxine (vitamin B6) may be prescribed with this medication to help prevent adverse effects of the isoniazid.

(4) If you miss a dose of this medication, take it as soon as possible. If it is almost time for the next dose, skip the missed dose and get back on your regular dosing schedule. DO NOT DOUBLE DOSE.

(5) Avoid alcohol with this medication. Alcohol can worsen liver problems sometimes associated with this medication.

(6) Check with your physician if you notice any weakness, clumsiness, numbness, tingling, burning, or pain in your hands and feet.

(7) This medication may cause dizziness and blurred vision. Be careful when driving or operating heavy machinery.

(8) If you are diabetic, this medication may cause false results with some urine sugar tests.

13. PYRAZINAMIDE, USP

Pharmacology

Antimycobacterial; still being investigated.

Pharmacokinetics

Absorption: well absorbed from gastrointestinal tract; peak concentration in 2 hours.

Distribution: widely distributed into body tissues and fluids; 50% protein bound.

Elimination: metabolized hepatically to active metabolite, then excreted in the urine; half-life is 9 to 10 hours.

Uses

Mycobacterium tuberculosis infections.

Adverse Reactions

Hepatotoxicity, inhibits renal excretion of urates, rash, nausea, vomiting, anorexia, arthralgia, acne, dysuria, photosensitivity.

Contraindications

Patients with severe hepatic damage.

Precautions

Check LFTs and uric acid levels closely.

Discontinue medication if signs of liver damage occur.

Use with caution in patients with renal failure or a history of gout.

Use with caution in patients with diabetes mellitus: management of the diabetes may be more difficult.

Usual Dosage

15 to 20 mg/kg per day po as a single daily dose.

Patient Instructions

(1) If you miss a dose of this medication, take it as soon as possible. If it is almost time for your next dose, skip the missed dose and get back on your regular dosing schedule. DO NOT DOUBLE DOSE.

(2) This medication may cause increased sensitivity to sunlight. Avoid overexposure to the sun until you know how you will react.

(3) If you are diabetic, this medication may cause false results with urine ketone tests.

14. RIFABUTIN[20]

Pharmacology

Antimycobacterial; probably inhibits DNA-dependent RNA polymerase, but may also interfere with the biosynthesis of DNA.

Pharmacokinetics

Absorption: well absorbed from the gastrointestinal tract; peak concentration in 30 minutes.

Distribution: widely distributed into body tissues and fluids; 25% protein bound.

Elimination: excreted in the urine and the bile.

Uses

Mycobacterium avium-intracellulare prophylaxis and treatment.

Adverse Reactions

Hepatotoxicity, nausea, vomiting, diarrhea, itching, leukopenia, thrombocytopenia, rash.

Contraindications

Hypersensitivity.

Precautions

Check CBC and LFTs closely to watch for toxicity.

Usual Dosage

Treatment: 300 mg po q.d. in combination with other agents.

Primary prophylaxis: 300 mg po q.d.

Patient Instructions

(1) If you miss a dose of this medication, take it as soon as possible. If it is almost time for your next dose, space the missed dose and the next dose 10 to 12 hours apart, then go back to your regular dosing schedule.

(2) If this medication upsets your stomach, take it with food.

(3) This medication may cause a rash, contact your physician if this occurs.

(4) This medication may cause bleeding problems. Be careful when using toothbrushes, dental floss, and toothpicks.

15. RIFAMPIN (various)

Pharmacology

Antibacterial; antimycobacterial; suppresses initiation of chain formation for RNA synthesis by inhibiting DNA-dependent RNA polymerase.

Pharmacokinetics

Absorption: well absorbed from gastrointestinal tract; peak concentration in 2 to 4 hours.

Distribution: widely distributed into most body tissues and fluids; 84% to 91% protein bound.

Elimination: metabolized hepatically and excreted mainly via the bile; half-life is 3 hours—decreases with continued use.

Uses

Mycobacterium tuberculosis and *Mycobacterium avium-intracellulare* infections.

Adverse Reactions

Epigastric distress, nausea, vomiting, abdominal cramps, diarrhea, headache, fatigue, liver toxicity, reddish orange coloration of body fluids, fever, confusion, dizziness, joint and muscle pain, bone marrow suppression, renal dysfunction.

Contraindications

Hypersensitivity.

Precautions

Imparts a red-orange color to urine, feces, sputum, sweat, and tears.

Check LFTs closely. Discontinue medication if liver toxicity occurs.

Drug Interactions

Hepatic microsomal enzyme induction: decreases concentration of methadone, oral antidiabetic agents, corticosteroids, digoxin, quinidine, dapsone, cyclosporine, chloramphenicol, oral anticoagulants, estrogens, and oral contraceptives.

Clofazimine: may decrease absorption of rifampin.

Ketoconazole: decreases concentration of ketoconazole.

Usual Dosage

10 mg/kg per day (maximum 600 mg) po or IV as a single daily dose.

Patient Instructions

(1) This medication is best taken with a full glass of water on an empty stomach (1 hour before or 2 hours after meals). If it upsets your stomach, you can take it with food.

(2) If you miss a dose of this medication, take it as soon as possible. If it is almost time for your next dose, skip the missed dose and then go back to your regular dosing schedule. DO NOT DOUBLE DOSE.

(3) Oral contraceptives containing estrogen may not work as well with this medication. Use a different means of birth control while taking this medication.

(4) Avoid alcohol with this medication, because liver problems may be more likely to occur.

(5) This medication may cause dizziness. Be careful when driving or operating heavy machinery.

(6) This medication will cause urine, stool, saliva, sputum, sweat, and tears to turn reddish orange to reddish brown. This effect may cause soft contact lenses to become permanently discolored; do not wear them while on therapy.

(7) This medication may cause bleeding problems. Be careful when using toothbrushes, dental floss, and toothpicks.

(8) Tell your physician that you are taking this medication before you have any medical tests: the results may be affected by the medication.

DRUG THERAPY FOR CYTOMEGALOVIRUS INFECTIONS

Foscarnet and ganciclovir appear to be equally effective against cytomegalovirus infections. Many physicians consider ganciclovir the drug of first choice, using foscarnet for patients who are intolerant of ganciclovir, whose CMV progresses while on ganciclovir, or who must continue on other bone marrow suppressive agents such as zidovudine.[21]

In one study comparing ganciclovir with foscarnet, patients on foscarnet therapy showed increased survival by a few months, possibly as a result of an antiretroviral action of foscarnet, but the rate of progression of retinitis was not different.[22]

16. FOSCARNET (Foscavir®)

Pharmacology

Antiviral; competitively inhibits viral DNA polymerase and also inhibits reverse transcriptase.

Pharmacokinetics

Absorption: not orally absorbed.

Distribution: appears to sequester in bone and cartilage; 14% to 17% bound to plasma protein; volume of distribution is 0.3 to 0.6 L/kg; variable CNS penetration with CNS levels ranging from 13% to 103% of plasma levels.

Elimination: excreted renally; half-life is approximately 3 hours and increases with the severity of renal impairment.

Uses

Cytomegalovirus infections.

Under investigation—herpes virus infections that are resistant to acyclovir.

HIV infection.

Adverse Reactions

Renal impairment (occurs to some degree in most patients; acute renal failure has occurred).

Changes in plasma minerals and electrolytes, including significant decreases in plasma-ionized calcium; hypokalemia, hypomagnesemia, and hypophosphatemia or hyperphosphatemia often occur and have caused seizures.

Other adverse reactions include fever, nausea, anemia, diarrhea, vomiting, and headache.

Contraindications

Hypersensitivity.

Precautions

Infuse solutions containing foscarnet only into veins with adequate blood flow to permit rapid dilution and distribution and avoid local irritation. Local irritation and ulcerations of penile epithelium have occurred in male patients receiving foscarnet, possibly related to the presence of drug in the urine. Adequate hydration with close attention to personal hygiene may minimize the occurrence of such events.

Closely monitor CBC. Monitor electrolyte levels and renal function 2 or 3 times per week during induction therapy and at least 1 time every 1 to 2 weeks during maintenance therapy.

Hydrate patient well before each dose. Prehydration or concurrent hydration with 1 liter of normal saline or D5W is recommended. NS or D5W may be infused simultaneously and through the same line as the foscarnet.

Drug Interactions

Nephrotoxic drugs: the elimination of foscarnet may be impaired by drugs that inhibit renal tubular secretion. Use foscarnet in combination with other nephrotoxic drugs such as amphotericin B, IV pentamidine, and aminoglycosides only if the potential benefits outweigh the risk to the patient.

Pentamidine: concurrent use of IV pentamidine and foscarnet may cause hypocalcemia.

Usual Dosage

Cytomegalovirus infections: 60 mg/kg IV q8h q.d. for 2 to 3 weeks, then 90 to 120 mg/kg IV q.d. indefinitely.

Herpes simplex infections resistant to acyclovir: 40 mg/kg IV q8h q.d. for 21 days.

Varicella-zoster infections resistant to acyclovir: 40 mg/kg IV q8h for 14 to 21 days.

Infuse each dose over 2 hours.

Adequate hydration is recommended to establish diuresis, both prior to and during treatment to minimize renal toxicity.

Dose must be adjusted according to the patient's renal function. See the package insert for guidelines.

Patient Instructions

(1) This drug is not a cure for retinitis. You may continue to experience progression of retinitis during or following treatment.

(2) A tingling sensation around your mouth, or numbness, pain, or tingling in your hands or feet may be a sign of electrolyte abnormalities. If you experience any of these feelings, stop your infusion and contact your physician.

(3) It is very important that you take in a lot of fluid before and during your foscarnet infusion to prevent kidney damage.

17. GANCICLOVIR (Cytovene®)[23]

Pharmacology

Antiviral; competitively inhibits DNA polymerase. Has 10 to 100 times greater activity than acyclovir against cytomegalovirus.

Pharmacokinetics

Absorption: minimal oral absorption.

Distribution: distributed well into lung and liver (approximates serum concentration); 38% enters CNS.

Elimination: excreted in the urine; half-life is 2.1 to 3.3 hours.

Uses

Cytomegalovirus infections.

Adverse Reactions

Severe neutropenia, diarrhea, nausea, phlebitis, testicular atrophy, thrombocytopenia, disorientation, psychosis, hepatitis, anorexia, rash, eosinophilia.

Contraindications

Hypersensitivity.

Precautions

Check CBC and LFTs closely to watch for toxicity.

Drug Interactions

Cytotoxic drugs: cytotoxic drugs that inhibit replication of rapidly dividing cell populations, such as bone marrow, spermatogonia, and germinal layers of skin and GI mucosa, may have additive toxicity when given with ganciclovir. Use drugs such as dapsone, pentamidine, flucytosine, vincristine, vinblastine, doxorubicin HCl, amphotericin B, trimethoprim/sulfamethoxazole, and other nucleoside analogues along with ganciclovir only when the potential benefit outweighs the risk to the patient.

Imipenem-cilastatin: combination may cause seizures.

Nephrotoxic drugs: combination may cause increase in S_{cr}. This has been seen with amphotericin B and cyclosporine.

Probenecid: may reduce renal clearance of ganciclovir.

Zidovudine: additive granulocytopenia. Hold zidovudine during induction treatment with ganciclovir; reinstitute with maintenance therapy and monitor CBC closely.

Usual Dosage

Induction: 5 mg/kg IV (infuse over 1 hour) q12h for 14 days.

Maintenance: 5 mg/kg IV 5 days per week indefinitely.

Patient Instructions

(1) This medication should be given over 1 hour.

(2) This medication may cause a rash or diarrhea; contact your physician if this occurs.

(3) This medication may cause bleeding problems. Be careful when using toothbrushes, dental floss, and toothpicks.

(4) This medication may or may not prevent the progression of this infection. For best results, it must be administered without fail.

Drug Therapy for *Toxoplasma gondii* Infection

Pyrimethamine plus sulfadiazine is the treatment of choice for *Toxoplasma gondii*. Although clindamycin is not indicated for treatment of *Toxoplasma gondii* infections, it is often used with pyrimethamine as the alternative regimen for patients who cannot tolerate sulfadiazine.

18. Pyrimethamine (Daraprim®)

Pharmacology

Folic acid antagonist.

Pharmacokinetics

Absorption: well absorbed after oral administration. Peak plasma concentrations occur in 2 to 5 hours.

Distribution: distributed mainly to kidneys, lung, liver, and spleen; 87% bound to plasma proteins.

Elimination: hepatically metabolized. Half-life is 4 days.

Uses

Toxoplasma gondii infections.

Adverse Reactions

Megaloblastic anemia, leukopenia, thrombocytopenia, pancytopenia, hematuria, anorexia, vomiting, atrophic glossitis.

Vomiting may be minimized by giving the dose with meals.

Contraindications

Hypersensitivity; documented megaloblastic anemia due to folate deficiency.

Precautions

Perform semiweekly CBC.

Use a lower initial dose in patients with convulsive disorders to avoid potential CNS toxicity.

Pyrimethamine may precipitate hemolytic anemia in patients with G6PD deficiency.

Drug Interactions

Antifolic drugs (e.g., methotrexate, sulfonamides, TMP/SMX) and other drugs causing neutropenia: concurrent use may increase the risk of bone marrow suppression. Monitor CBC.

Usual Dosage

Treatment: 100 mg po on day 1 (loading dose), then 50 to 75 mg po q.d. plus sulfadiazine 100 mg/kg (4 to 8 g) po or IV q.d. plus folinic acid 10 mg po q.d. for 4 to 6 weeks.

Maintenance therapy: 50 mg po q.d. plus sulfadiazine 4 to 8 g po q.d. plus folinic acid 10 mg po q.d.

Patient Instructions

(1) This medication may cause anorexia or vomiting. Take it with food or meals to help prevent these side effects.

(2) Contact your physician if you develop a skin rash or sore throat.

(3) It is very important that you make all of your appointments for blood counts to prevent possible side effects of this drug.

19. SULFADIAZINE (various)

Pharmacology

Competitively inhibits dihydrofolic acid synthesis.

Pharmacokinetics

Absorption: readily absorbed; bioavailability is 70% to 100%.

Distribution: distributed throughout all body tissues and readily enters the CSF. Wide interpatient variations in serum levels occur from identical doses.

Elimination: metabolized hepatically and excreted renally. Patients who are slow acetylators have an increased risk of toxicity from sulfonamide accumulation.

Uses

Toxoplasma gondii infections.

Adverse Reactions

Allergic reactions (skin rash, drug fever, pruritus, photosensitization); periarteritis nodosa and SLE; Stevens-Johnson syndrome; serum sickness syndrome; myocarditis; neurotoxicity (psychosis, neuritis); hepatic toxicity; blood dyscrasias (usually agranulocytosis); crystalluria; nausea and vomiting; headache; dizziness; lassitude; mental depression; acidosis; sulfhemoglobin; hemolytic anemia in G6PD-deficient patients.

Contraindications

Hypersensitivity to sulfonamides or chemically related drugs; pregnancy at term; lactation; infants less than 2 months of age; porphyria; hypersensitivity to salicylates.

Precautions

Give sulfonamides with caution to patients with severe allergy or bronchial asthma. If toxicity or hypersensitivity reactions occur, discontinue immediately.

Hemolytic anemia, frequently dose related, may occur in G6PD-deficient patients.

Drug Interactions

Oral anticoagulants: enhanced anticoagulation.

Cyclosporine: cyclosporine concentrations are increased and the risk of nephrotoxicity may be increased.

Phenytoin: serum phenytoin levels may be increased.

Methotrexate: the risk of methotrexate-induced bone marrow suppression may be enhanced.

Sulfonylureas: increased sulfonylurea half-lives and hypoglycemia have occurred.

Usual Dosage

Treatment: pyrimethamine 100 mg po on day 1 (loading dose), then 50 to 75 mg po q.d. plus sulfadiazine 200 mg/kg (4 to 8 g) po or IV q.d. plus folinic acid 10 mg po q.d. for 4 to 6 weeks.

Maintenance therapy: pyrimethamine 50 mg po q.d. plus sulfadiazine 4 to 8 g po q.d. plus folinic acid 10 mg po q.d.

Patient Instructions

(1) Take this medication on an empty stomach with a full glass of water.

(2) Avoid prolonged exposure to sunlight; photosensitivity may occur. If you are outside, wear protective clothing and apply sunscreen to exposed areas.

(3) Contact your physician if you experience blood in your urine, rash, ringing in ears, difficulty breathing, fever, sore throat, or chills.

DRUG THERAPY FOR HERPES VIRUS INFECTIONS

Acyclovir remains the only *approved* drug for the treatment of herpes simplex and zoster infections, although foscarnet is being used to treat acyclovir-resistant herpes virus infections.

20. ACYCLOVIR (Zovirax®)

Pharmacology

Antiviral; inhibits DNA polymerase of the virus.

Pharmacokinetics

Absorption: variable and incomplete; 15% to 30% absorbed. Peak concentration in 1.5 to 2.5 hours.

Distribution: widely distributed into body tissues and fluids; 9% to 33% protein bound.

Elimination: partially metabolized hepatically, but mainly excreted in the urine; half-life is 2.1 to 3.5 hours.

Uses

Herpes simplex viruses 1 and 2.

Varicella-zoster infections.

Adverse Reactions

IV: local reactions at IV site, renal dysfunction, bone marrow suppression.

Oral: headache, vertigo, fatigue, insomnia, irritability, depression, nausea, vomiting, anorexia, rash.

Contraindications

Hypersensitivity.

Precautions

Use with caution in patients with preexisting renal disease, dehydration, or concomitant use of nephrotoxic medications.

Drug Interactions

Probenecid: decreases clearance of acyclovir.

Usual Dosage

Herpes simplex:

> Treatment: 200 mg po 5 times a day; 5 mg/kg IV q8h for 10 days.

> Chronic prophylaxis of recurrent episode: 400 mg twice daily indefinitely.

Varicella-zoster: 800 mg po 5 times a day; 10 to 12 mg/kg IV q8h for 7 to 14 days.

Dosage adjustment is required for patients with renal dysfunction. Please refer to the manufacturer's prescribing information for specific guidelines.

Patient Instructions

(1) This medication may be taken with food.

(2) If you miss a dose of this medication, take it as soon as possible. If it is almost time for the next dose, skip the missed dose and get back to your regular dosing schedule. DO NOT DOUBLE DOSE.

(3) Areas affected by the virus should be kept as clean as possible. Also, wear loose-fitting clothes to avoid irritation.

C. DRUGS LICENSED AND BEING USED FOR TREATMENT OR PROPHYLAXIS OF OPPORTUNISTIC INFECTIONS OUTSIDE INDICATION

1. AZITHROMYCIN (Zithromax®)

Pharmacology

Azalide antibiotic, a subclass of the macrolides. Acts by binding to the 50S ribosomal subunit, thus interfering with microbial protein synthesis.

Pharmacokinetics

Absorption: rapidly absorbed; approximately 40% bioavailability. Food decreases absorption.

Distribution: widely distributed throughout the body. Rapid distribution into tissues and high concentration within cells result in significantly higher concentrations in tissues than in plasma or serum. Only very low concentrations have been detected in the CNS. Protein binding is variable, ranging from 51% at 0.02 mcg/mL to 7% at 2 mcg/mL.

Elimination: 4.5% excreted unchanged in the urine; primarily excreted unchanged in bile; half-life is 68 hours.

Uses

Mycobacterium avium-intracellulare infections.

Adverse Reactions

Nausea, vomiting, diarrhea, abdominal pain.

Contraindications

Hypersensitivity to any macrolide antibiotic.

Drug Interactions

Didanosine and aluminum- and magnesium-containing antacids: reduce the peak serum levels but not the extent of azithromycin absorption.

Theophylline: effect of azithromycin on theophylline levels is not known. However, concurrent use of macrolides with theophylline has been associated with increased serum levels of theophylline. Carefully monitor theophylline levels.

Warfarin: effect of azithromycin on warfarin levels is not known. However, concurrent use of macrolides and warfarin has been associated with increased anticoagulant effects. Carefully monitor warfarin levels.

Food: decreases the absorption of azithromycin, reducing the maximum concentration by 52% and bioavailability by 43%. Take on an empty stomach (1 hour before or 2 hours after meals).

Usual Dosage

500 to 1,000 mg po q.d. in combination with other agents.

Patient Instructions

(1) Take this medication on an empty stomach at least 1 hour before or 2 hours after meals.

(2) Do not take antacids at the same time you take this medication.

2.   CIPROFLOXACIN (Cipro™)

Pharmacology

Antibacterial; antimycobacterial; inhibits DNA topoisomerase (DNA gyrase), which is necessary for bacterial DNA replication and some aspects of transcription, repair, recombination, and transposition.

Pharmacokinetics

Absorption: well absorbed from the gastrointestinal tract; peak concentration in 0.5 to 2.3 hours.

Distribution: widely distributed into body tissues and fluids; 16% to 43% protein bound.

Elimination: metabolized hepatically (10% to 15%), excreted renally (15% to 50%), and eliminated in the feces (20% to 40%); half-life is 3 to 5 hours.

Uses

Mycobacterium tuberculosis and *Mycobacterium avium-intracellulare* infections.

Adverse Reactions

Nausea, vomiting, diarrhea, abdominal pain, headache, restlessness, rash, renal dysfunction, increase in liver function test values, photosensitivity, CNS disturbances.

Contraindications

Hypersensitivity.

Children: drug shown to cause arthropathy in immature animals.

Precautions

Use cautiously in patients with known or suspected CNS disorders: ciprofloxacin can sometimes cause CNS disturbances.

Drug Interactions

Antacids: decrease absorption of ciprofloxacin.

Probenecid: decreases excretion of ciprofloxacin.

Theophylline: may increase theophylline levels by 25% to 30%.

Usual Dosage

500 to 750 mg po q12h.

Patient Instructions

(1) This medication is best taken on an empty stomach with a full glass of water.

(2) If you miss a dose of this medication, take it as soon as possible. If it is almost time for your next dose, skip the missed dose and go back to your regular dosing schedule. DO NOT DOUBLE DOSE.

(3) If you are taking aluminum or magnesium antacids, do not take them at the same time with this medication—take 2 hours before or after dose.

(4) This medication may cause increased sensitivity to sunlight. Avoid over-exposure to sunlight until you know how you will react.

(5) This medication may cause blurred vision, drowsiness, and dizziness. Be careful when driving or operating heavy machinery.

3. CLARITHROMYCIN (Biaxin®)

Pharmacology

Azalide antibiotic, a subclass of the macrolides. Acts by binding to the 50S ribosomal subunit, thus interfering with microbial protein synthesis.

Pharmacokinetics

Absorption: rapidly absorbed; approximately 50% bioavailability. Food delays onset of absorption and formation of metabolite, but does not affect the extent of bioavailability. May take without regard to meals.

Distribution: metabolized to active metabolite (14-OH clarithromycin). Clarithromycin and the 14-OH clarithromycin metabolite distribute readily into body tissues and fluids. No data are available on CSF penetration.

Because of high intracellular concentrations, tissue concentrations are higher than serum concentrations.

Elimination: excreted renally; half-life is 3 to 7 hours.

Uses

Mycobacterium avium-intracellulare infections.

Adverse Reactions

Diarrhea, nausea, abnormal taste, dyspepsia, abdominal pain or discomfort, headache.

Contraindications

Hypersensitivity to any macrolide antibiotics.

Drug Interactions

Carbamazepine: may increase concentrations of carbamazepine. Monitor carbamazepine levels.

Theophylline: may increase concentrations of theophylline. Monitor theophylline levels.

Usual Dosage

500 to 1,000 mg po b.i.d. in combination with other agents.

Patient Instructions

You may take this medication without regard to meals.

4.   CLINDAMYCIN (Cleocin®)

Pharmacology

Antibacterial; appears to inhibit protein synthesis by binding to the 50S ribosomal subunits.

Pharmacokinetics

Absorption: well absorbed from the gastrointestinal tract; peak concentration in 45 to 60 minutes.

Distribution: well distributed into body tissues; 93% protein bound.

Elimination: partially metabolized hepatically and excreted in urine, bile, and feces; half-life is 2 to 3 hours.

Uses

Pneumocystis carinii pneumonia.

Toxoplasma gondii infections.

Adverse Reactions

Nausea, vomiting, abdominal pain, tenesmus, bloating, anorexia, unpleasant or metallic taste, diarrhea, *Clostridium difficile*–associated colitis, rash, thrombophlebitis, increase in liver function test values.

Contraindications

Hypersensitivity.

Precautions

If persistent diarrhea develops, discontinue medication or, if necessary, continue with close observation.

Check LFTs and renal function tests while on long-term therapy.

Capsules contain tartrazine, which may cause allergic reactions.

Use with caution in patients with GI disease (especially colitis), severe hepatic impairment, and severe renal impairment.

Drug Interactions

Erythromycin: *in vitro* antagonism of bactericidal activity has been observed.

Usual Dosage

Treatment of PCP: 300 to 600 mg po q6h plus primaquine 30 mg (base) po q.d. for 21 days.

Treatment of toxoplasmosis: 1,200 to 2,400 mg po daily plus pyrimethamine 200 mg (load), then 50 mg po q.d. plus 10 mg folinic acid po q.d. indefinitely.

Patient Instructions

(1) If you miss a dose of this medication, take it as soon as possible. If it is almost time for the next dose and you are taking 3 or more doses per day, space the missed dose and next dose 2 to 4 hours apart or double the next dose, then go back to your regular dosing schedule.

(2) If this medication upsets your stomach, take it with food.

(3) This medication may cause severe diarrhea or rash. If this occurs, contact your physician before resuming therapy.

(4) This medication contains tartrazine in its formulation. If you have an allergy to this compound or to aspirin, let your physician know.

5. CLOFAZIMINE (Lamprene®)

Pharmacology

Antimycobacterial; appears to bind preferentially to mycobacterial DNA and inhibit replication and growth.

Pharmacokinetics

Absorption: variable and incomplete (40% to 75%); peak concentration in 4 to 12 hours.

Distribution: distributed primarily to fatty tissue and cells of the reticulo-endothelial system; also taken up by macrophages.

Elimination: excreted principally in the feces; half-life is 8 days.

Uses

Mycobacterium avium-intracellulare infections.

Adverse Reactions

Pink to brownish black skin discoloration; ichthyosis and dry skin; pruritus; rash; red-brown discoloration of conjunctiva, cornea, and lacrimal fluid; abdominal pain; diarrhea; nausea, vomiting; constipation; dizziness; drowsiness; headache; depression.

Contraindications

None.

Precautions

Use with caution in patients with GI symptoms such as abdominal pain and
   diarrhea. If patient develops colicky or burning abdominal pain, nausea,
   vomiting, or diarrhea, dosage should be reduced or discontinue the medication.

Usual Dosage

100 to 200 mg po q.d.

Patient Instructions

(1) If you miss a dose of this medication, take it as soon as possible. If it is
   almost time for your next dose, skip the missed dose and get back on
   your regular dosing schedule. DO NOT DOUBLE DOSE.

(2) This medication should be taken with food.

(3) If you have diabetes, this medication may cause false test results with
   some blood sugar tests.

(4) This medication may cause dizziness or drowsiness. Be careful when
   driving or operating heavy machinery.

(5) This medication may cause increased sensitivity to sunlight. Avoid overexposure to sunlight until you know how you will react.

(6) This medication may cause dry, rough, or scaly skin. A skin cream,
   lotion, or oil may help to treat this problem.

6. DAPSONE, USP

Pharmacology

Probably inhibits folic acid synthesis in susceptible organisms.

Pharmacokinetics

Absorption: almost completely absorbed from gastrointestinal tract; peak
   concentration in 2 to 8 hours.

Distribution: well distributed into most body tissues; 50% to 90% protein
   bound.

Elimination: metabolized hepatically and excreted in the urine; half-life is 20
   to 30 hours.

Uses

Treatment and prophylaxis of *Pneumocystis carinii* pneumonia.

Adverse Reactions

Hemolytic anemia (especially in patients with G6PD deficiency), methemoglobinemia, leukopenia, rash, peripheral neuropathy, insomnia, headache,
nervousness, vertigo, nausea, vomiting, liver toxicity, renal toxicity, vision
changes, tinnitus, fever, photosensitivity.

Contraindications

Hypersensitivity.

Precautions

Caution in administering medication in patients with severe anemia, G6PD
deficiency, or those receiving other hemolytic medications.

Check CBC and LFTs frequently.

Drug Interactions

Drugs associated with similar hematologic effects—pyrimethamine, nitrofurantoin, primaquine.

The buffers in didanosine interfere with the absorption of drugs that require
an acidic pH for absorption (e.g., ketoconazole, dapsone). Administer
such drugs at least 2 hours away from didanosine.

Rifampin: reportedly decreases dapsone concentrations by inducing liver
enzymes.

Usual Dosage

Treatment: 100 mg po q24h plus 20 mg/kg per day divided q6h of trimethoprim for 21 days.[24]

Prophylaxis: 100 mg po 2 times per week, 50 mg po q.d. or 25 mg po b.i.d.

Patient Instructions

(1) If you develop a rash, discontinue medication and consult your physician.

(2) If you miss a dose of this medication, take it as soon as possible; if it is almost time for your next dose, skip the missed dose and get back on your regular dosing schedule. DO NOT DOUBLE DOSE.

(3) Try to take this medication on an empty stomach, but if stomach upset occurs, take it with food.

(4) This medication may cause bleeding problems. Be careful when using toothbrushes, dental floss, and toothpicks.

(5) This medication may cause light-headedness or dizziness. Be careful when driving or operating heavy machinery.

(6) This medication may cause increased sensitivity to sunlight. Use caution with overexposure to sunlight until you know how you will react.

7. PRIMAQUINE

Pharmacology

Antimalarial; action unknown.

Pharmacokinetics

Absorption: well absorbed from gastrointestinal tract; peak concentration in 6 hours.

Distribution: appears to be widely distributed.

Elimination: metabolized hepatically and small amount of drug excreted unchanged in the urine; half-life is 3.7 to 9.6 hours.

Uses

Pneumocystis carinii pneumonia.

Adverse Reactions

Hemolytic anemia (especially if G6PD deficient), methemoglobinemia, leukocytosis, leukopenia, nausea, vomiting, epigastric distress, abdominal cramps, headache, visual changes, pruritus.

Contraindications

Acutely ill patients with a systemic disease that tends to produce granulo-cytopenia (e.g., rheumatoid arthritis, systemic lupus erythematosus).

Patients receiving other potentially hemolytic drugs or agents capable of depressing bone marrow.

Precautions

Check CBC closely due to hematologic effects of the drug.

Discontinue drug if marked darkening of the urine or sudden decrease in hemoglobin occur.

Usual Dosage

30 mg (base) q.d. plus 300 to 600 mg clindamycin q6h for 21 days.

Patient Instructions

(1) If this medication upsets your stomach, you may take it with food or antacids.

(2) If you miss a dose of this medication, take it as soon as possible; if it is almost time for your next dose, skip the missed dose and get back on your regular dosing schedule. DO NOT DOUBLE DOSE.

(3) This medication may cause dizziness. Use caution while driving or operating heavy machinery.

(4) This medication may cause bleeding problems. Be careful when using toothbrushes, dental floss, and toothpicks.

D. DRUGS IN DEVELOPMENT

1. EFLORNITHINE[25]

Pharmacology

Antiprotozoal; inhibits ornithine decarboxylase, which affects DNA synthesis by controlling the rate of movement of the DNA replication fork and also by regulating protein synthesis.

Pharmacokinetics

Data in humans lacking.

Absorption: unknown.

Distribution: Vd = 0.43 L/kg.

Elimination: excreted in the urine; half-life is 3.6 hours.

Uses

Pneumocystis carinii pneumonia.

Adverse Reactions

Thrombocytopenia, leukopenia, anemia, diarrhea, alopecia, loss of high-frequency hearing, seizures, increase in liver function tests, rash.

Contraindications

Investigators recommend: WBC < 2,000; platelet count < 30,000; serum creatinine > 2; life expectancy < 5 days.

Precautions

Check CBC and LFTs closely: if bone marrow suppression occurs, discontinue medication; when counts return, initiate therapy at half normal dose.

Check for diarrhea: if dehydration occurs, discontinue medication to allow recovery, then initiate therapy at half normal dose.

Usual Dosage

100 mg/kg IV q6h for 14 days, then 75 mg/kg po q6h to maximum 30 g/day.

Patient Instructions

(1) This medication may cause a rash or severe diarrhea; contact your physician if this occurs.

(2) This medication may cause bleeding problems. Be careful when using toothbrushes, dental floss, and toothpicks.

2. TRIMETREXATE (investigational)[26]

Pharmacology

Antiprotozoal; potent inhibitor of dihydrofolate reductase; 1,500 times more potent than trimethoprim.

Pharmacokinetics

Data in humans lacking.

Absorption: not absorbed orally.

Distribution: unknown.

Elimination: unknown; half-life is 11 hours.

Uses

Pneumocystis carinii pneumonia.

Adverse Reactions

Neutropenia, thrombocytopenia, rash, increased liver function test values, increased serum creatinine, peripheral neuropathy.

Contraindications

Hypersensitivity.

Precautions

Check CBC and platelet count closely—if neutrophil count < 1,000 and platelet count < 100,000, may want to decrease dose to 15 mg/m^2 for 4 days (counts should rise in 3 days).

Check renal function tests and LFTs for signs of toxicity.

Usual Dosage

Trimetrexate 30 mg/m^2 IV for 21 days, given with leucovorin 20 mg/m^2 IV po q6h for 23 days.

Patient Instructions

(1) This medication may cause a rash; contact your physician if this occurs.

(2) This medication may cause bleeding problems. Be careful when using toothbrushes, dental floss, and toothpicks.

(3) Leucovorin is given with this medication to prevent harmful side effects. It is important to take this medication as prescribed without fail.

SUMMARY

We have discussed the role of the pharmacist in caring for the patient with HIV infection, and we have discussed the drug development process. We have presented monographs on antiretroviral drugs and the drugs used to treat opportunistic infections. In chapter 3, we discussed new medications being investigated for the treatment of primary HIV infection. There is still no cure for HIV infection, but we have reasons to be optimistic about the future.

We now have a therapeutic regimen to offer asymptomatic patients: we know that they can benefit from zidovudine therapy if their CD4 counts are below 500 cells per mm^3. Also, many new therapies for HIV infection are being investigated.

Additionally, there are exciting new drugs for opportunistic infections being developed. Research in the area of HIV infection is proceeding rapidly, and pharmacists are challenged to keep up with this new information and to be able to give their patients and fellow health care workers the best information and advice possible.

ANSWERS TO REVIEW QUESTIONS

I & II

1.   a
2.   d
3.   a
4.   c
5.   d

REFERENCES

1. Blaschke TF, Nies AS, Mamelok RD. Principles of therapeutics. In: Gilman AG, Goodman LS, Rall TW, et al (eds): *Goodman and Gilman's The Pharmacological Basis of Therapeutics.* 7th ed. New York, NY: Macmillan; 1985:49–65.

2. McEvoy GK, ed. *AHFS Drug Information 1992.* Bethesda, MD: American Society of Hospital Pharmacists; 1992.

3. *USP DI (v2) Advice for the Patient, 1992,* 12th ed. Rockville, MD: United States Pharmacopeial Convention, Inc; 1992.

4. Olin BR, ed. *Drug Facts and Comparisons, Updated Monthly.* St. Louis, MO: JB Lippincott Company.

5. Sanford JP, Sande MA, Gilbert DN, Gerberding JL. *The Sanford Guide to HIV/AIDS Therapy.* Dallas, TX: Antimicrobial Therapy, Inc; 1992.

6. Cotton DJ, Freidland GH, ed. Key clinical trials of antiretroviral drugs. *AIDS Clin Care.* July 1992;4(7):52.

7. Unadkat JD, Collier AC, Crosby SS, et al. Pharmacokinetics of oral zidovudine (azidothymidine) in patients with AIDS when administered with and without a high-fat meal. *AIDS.* March 1990;4(3):229–232.

8. Fischl MA, Parker CB, Pettinelli C, et al. A randomized controlled trial of a reduced daily dose of zidovudine in patients with the acquired immunodeficiency syndrome. *N Engl J Med.* October 11, 1990;323(15): 1009–1014.

9. Fischl MA, Richman DD, Hansen N, et al. The safety and efficacy of zidovudine (AZT) in the treatment of subjects with mildly symptomatic human immunodeficiency virus type 1 (HIV) infection: a double-blind, placebo-controlled trial. *Ann Intern Med.* May 15, 1990;112:727–737.

10. Volberding PA, Lagakos SW, Koch MA, et al. Zidovudine in asymptomatic human immunodeficiency virus infection: a controlled trial in persons with fewer than 500 CD4-positive cells per cubic millimeter. *N Engl J Med.* April 5, 1990;322(14):941–949.

11. Olin BR, Hebel SK, Connell SI, et al, eds. *Drug Facts and Comparisons.* St. Louis, MO: JB Lippincott Company; 1991:1782.

12. Kahn JO, Lagakos SW, Richman DD. A controlled trial comparing continued zidovudine with didanosine in human immunodeficiency virus infection. *N Engl J Med.* August 27, 1992;327(9):581–587.

13. Cotton DJ, Freidland GH, eds. ddC/AZT approved, clinical benefit unknown. *AIDS Clin Care.* August 1992;4(8):68.

14. Bozzette SA, Sattler FR, Chiu J, et al. A controlled trial of early adjunctive treatment with corticosteroids for *Pneumocystis carinii* pneumonia in the acquired immunodeficiency syndrome. *N Engl J Med.* November 22, 1990; 323(21):1451–1457.

15. Falloon J, Kovacs J, Hughes W. A preliminary evaluation of 566C80 for the treatment of pneumocystis pneumonia in patients with the acquired immunodeficiency syndrome. *N Engl J Med.* November 28, 1991;325(22): 1534–1538.

16. NebuPent™ prescribing information. *Physicians' Desk Reference.* 46th ed. Montvale, NJ: Medical Economics Data; 1992.

17. Ruskin J, LaRiviere M. Low-dose co-trimoxazole for prevention of *Pneumocystis carinii* pneumonia in human immunodeficiency virus disease. *Lancet.* February 23, 1991;337:468–471.

18. Saag MS, Dismukes WE. Azole antifungal agents: emphasis on new triazoles. *Antimicrob Agents Chemother.* January 1988;32(1):1–8.

19. Stansell J. Update: treating cryptococcal meningitis. *AIDS Clin Care.* January 1991;3(1):6.

20. O'Brien RJ, Lyle MA, Snider DE Jr. Rifabutin (ansamycin LM 427): a new rifamycin-S derivative for the treatment of mycobacterial diseases. *Rev Infect Dis.* May–June 1987;9(3):519–530.

21. Jacobson MA, Drew WL, Feinberg J, et al. Foscarnet therapy for ganciclovir-resistant cytomegalovirus retinitis in patients with AIDS. *J Infect Dis.* June 1991;163:1348–1351.

22. Studies of Ocular Complications of AIDS Research Group, AIDS Clinical Trials Group. Mortality in patients with the acquired immunodeficiency syndrome treated with either foscarnet or ganciclovir for cytomegalovirus retinitis. *N Engl J Med.* January 23, 1992; 326(4):213–220.

23. Jacobson MA, Mills J. Serious cytomegalovirus disease in the acquired immunodeficiency syndrome (AIDS). *Ann Intern Med.* April 1988;108(4): 585–594.

24. Infectious Disease Clinics of North America. Medical management of AIDS. Philadelphia, PA: WB Saunders Co; 1988;2(2).

25. Sahai J, Berry AJ. Eflornithine for the treatment of *Pneumocystis carinii* pneumonia in patients with the acquired immunodeficiency syndrome: a preliminary review. *Pharmacotherapy*. 1989;9(1):29–33.

26. Allegra CJ, Chabner BA, Tuazon CU, et al. Trimetrexate for the treatment of *Pneumocystis carinii* pneumonia in patients with the acquired immuno-deficiency syndrome. *N Engl J Med*. October 15, 1987;317(16):978–985.

PHARMACY CONTINUING EDUCATION POSTTEST

DIRECTIONS. To receive pharmacy CE credit for this program, read the Test Grading Options section that follows this pharmacy continuing education posttest. Select the posttest submission method you prefer and follow the instructions provided.

1. Which of the following is *not* a documented method of transmission for the virus that causes AIDS?

    a. contamination of food products
    b. cross-placental infection from mother to fetus
    c. heterosexual intercourse
    d. transfusion of infected blood products

2. The cell that suffers the most damage in HIV infection is the

    a. B cell.
    b. macrophage.
    c. T helper/inducer cell.
    d. T suppressor cell.

3. The major function of the immune system that suffers damage in AIDS is the ability to

    a. attach antibodies to antigens.
    b. distinguish "self" from foreign protein.
    c. initiate a cell-mediated immune response.
    d. remove cellular debris.

4. The major action of the cellular immune system is the activation of

    a. B lymphocytes.
    b. plasma cells.
    c. stem cells.
    d. T lymphocytes.

5. The major function of B lymphocytes is the production of

    a. antigens.
    b. antibodies.
    c. lymphokines.
    d. plasma cells.

6. Which of the following is *not* a result of HIV infection of a host cell?

    a. It can cause the functional impairment of CD4 lymphocytes.
    b. It can form buds that break off from the host cell.
    c. It kills the host cell and infects new cells.
    d. It reproduces new virus cells by mitotic division.

7. Cells that express CD4 antigen on their cell surface

    a. are immune to infection by HIV.
    b. are present only during active HIV infection.
    c. include T cells, monocytes, and macrophages.
    d. selectively kill the AIDS virus.

8. Monoclonal antibodies are

    a. a sign of a failing immune system.
    b. less efficient than polyclonal antibodies at combining with their specific antigen.
    c. produced in response to a single epitope.
    d. the most common antibodies produced in HIV infection.

9. All of the following are common side effects of zidovudine *except*

    a. anemia.
    b. granulocytopenia.
    c. macrocytosis.
    d. thrombocytopenia.

10. What is the main advantage of didanosine over zidovudine that we have seen to date?

    a. Didanosine causes less peripheral neuropathy than zidovudine.
    b. Didanosine has been shown to attack the HIV virus *in vitro*.
    c. Didanosine has not caused the hematologic toxicities that have been seen with zidovudine.
    d. Didanosine will probably be much less expensive than zidovudine.

11. A patient's risk of developing clinical AIDS

    a. increases as CD4 cell count decreases.
    b. increases as CD4 cell count increases.
    c. increases only when CD4 cell count drops below 200.
    d. is unrelated to CD4 cell count.

12.   The FDA has approved zidovudine for

       a. patients with AIDS.
       b. patients with AIDS and advanced AIDS-related complex.
       c. HIV-positive patients who have CD4 counts of 500 cells/mm^3 or less.
       d. any patient with a CD4 count of 500 cells/mm^3 or less.

13.   The toxicities of didanosine include all of the following *except*

       a. hepatitis.
       b. peripheral neuropathy.
       c. pancreatitis.
       d. thrombocytopenia.

14.   Experimental therapies being investigated for the treatment of HIV infec-
       tion include

       a. reverse transcriptase inhibitors.
       b. inhibitors of other elements in the virus life cycle such as HIV
           protease.
       c. immune-based therapies.
       d. all of the above.

15.   *Pneumocystis carinii* pneumonia

       a. is caused by a virulent form of bacteria.
       b. is usually fatal.
       c. may initially present with mild cough and malaise.
       d. rarely occurs in conjunction with other infections.

16.   A patient who is seropositive for HIV and presents with retinitis is most
       probably suffering from

       a. cytomegalovirus infection.
       b. diabetic retinopathy.
       c. toxoplasmosis.
       d. zidovudine toxicity.

17.   Defining AIDS as a legal handicap implies that

       a. AIDS-affected employees can be considered handicapped in their
           ability to perform their jobs.
       b. AIDS-affected employees may not be fired because of their disease.
       c. medical care must be given under certain circumstances.
       d. workers with AIDS must be given a medical leave of absence.

18. Which of the following statements about informed consent is true?

    a. It assumes that the patient has received adequate teaching about the procedure and its possible consequences.
    b. It can be obtained after the test has been performed, but before the results are known.
    c. It implies that the patient gives medical staff permission to disclose results to family members.
    d. It must always be obtained before performing a test for HIV antibodies.

19. Which of the following groups is usually *not* subject to involuntary testing?

    a. applicants for immigration
    b. health care professionals
    c. prison inmates
    d. prostitutes

20. An employer who determines that a health care worker is HIV positive

    a. may terminate employment based on anticipated disability.
    b. must base decisions about transfer on actual risk of HIV transmission.
    c. must transfer other workers away from that worker if they request transfer.
    d. must transfer that worker away from direct patient care.

21. Which of the following statements about the use of condoms is *not* true?

    a. The addition of a petroleum-based lubricant will lessen the chance of the condom tearing.
    b. The use of spermicide may add additional protection.
    c. The user should be careful not to touch the condom with sharp fingernails.
    d. The user should put on the condom before beginning fellatio or anal intercourse.

22. Which of the following are mechanisms used by the FDA to expedite the evaluation of promising new treatments for HIV infection?

    a. treatment IND
    b. import of foreign drugs
    c. expedited review of phase II and III studies
    d. both a and c

23.   Which of the following is *not* an expected toxicity of zidovudine?

a. anemia
b. nephrotoxicity
c. neutropenia
d. pigmentation of fingernails and toenails

24.   Which one of these drugs is *not* used as prophylaxis against *Pneumocystis carinii* pneumonia?

a. aerosolized pentamidine
b. dapsone
c. rifampin
d. trimethoprim/sulfamethoxazole

25.   Which of the following is *not* an expected side effect of IV pentamidine therapy?

a. hypercalcemia
b. hypoglycemia
c. hypotension
d. leukopenia

26.   Which of the following is *not* an expected toxicity of trimethoprim/ sulfamethoxazole therapy?

a. bone marrow suppression
b. hypotension
c. peripheral neuropathy
d. rash

27.   You should instruct your patients who are taking ketoconazole to do which one of the following?

a. Avoid taking the drug concomitantly with zidovudine because of the chance of increased hematologic toxicity.
b. Do not take the drug and check with their physician if they are G6PD deficient.
c. Take each dose on an empty stomach.
d. Take each tablet with an antacid to increase absorption.

28.   What is the recommended dose of aerosolized pentamidine for prophylaxis against *Pneumocystis carinii* pneumonia?

a. 60 mg weekly
b. 150 mg once every two weeks
c. 300 mg once every two weeks
d. 300 mg once every four weeks

29. Which of the following drugs is *not* used as treatment for *Mycobacterium avium-intracellulare* infections?

   a. clarithromycin
   b. ciprofloxacin
   c. clindamycin
   d. rifampin

30. What is the oral dose of acyclovir for varicella-zoster infections?

   a. 200 mg 5 times a day
   b. 200 mg q4h, 6 times a day
   c. 400 mg 5 times a day
   d. 800 mg 5 times a day

31. Which of the following side effects has *not* been reported for fluconazole?

   a. abdominal pain
   b. abnormal liver function tests
   c. headache
   d. peripheral neuropathy

32. Foscarnet is a drug used to treat which opportunistic infection?

   a. cytomegalovirus infection
   b. *Mycobacterium avium-intracellulare* infection
   c. *Pneumocystis carinii* pneumonia
   d. systemic fungal infection

33. Ciprofloxacin is being used to treat which opportunistic infection?

   a. cytomegalovirus infection
   b. *Mycobacterium avium-intracellulare* infection
   c. *Pneumocystis carinii* pneumonia
   d. *Toxoplasma gondii* infection

34. What is the mechanism of action of zidovudine?

   a. inhibits assembly of viral proteins
   b. inhibits reverse transcriptase
   c. inhibits uncoating of the virus
   d. inhibits viral binding

35. What is the usual dose of dapsone/trimethoprim for treatment of *Pneumocystis carinii* pneumonia?

    a. dapsone 100 mg q.d. + trimethoprim 20 mg/kg q6h
    b. dapsone 100 mg q.d. + trimethoprim 20 mg/kg per day as a single dose
    c. dapsone 100 mg po q24h + trimethoprim 20 mg/kg per day, divided q6h
    d. dapsone 100 mg q6h + trimethoprim 20 mg/kg q6h

36. Which precautions should physicians follow when prescribing ethambutol?

    a. Avoid prescribing for patients who have G6PD deficiency.
    b. Check visual function, renal function, LFTs, and CBC closely.
    c. Discontinue medication if persistent diarrhea develops.
    d. Warn patient that this medication imparts a red-orange color to urine, feces, sputum, sweat, and tears.

37. Clofazimine is used to treat which AIDS-related opportunistic infection?

    a. cryptococcal meningitis
    b. *Mycobacterium avium-intracellulare* infection
    c. *Pneumocystis carinii* pneumonia
    d. toxoplasmosis

TEST GRADING OPTIONS

To make it as convenient as possible for you to complete this program, Glaxo offers you three choices for having your test graded: **Phone-in Grading, Mail-in Grading, Computer Telecommunications Grading, and Facsimile Grading.**

To assist you in selecting the type of grading service that best suits your needs, consider the following:

Phone-in Grading:

- Your call is answered by a trained and courteous operator.
- Your certificate is dated the same day as your call.
- You get your test score immediately over the phone. If your score is over 70%, you are informed of the correct answers to any incorrect responses.
- See the instructions on the following page.

Mail-in Grading:

- Your test will be processed promptly upon receipt.
- Simply enclose a check or money order with your completed answer sheet.
- Use the special scannable form contained in the envelope at the end of the book.
- See the instructions on the scannable form.

For your convenience, additional scannable forms are available upon request by calling 516-563-1604, Monday–Friday, 10 a.m. to 5 p.m. (EST).

Computer Telecommunications Grading:

If you have a copy of the HELIX OnLAN PC or OnLAN Mac, you can access Glaxo's HELIX Network via your local CompuServe number, allowing you to take your test on-line 24 hours a day, 365 days per year:

- Dial into HELIX.
- Select menu item "Glaxo C.E. Tests."
- Select the test you wish to take.
- Complete your test and provide your charge card information.
- Your certificate will arrive within two weeks.

If you have not yet enrolled in HELIX, see a Glaxo sales representative for an enrollment brochure or call 1-800-85-HELIX to obtain free membership and software.

Facsimile Grading:

- Your fax is received by a trained operator.
- If your fax is received before 2 p.m. (EST), your certificate is dated the same business day.
- You can fax your completed answer sheet at your convenience 24 hours per day.
- See the instructions on the Facsimile-Grading Posttest Answer Sheet.

Phone-in Grading Instructions:

To use the **Phone-in Grading** service, call 1-800-327-9263, 10 a.m. to 5 p.m. (EST) Monday–Friday. Please have the following ready when you call:

1) **The posttest answers**
2) **Your Social Security number**
3) **Credit card name, number, and expiration date**

For Phone-in Grading, you can use your **Visa, MasterCard, or American Express** card to pay the $10.00 per test processing fee. Your call will be answered by a trained and courteous operator who will assist you and process your certificate the same day.

NOTE: **Pharmacists wishing to use this course to meet the mandatory AIDS education requirement in Florida *must* complete the program "Florida Law on AIDS" and use the answer sheet on page 329.**

FACSIMILE GRADING POSTTEST ANSWER SHEET

Care and Management of Patients with HIV Infection
ACPE ID# 686-342-92-041   Credit: 0.7 CEU
Please print clearly the information requested below.

SOCIAL SECURITY NO. ☐☐☐ – ☐☐ – ☐☐☐☐

Name ☐☐☐☐☐☐☐☐☐☐☐☐☐ ☐ ☐☐☐☐☐☐☐☐☐☐☐☐☐☐☐
First   M.I.   Last

Home Address ☐☐☐☐☐☐☐☐☐☐☐ ☐☐☐☐☐☐☐☐☐☐☐☐☐☐☐☐

☐☐☐☐☐☐☐☐☐☐☐☐☐ ☐☐ ☐☐☐☐☐ – ☐☐☐☐
City   State   Zip Code

Home Phone (   ) – ☐☐☐ – ☐☐☐☐   **Bus. Phone (   ) –** ☐☐☐☐☐☐☐

Are you licensed in Alabama?   Yes _____   No _____   Alabama License No. _____

Other states licensed in: _____

You may fax your completed answer sheet to **(516) 563-1907**, 24 hours a day. You may use your charge card to pay the $10.00 per test processing fee. Please provide the following information.

Credit Card Name: ☐VISA   ☐MC   ☐Am. Exp.

Number: ☐☐☐☐☐☐☐☐☐☐☐☐☐☐☐☐☐☐☐☐☐☐☐☐

Expiration date: _____/_____

Your signature: _____

Your fax number: _____

If your fax is received before 2 p.m. (EST), your certificate is dated the same business day.

Please be sure your Social Security number is given as requested above. Credit will be granted for the successful completion of this program up to November 1, 1995.

For each question, decide on the best answer, and place an X through that letter. If you change an answer, be sure to erase completely. Mark only **one** answer for each question.

1.	A B C D	14.	A B C D	27.	A B C D
2.	A B C D	15.	A B C D	28.	A B C D
3.	A B C D	16.	A B C D	29.	A B C D
4.	A B C D	17.	A B C D	30.	A B C D
5.	A B C D	18.	A B C D	31.	A B C D
6.	A B C D	19.	A B C D	32.	A B C D
7.	A B C D	20.	A B C D	33.	A B C D
8.	A B C D	21.	A B C D	34.	A B C D
9.	A B C D	22.	A B C D	35.	A B C D
10.	A B C D	23.	A B C D	36.	A B C D
11.	A B C D	24.	A B C D	37.	A B C D
12.	A B C D	25.	A B C D		
13.	A B C D	26.	A B C D		

To avoid delay, please be sure to include the proper credit card information.

This CE program is sponsored by Glaxo Inc. as an educational service to keep today's pharmacist abreast of a rapidly changing health care environment. Address all inquiries to: Barbara Mitchell, Manager, Pharmacy Education, Glaxo Inc., Five Moore Drive, RTP, NC 27709.

Each participant achieving a grade of 70% or above will receive a participation certificate indicating the number of CE credits earned. Please allow three weeks for processing. This certificate should be kept in a safe place and used as documentation of CE credits earned. A participant obtaining a grade below 70% will be notified and permitted to retake the exam one time at no extra cost.

How long did it take you to complete this CE activity? _____

SURVEY QUESTIONS

1. Highest degree earned: (Check one.) ☐ BS Pharmacy ☐ BS (Other) ☐ PharmD
☐ PhD ☐ Other _____

2. How long ago did you complete your last degree: (Check one.)

☐ Less than 1 yr ☐ 1–5 yrs ☐ 6–10 yrs ☐ 11–20 yrs ☐ 21–30 yrs ☐ More than 30 yrs

3. Area of practice: (Check all applicable.)

☐ Independent ☐ Teaching/Research ☐ Medical sales rep.
☐ Chain ☐ Industry/Research ☐ Wholesale
☐ Hospital or institution ☐ Other _____

4. I found the program: (Circle the appropriate number/level.)

Not Practical	1	2	3	4	5	Very Practical
Poorly Written	1	2	3	4	5	Expertly Written
Difficult to Understand	1	2	3	4	5	Easily Understood

5. The examination was: (Circle the appropriate number/level.)

Too Short	1	2	3	4	5	Too Long
Too Difficult	1	2	3	4	5	Too Easy
Poorly Written	1	2	3	4	5	Clearly Written

6. Please check any of the following topics that you feel would be of interest for future CE programs.

☐ Drug Interactions
☐ Drugs and Nutritional Disorders
☐ Drugs and the Geriatric Patient
☐ Pharmacokinetics/Biopharmaceutics
☐ Drugs and Cancer
☐ Drugs and Infectious Diseases
☐ Drugs and Dermatologic Disorders
☐ Basic Pharmacology of Selected
Drug Categories. Any special
categories: _____

☐ Drugs and Cardiovascular Diseases
☐ Rational Approaches to Drug Selection
☐ Drug-induced Diseases
☐ Drugs and Their Side Effects
☐ Drugs and Respiratory Diseases
☐ Drugs and Gastrointestinal Disorders
☐ Drugs and Sexually Transmitted Diseases
☐ Please list other topics of interest or
concern: _____

FLORIDA LAW ON AIDS:

A Supplement to
Care and Management of Patients with HIV Infection

By David B. Brushwood, BS Pharm, JD

Glaxo Inc. is approved by the American Council on Pharmaceutical Education as a provider of continuing pharmaceutical education.

ACPE ID No.: 686-342-92-016, 0.1 CEU (1 Contact Hour) and
ACPE ID No.: 686-342-92-041, 0.7 CEU (7 Contact Hours)

Florida Program ID No.: PSA-94-006, 0.8 CEU (8 Contact Hours)

Florida PSA-94-006 includes chapters 1, 2, 3, 4, and 6 of *Care and Management of Patients with HIV Infection* and the one-hour supplement "Florida Law on AIDS."

CONTENTS

Introduction 313
Special Note to Florida Registered Pharmacists 313
Objectives 314
   I.   The Legal Requirement for Continuing Education
       on HIV/AIDS in Florida 315
  II.   Florida Law on AIDS and Its Impact on Testing 316
 III.   Florida Law on AIDS and Its Impact on the Confidentiality
      of Test Results 319
 IV.   Florida Law on AIDS and Its Impact on the Treatment
      of Patients 322
Summary 325
Posttest 326
Mail-in Grading Posttest Answer Sheet 329

INTRODUCTION

This text is designed to provide accurate, authoritative information on current Florida law as it pertains to HIV/AIDS. It is published with the understanding that the writer is not engaged in rendering legal or other professional service. If legal advice or other expert assistance is required, the services of a competent professional should be sought.

Chapter 4 of *Care and Management of Patients with HIV Infection* provides a thorough overview of the general national approach to legal issues regarding the treatment of patients with HIV infection. This supplement provides specifics concerning Florida law. Information in this supplement concerning current Florida law on AIDS and its impact on testing, confidentiality of test results, and treatment of patients, taken together with information in the book *Care and Management of Patients with HIV Infection*, meets the requirement that Florida pharmacy licensees participate in a continuing education course on HIV/AIDS. A supplement such as this one is necessary for Florida pharmacy practitioners, because certain areas of Florida law on HIV infection are both more extensive and more precise than general national requirements.

SPECIAL NOTE TO FLORIDA REGISTERED PHARMACISTS

In order to meet the Florida mandatory AIDS education requirements, pharmacists registered in Florida must complete the seven-hour program (chapters 1, 2, 3, 4, and 6) *and* this supplemental one-hour program, "Florida Law on AIDS." The combination of the seven-hour course and the one-hour supplement constitutes an eight-hour program (Florida program number PSA-94-006, expiration date December 31, 1994).

Pharmacists who wish to meet the mandatory Florida AIDS education requirement *must* use the posttest answer sheet located on page 329. This answer sheet is comprehensive of the posttest questions at the end of chapter 6 and the posttest questions at the end of this supplement.

OBJECTIVES

Objectives presented here are intended to focus the reader's attention on expected learning outcomes.

On completion of this supplement, the reader should be able to:

1. Explain the legal requirement for continuing education on HIV/AIDS in Florida.

2. Describe the current Florida law on AIDS and its impact on testing.

3. Describe the current Florida law on AIDS and its impact on the confidentiality of test results.

4. Describe the current Florida law on AIDS and its impact on the treatment of patients.

I. THE LEGAL REQUIREMENT FOR CONTINUING EDUCATION ON HIV/AIDS IN FLORIDA

The Florida legislature has established a requirement that pharmacy licensees subject to regulation by the Department of Health and Rehabilitative Services complete an educational course on HIV/AIDS as a condition of relicensure. The course must contain at least these five components: (1) Education on the modes of transmission, (2) Infection control procedures, (3) Clinical management, (4) Prevention of HIV and AIDS, and (5) Information on current Florida law on AIDS and its impact on testing, confidentiality of test results, and treatment of patients. Failure to complete the requirement is grounds for disciplinary action, and anyone failing to comply must still complete the course in addition to being subject to administrative discipline. Applicants for initial licensure must also complete the HIV/AIDS course requirement.

Legislative reaction to the spread of HIV/AIDS is not surprising, considering the enormous legal dimensions to a disease that presents challenging, but by no means unprecedented, medical problems. In fact, AIDS is unique as a disease primarily because of its political characteristics. In other ways it is similar to infectious diseases that are not subject to such extensive legislative attention. AIDS can be sexually transmitted, but so can syphilis, hepatitis, and herpes. AIDS can be transmitted by the exchange of blood, but so can hepatitis and yellow fever. AIDS is fatal, but smallpox, Legionnaire's disease, and plague can also be fatal. AIDS is caused by a virus, but so are yellow fever, smallpox, and herpes. The uniqueness of AIDS is due to its being currently controllable primarily through programs that produce social change, rather than through technological advances. The law is an instrument of social change, and the legislature has recognized its special role as lawmaker in addressing this unusual public health problem.

It may seem unnecessary to say that legislatures are, above all, political. Yet realization of this primary character of the legislature can explain why such extraordinary steps have been taken to protect Floridians from AIDS, and why health care providers are specifically required to learn about the law and AIDS. AIDS has been a political disease since it was discovered, and it has become more political over time. The Florida legislature has participated in the politics of AIDS not by choice but by necessity. The content of the Florida AIDS law reflects a considered approach to a public health problem that might otherwise be hampered by bigotry, prejudice, and ignorance. The Florida AIDS law assures that the normal medical treatment and research process will be influenced by medical considerations alone, and not by extraneous factors that produce poor judgment based on irrelevant matters.

II. FLORIDA LAW ON AIDS AND ITS IMPACT ON TESTING

Patients may be tested for HIV antibody as a component of their diagnosis and treatment, and this testing is relatively noncontroversial. There are also voluntary programs to test individuals who are not patients under treatment, but who wish to know whether they are HIV positive. Voluntary testing raises some controversy due to the psychological effects of knowing one's own seropositivity and the social effects of others knowing that one is seropositive. Perhaps the greatest level of controversy is associated with proposals that patients and/or health care providers be routinely screened for HIV to protect themselves and each other from transmission. Policy makers have not embraced this approach. The use of universal precautions that result in treating all patients as if they were HIV-positive weakens the force of arguments favoring routine screening of patients and health care providers.

Because of the controversy associated with HIV testing, the Florida legislature has established requirements concerning testing for HIV. The legislature bases its requirements on its determination that the use of tests designed to reveal HIV infection can be a valuable tool in protecting the public health. Despite the many good reasons to be tested for HIV infection, the Florida legislature observed that many members of the public are deterred from seeking such a test because they misunderstand the nature of the test and/or fear that the results will be disclosed without their consent. The Florida legislation is designed to overcome barriers to the effective use of HIV testing as a public health measure.

Several important definitions are specifically delineated by the Florida legislature. They are:

- *HIV test* means a test ordered after July 6, 1988, to determine the presence of the antibody or antigen to human immunodeficiency virus or the presence of human immunodeficiency virus infection.

- *HIV test result* means a laboratory report of a human immunodeficiency virus test result entered into a medical record on or after July 6, 1988, or any report of a human immunodeficiency virus test. As used in this section, the term *HIV test result* does not include test results reported to a health care provider by a patient.

- *Significant exposure* means:

    1. Exposure to blood or body fluids through needle-stick, instruments, or sharps.

    2. Exposure of mucous membranes to visible blood or body fluids, to which universal precautions apply according to the National Centers for Disease Control, including, without limitations, the following body fluids:

        a. Blood

        b. Semen

        c. Vaginal secretions

        d. Cerebrospinal fluid (CSF)

        e. Synovial fluid

        f. Pleural fluid

        g. Peritoneal fluid

        h. Pericardial fluid

        i. Amniotic fluid

        j. Laboratory specimens that contain HIV (e.g., suspensions of concentrated virus)

    3. Exposure of skin to visible blood or body fluids, especially when the exposed skin is chapped, abraded, or afflicted with dermatitis or the contact is prolonged or involves an extensive area.

- *Test subject* or *subject of the test* means the person upon whom an HIV test is performed, or the person who has legal authority to make health care decisions for the test subject.

Bearing in mind these particularized definitions, the legislature has required that no person order a test without making available to the person tested, prior to the test, information regarding measures for the prevention of HIV transmission, exposure to HIV, and the transmission of HIV. At the time an HIV test is ordered, the person ordering the test must schedule a return visit with the test subject for the purpose of disclosing the test results and conducting posttest counseling.

Under Florida law, no test result may be determined as positive, and no positive test result may be revealed to any person, without corroborating or confirmatory tests being conducted. However, preliminary test results may be released to licensed physicians or certain medical personnel who have a "need to know" the results.

No test result may be revealed to the person upon whom the test was performed without affording that person the immediate opportunity for individual face-to-face counseling about:

1. The meaning of the test results.

2. The possible need for additional testing.

3. Measures for the prevention of the transmission of HIV.

4. The availability in the geographic area of any appropriate health care services, including mental health care, and appropriate social and support services.

5. The benefits of locating and counseling any individual by whom the infected individual may have been exposed to HIV infection, and any individual whom the infected individual may have exposed to HIV infection.

6. The availability, if any, of the services of public health authorities with respect to locating and counseling any individual described in paragraph 5 immediately above.

III. FLORIDA LAW ON AIDS AND ITS IMPACT ON THE CONFIDENTIALITY OF TEST RESULTS

Confidentiality is a general rule in health care. Respect for individual privacy is one reason why health care providers are always careful not to disclose private facts about patients. In addition, because it is beneficial to the public for individuals with infectious diseases to seek medical assistance, information about infectious diseases is held confidential, since otherwise infected individuals might not risk public disclosure of health-related information by health care providers. In Florida, HIV infection is considered to be highly confidential. This means that it is particularly important not to disclose information about HIV seropositivity because of the particularly strong public reaction to an infected individual that disclosure of the information might cause.

Confidentiality has never been an absolute right. There have always been circumstances in which greater good can be done by breaching confidentiality than by respecting it. While some scholars and practitioners believe that confidentiality is so fundamental that it should always be respected, the prevailing view is that when a breach of confidentiality would save the patient or others from great harm, there is a duty to breach confidentiality. This prevailing view has been adopted by the Florida legislature in the requirements relating to the confidentiality of the results of AIDS testing.

The general rule in Florida is that the identity of any person upon whom a test has been performed and the test results are confidential. No person who has obtained a test result, or has knowledge of a test result, may disclose or be compelled to disclose the identity of any person upon whom a test is performed or the results of such a test. The confidentiality requirement extends to a prohibition on disclosure in any manner which permits identification of the subject of the test.

The general rule of confidentiality of HIV testing and test results is subject to several specific exceptions listed by the Florida legislature. Under the exceptions to confidentiality, a person may disclose the identity of an individual who has been tested, or the results of a test, to the following persons:

1. The subject of the test or the subject's legally authorized representative.

2. Any person designated in a legally effective written release of the test results executed prior to or after the test by the subject of the test, or by the subject's legally authorized representative.

3. An employee of a health facility, if the facility is authorized to obtain the test results, and if the employee both (a) participates in the provision of patient care, and (b) has a need to know the information.

4.   Health care providers consulting between themselves or with health care facilities to determine diagnosis and treatment.

5.   The Department of Health and Rehabilitative Services.

6.   Health facility staff committees, for the purposes of conducting program monitoring, program evaluation, or service reviews.

7.   Authorized medical or epidemiological researchers, who may not further disclose any identifying characteristics or information.

8.   A person allowed access by order of a court or by order of a worker's compensation judge.

9.   Persons involved with child-caring agencies or family foster homes, or adoptive parents of tested individuals.

10. Medical personnel who have been subject to a significant exposure during the course of medical practice.

The Florida legislature has addressed the subject of immunity from civil or criminal liability for the disclosure or nondisclosure of information about HIV infection by practitioners regulated through the Division of Medical Quality Assurance of the Department of Health and Rehabilitative Services. These requirements serve as guidelines for all health care professionals concerning the possibility of liability (either civil or criminal) for disclosure or nondisclosure.

The law states that there shall be no criminal or civil liability for the disclosure of otherwise confidential information about a positive test for HIV to a patient's sexual partner or a patient's needle-sharing partner under the following circumstances:

1.   If a patient discloses to a health care provider the identity of a sexual partner or a needle-sharing partner.

2.   The health care provider recommends that the patient notify the sexual partner or the needle-sharing partner of the positive test and refrain from engaging in sexual or drug activity in a manner likely to transmit the virus and the patient refuses, and the health care provider informs the patient of his or her intent to inform the sexual partner or needle-sharing partner.

3.   If pursuant to a perceived civil duty or the ethical guidelines of the profession, the health care provider reasonably and in good faith advises the sexual partner or the needle-sharing partner of the patient of the positive test and facts concerning the transmission of the virus.

Florida law also indicates that health care providers will not be civilly or criminally liable if they know of a positive test result for HIV, but fail to disclose the information to a sexual partner or a needle-sharing partner of the patient. While this part of the law specifically applies to practitioners regulated through the Division of Medical Quality Assurance of the Department of Health and Rehabilitative Services, it can probably be generalized to all health care professionals.

IV. FLORIDA LAW ON AIDS AND ITS IMPACT ON THE TREATMENT OF PATIENTS

The specifics of Florida AIDS law are directed particularly at testing and have only peripheral application to patient care. Nevertheless, there are some aspects of the Florida AIDS law that can impact on patient care directly, or perhaps indirectly through their relevance to testing.

One important legal requirement relating to treatment of patients is the Florida law that prohibits the sale of self-testing kits designed to tell persons their status concerning HIV or AIDS, or related disorders or conditions. This law is contrary to the trend toward increased use of self-diagnostic kits (pregnancy, diabetes, etc.) that patients have begun to use more often now than in the past. The apparent belief is that self-treatment is not appropriate for AIDS or HIV infection, and therefore self-diagnosis should not be permitted. This approach is probably used because of the severe psychological consequences of discovering that one has tested positive for HIV antibodies.

Florida law also is relevant to the treatment of patients with HIV/AIDS in that the law makes it illegal to require that taking or submitting to an HIV-related test is a condition of receiving medical services. The medical services that may not be conditioned on the taking of, or submitting to, an HIV-related test include admission into any licensed health care facility, or the purchasing or obtaining of any service or product for which the provider must be licensed. This area of the law is modified so as not to prohibit any physician in good faith from declining to provide a particular treatment requested by a patient if the appropriateness of that treatment can only be determined through an HIV-related test.

Florida law specifies the requirements applicable to a health care facility that conducts, or holds itself out to the public as conducting, a testing program for HIV/AIDS. These requirements include registration with the Department of Health and Rehabilitative Services and compliance with other applicable legal requisites. In particular, a testing program must be directed by a person with experience in the counseling of persons with AIDS. All medical care must be supervised by a licensed physician. All requirements relating to testing, confidentiality, and informed consent must be observed.

The informed consent requirements are perhaps the most important aspect of the Florida AIDS law as it relates to the treatment of patients. Informed consent is a widely accepted and recognized requirement for patient care. As the phrase indicates, there are two components to informed consent, the "informed" component and the "consent" component. Informed consent requires that a patient be told about a proposed procedure, including a description of the benefits and risks of the procedure, and that a patient be given an opportunity to decide whether he or she wants to have the procedure done. A patient must give permission before a procedure can be done on the patient. The primary objective of informed consent is to involve the patient in his or her care, with the goal of increased quality of care through patient participation.

There are circumstances under which the requirement of informed consent does not apply in general patient care. One such circumstance is the emergency situation, in which consent is inferred by the circumstances. Another circumstance is presumed consent, which occurs when actions indicate that consent has been given, but words are not specifically spoken. And there is the "therapeutic privilege," a narrow exception to the general requirement of informed consent, which permits a care provider to not fully inform the patient of relevant risks because being fully informed would be detrimental to the patient.

Under Florida law, no person may perform a test designed to identify HIV, or its antigen or antibody, without first obtaining the informed consent of the person upon whom the test is being performed. Informed consent must be preceded by an explanation of the right to confidential treatment of information identifying the subject of the test and the results of the test. Consent need not be in writing, provided there is documentation in the medical record that the test has been explained and that consent has been obtained. Informed consent must be obtained from a legal guardian or other person authorized by law when the patient is not competent or is otherwise unable to make an informed judgment.

There are several exceptions to the requirement of informed consent to HIV testing under Florida law. They are:

1.   When testing for sexually transmissible diseases as authorized by law.

2.   Medical emergencies, when test results are necessary for appropriate emergency care and the patient is unable to consent.

3.   When, in the opinion of the attending physician, informed consent would be detrimental to the patient.

4.   HIV testing as part of an autopsy for which consent was obtained.

5.   After a sexual battery where a blood sample has been taken from the defendant.

6.   When an HIV test is mandated by court order.

7.   For epidemiological research consistent with institutional review boards.

8.   For an infant, when the parents cannot be contacted.

Florida law on AIDS also addresses the need to obtain informed consent for the performance of an HIV test on a patient who comes into contact with medical personnel in such a way that a significant exposure has occurred. If a blood sample has already been taken voluntarily, then the following rules apply:

1. The patient must be requested to consent to an HIV test.

2. Reasonable efforts must be made to locate the patient, if the patient is not readily available.

3. Costs of the test must be borne by the medical personnel, or the employer.

4. The medical personnel must be tested also, or provide evidence of a negative test within six months.

5. If all conditions are met, then no informed consent is necessary.

6. If no blood has been voluntarily drawn from the patient, and medical personnel have a significant exposure during treatment of a medical emergency, then the same rules apply, and a blood test may be done during the course of treatment for the emergency.

A particularly important part of the Florida law on HIV/AIDS applies to minors' consent to treatment. It specifies that a health care professional may provide treatment for sexually transmissible diseases to any minor. The consent of the parents or guardians of a minor is not a prerequisite for an examination or treatment of a minor. Even the fact of consultation, examination, and treatment of a minor for a sexually transmissible disease is confidential. This information may not be divulged to a parent or guardian by any direct means, or by indirect means such as sending a bill for services rendered.

SUMMARY

The structure of Florida law on HIV/AIDS encourages voluntary testing by those who think they may be infected. This goal of voluntary testing is sought through legal controls placed on testing by individuals and institutions to assure accuracy and confidentiality of test results. Florida law declares that persons infected or perceived to be infected with HIV may not be discriminated against based on their seropositive status. The result of this approach should be to encourage as many people as possible to discover their HIV infection and take necessary steps to assure that others are not infected.

The Florida statute on AIDS has been amplified through regulations promulgated by the Department of Health and Rehabilitative Services. Particularly noteworthy within those regulations is the definition of "need to know." There are several types of persons who are deemed to have a need to know the results of a patient's HIV-related test under Florida law. These include individuals involved with the business operations of a health care facility (financial staff, transcribers, etc.), individuals responsible for patient care (licensed professionals and others on the health care team), and students or teachers who use a facility for education.

The Florida legislature and the Florida Department of Health and Rehabilitative Services have very broad powers to protect the public health. However, the United States Constitution limits the extent to which state authority may be used to achieve the state's legitimate purposes. A state must use the least restrictive alternative in light of the constitutional requirements. For this reason, Florida law has concentrated on measures designed to encourage those who may be suffering from HIV/AIDS to come forward and be tested. The law attempts to remove barriers that may exist to voluntary testing. In this way, public health can be protected without unduly infringing individual rights.

POSTTEST

DIRECTIONS. To receive pharmacy CE credit for this program, use the posttest answer sheet on page 329. Indicate your answers to questions 1 through 37 located at the end of chapter 6 and to questions 38 to 45. Follow the instructions on the posttest answer sheet.

38. Which of the following subjects is specifically required by law to be included in educational courses on HIV/AIDS in Florida?

    a. drug therapy
    b. current Florida law
    c. diagnosis
    d. social aspects

39. In what way is AIDS unique as a disease?

    a. Its political aspects.
    b. It is sexually transmitted.
    c. It is fatal.
    d. It is caused by a virus.

40. Despite many good reasons to be tested for HIV infection, the Florida legislature observed that many members of the public

    a. are deterred from seeking such a test.
    b. misunderstand the nature of the test.
    c. fear that results of such a test will be disclosed.
    d. all of the above.

41. Prior to an HIV-related test, the person being treated must be given

    a. a complete physical.
    b. a lecture regarding the evils of drug abuse.
    c. information concerning the transmission of HIV.
    d. a prescription for AZT.

42. Individuals who undergo an HIV-related test have an absolute right of confidentiality in Florida.

    a. true
    b. false

43. Florida health care providers will not suffer criminal or civil liability for disclosing a positive test for HIV to a patient's sexual partner if

    a. the partner's identity was disclosed by the patient.
    b. the patient knows of the health care provider's intent to disclose.
    c. the health care provider acts in good faith.
    d. all of the above.

44. Informed consent to treat minors for sexually transmissible diseases

    a. must be obtained from the minor's parents.
    b. must be obtained from the minor's legal guardian.
    c. must be obtained from a court of law.
    d. none of the above.

45. The structure of Florida law on HIV/AIDS

    a. encourages voluntary testing.
    b. punishes those with AIDS.
    c. deters drug abuse.
    d. promotes morality.

MAIL-IN GRADING POSTTEST ANSWER SHEET

Care and Management of Patients with HIV Infection
and Florida Law on AIDS
ACPE ID No. 686-342-92-016   Credit: 0.1 CEU
ACPE ID No. 686-342-92-041   Credit: 0.7 CEU
Florida ID No. PSA-94-006
Please print clearly the information requested below.

SOCIAL SECURITY NO. ☐☐☐ – ☐☐ – ☐☐☐☐

Name ☐☐☐☐☐☐☐☐☐☐☐☐ ☐ ☐☐☐☐☐☐☐☐☐☐☐☐☐☐
First   M.I. Last

Home
Address ☐☐☐☐☐☐☐☐☐☐☐☐☐☐☐☐☐☐☐☐

☐☐☐☐☐☐☐☐☐☐☐☐ ☐☐ ☐☐☐☐☐ – ☐☐☐
City   State Zip Code

Home Phone ( ) – ☐☐☐ – ☐☐☐☐   Bus. Phone ( ) – ☐☐☐☐☐☐☐

Are you licensed in Alabama? Yes _____ No _____ Alabama License No. _____

Other states licensed in: _____

To use the Mail-in Grading service, carefully complete the answer sheet and enclose a check
or money order for **$10.00 payable to Program Management Services, Inc.** and mail to:

> **Program Management Services, Inc.**
> **PO Box 490**
> **East Islip, NY 11730**

To avoid delay, please be sure to enclose the proper remittance.

**Please be sure your Social Security number is given as requested above. Credit will be granted for the
successful completion of this program up to December 31, 1994.**

For each question, decide on the best answer, and place an X through that letter. If you change an answer,
be sure to erase completely. Mark only **one** answer for each question.

1.	A B C D	16.	A B C D	31.	A B C D
2.	A B C D	17.	A B C D	32.	A B C D
3.	A B C D	18.	A B C D	33.	A B C D
4.	A B C D	19.	A B C D	34.	A B C D
5.	A B C D	20.	A B C D	35.	A B C D
6.	A B C D	21.	A B C D	36.	A B C D
7.	A B C D	22.	A B C D	37.	A B C D
8.	A B C D	23.	A B C D	38.	A B C D
9.	A B C D	24.	A B C D	39.	A B C D
10.	A B C D	25.	A B C D	40.	A B C D
11.	A B C D	26.	A B C D	41.	A B C D
12.	A B C D	27.	A B C D	42.	A B C D
13.	A B C D	28.	A B C D	43.	A B C D
14.	A B C D	29.	A B C D	44.	A B C D
15.	A B C D	30.	A B C D	45.	A B C D

To avoid delay, please be sure to enclose proper remittance.

This CE program is sponsored by Glaxo Inc. as an educational service to keep today's pharmacist abreast of a rapidly changing health care environment. Address all inquiries to: Barbara Mitchell, Manager, Pharmacy Education, Glaxo Inc., Five Moore Drive, RTP, NC 27709.

Each participant achieving a grade of 70% or above will receive a participation certificate indicating the number of CE credits earned. Please allow three weeks for processing. This certificate should be kept in a safe place and used as documentation of CE credits earned. A participant obtaining a grade below 70% will be notified and permitted to retake the exam one time at no extra cost.

How long did it take you to complete this CE activity? _____

SURVEY QUESTIONS

1.   Highest degree earned: (Check one.) ☐ BS Pharmacy ☐ BS (Other) ☐ PharmD
     ☐ PhD ☐ Other _____

2.   How long ago did you complete your last degree: (Check one.)

     ☐ Less than 1 yr ☐ 1–5 yrs ☐ 6–10 yrs ☐ 11–20 yrs ☐ 21–30 yrs ☐ More than 30 yrs

3.   Area of practice: (Check all applicable.)

     ☐ Independent   ☐ Teaching/Research   ☐ Medical sales rep.
     ☐ Chain   ☐ Industry/Research   ☐ Wholesale
     ☐ Hospital or institution ☐ Other _____

4.   I found the program: (Circle the appropriate number/level.)

Not Practical	1	2	3	4	5	Very Practical
Poorly Written	1	2	3	4	5	Expertly Written
Difficult to Understand	1	2	3	4	5	Easily Understood

5.   The examination was: (Circle the appropriate number/level.)

Too Short	1	2	3	4	5	Too Long
Too Difficult	1	2	3	4	5	Too Easy
Poorly Written	1	2	3	4	5	Clearly Written

6.   Please check any of the following topics that you feel would be of interest for future CE programs.

     ☐ Drug Interactions   ☐ Drugs and Cardiovascular Diseases
     ☐ Drugs and Nutritional Disorders   ☐ Rational Approaches to Drug Selection
     ☐ Drugs and the Geriatric Patient   ☐ Drug-induced Diseases
     ☐ Pharmacokinetics/Biopharmaceutics   ☐ Drugs and Their Side Effects
     ☐ Drugs and Cancer   ☐ Drugs and Respiratory Diseases
     ☐ Drugs and Infectious Diseases   ☐ Drugs and Gastrointestinal Disorders
     ☐ Drugs and Dermatologic Disorders   ☐ Drugs and Sexually Transmitted Diseases
     ☐ Basic Pharmacology of Selected   ☐ Please list other topics of interest or
       Drug Categories. Any special   concern: _____
       categories: _____

CARE AND MANAGEMENT OF PATIENTS WITH HIV INFECTION

Chapter 7: The Role of the Nurse in the Care of Patients with HIV Infection

Anthony Adinolfi, RN, MSN (Candidate)
Nurse Clinician, Division of Infectious Diseases
AIDS Clinical Trials Unit
Duke University Medical Center

CONTENTS

Introduction 335
Objectives 335
Recommended Preparation 336
   I.   Historical Perspective of the Nurse's Role in AIDS 337
  II.   Overview of the Use of the Nursing Process 340
       A. Assessment 340
       B. Diagnosis (Nursing) 346
       C. Planning 347
       D. Implementation 348
       E. Evaluation 348
 III.   Application of the Nursing Process to Persons with AIDS 349
       A. Care of the Hospitalized Adult with AIDS 349
       B. Care of the Hospitalized Pediatric AIDS Patient 353
       C. Care of the AIDS Patient in the Home and Community 357
  IV.   How Do Nurses Help Each Other? 363
       A. Identifying the Problem 363
       B. Approaches to Dealing with Burnout 365
Summary 367
References 369
Recommended Follow-up 370
Nursing Continuing Education Posttest 372
Test Grading Options 380
Mail-in Grading Scannable Form . . . . end of book

INTRODUCTION

This chapter of *Care and Management of Patients with HIV Infection* is recommended for nurses and other health care professionals who desire a review of nursing care of the patient with HIV infection or AIDS. This chapter covers the role of the nurse in caring for patients with HIV infection as well as presents guidelines for protection of persons who care for such patients.

OBJECTIVES

Objectives presented here are intended to focus the reader's attention on expected learning outcomes.

On completion of the chapter, the reader should be able to:

1. Explain the historical perspectives of nursing in the care of persons with HIV infection.

2. Identify the role of the nurse in the care of persons with HIV infection.

3. Describe the application of the nursing process in caring for persons with HIV infection.

4. Explain the usefulness of NANDA taxonomy in the development of nursing diagnoses.

5. Integrate nursing diagnoses into nursing care planning for adults with HIV infection.

6. Integrate nursing diagnoses into nursing care planning for children with HIV infection.

7. Explain the nursing strategies in the care of adults and children with HIV infection in the home and community.

8. Evaluate the resources needed in caring for persons with HIV infection.

9. Identify strategies to help other nurses maintain coping skills and prevent burnout when caring for persons with HIV infection.

10. Identify strategies for reducing occupational transmission of HIV.

RECOMMENDED PREPARATION

Since this chapter contains a continuing education posttest that is comprehensive of chapters 1 through 4 as well as chapter 7, the reader is encouraged to review the first four chapters, which cover the pathophysiology, diagnosis, and treatment of acquired immunodeficiency syndrome and its associated infections.

I. HISTORICAL PERSPECTIVE OF THE NURSE'S ROLE IN AIDS

The reported incidence of acquired immunodeficiency syndrome (AIDS) in the United States has reached epidemic proportions. The number of people diagnosed is over 300,000, with probably five times as many people infected with the human immunodeficiency virus (HIV). The health care system is being stretched to the limit to provide primary, secondary, and tertiary care to those in need. The nation's clinics, hospitals, and home-based care systems must be able to meet this challenge in the '90s.

As nurses, we must be ready to cope with AIDS and HIV. Our best weapon is knowledge: the facts about transmission, pathophysiology, and treatment. We must comprehend the significant role that family and friends play in caring for the person with AIDS (PWA) and be able to support them. We must become advocates for AIDS patients, who have limited power in dealing with a devastating disease, an inadequate health care delivery system, and a society that blames them for their illness.

There have been nurses since the beginning of the AIDS epidemic who have been spokespersons for PWAs—advocates, change-agents, and veritable saints. Nurses have been at the bedsides, but they have also been in administrators' offices and on Capitol Hill making a difference. Although there have been many nurses visible in AIDS care, five nurses are described here to illustrate how nurses have provided leadership, shown compassion, and set standards of care in providing services to PWAs.

In December 1983, the first person with Kaposi's sarcoma (KS) to announce publicly that he had AIDS was a registered nurse.[1] His name was Bobbi Campbell, and he was the sixteenth person diagnosed with AIDS in San Francisco. He went public to "heighten awareness" of this new and frightening disease. Bobbi helped to enlighten both the country, and, especially, the citizens of San Francisco. He helped to establish a support group for people with KS, and he started a process to identify the needs of PWAs that could be met through community, city, and county resources. Bobbi provided guidance to many people with AIDS so that they could obtain necessary resources and thus feel a sense of power, an important feeling when dealing with this devastating illness.

An innovative and model approach to the inpatient care of PWAs was spearheaded by Cliff Morrison, RN, a clinical specialist at San Francisco General Hospital (SFGH).[1] Cliff evaluated the need for specialized care for PWAs and organized what would become the first inpatient unit for treating them. He concluded that a nursing care unit should be run by nurses and that patients should have input into decisions involving their care. Ward 5B at SFGH has become the model for AIDS care throughout the world. Since admitting its first dozen patients, the unit has very rarely had empty beds. The idea of a nursing-managed inpatient unit, with patients assisting in decision making, has ensured that patients have had access to all available resources, including the most up-to-date psychosocial, medical, nursing, and spiritual interventions.

Patients have always needed a place to go after discharge. Many PWAs, however, have had nowhere to go after leaving the hospital because of the stigma of having AIDS, because of family and friends lacking knowledge or fearing the disease, or because of limited financial resources. The Shanti Project in San Francisco had already been organized to provide hospice care for terminally ill cancer patients. When AIDS appeared, Shanti redirected its mission to provide care to those with AIDS. As of 1981, the San Francisco AIDS Home Care and Hospice Program, along with the Visiting Nurse Association of San Francisco, began to identify patients with AIDS and to provide care. These home-health agencies realized that patients could receive most of their care in the home, a much more pleasant experience than inpatient care. The director of the Shanti Project was Helen Schietinger, RN. Through her own example, Helen demonstrated the ability to provide well-organized outpatient care that was efficient and compassionate and that included the most important component: a warm smile and gentle touch.

Jeanne Parker Martin, RN, the director of the AIDS Home Care and Hospice Program, helped develop the manual that is used widely in caring for PWAs at home. Under Jeanne's supervision, her home care program has grown to be the largest in the world. Even today, Jeanne has enthusiasm and confidence that home care is the model for AIDS care delivery.

In the area of education, a New York City nurse, JoAnne Bennett, RN, has worked as a volunteer with the Gay Men's Health Crisis (GMHC), one of the first volunteer groups to provide education and information about AIDS to the public. GMHC has also provided support to PWAs, their families, and their friends. JoAnne has provided guidance and leadership in the area of nursing education by writing articles for nursing journals, identifying needs of PWAs, and helping design innovative approaches in patient care.

These five nurses that have been highlighted in the history of nursing in the AIDS epidemic are not unique. Nurses at every level of care have met the needs of PWAs: nursing administrators setting policies and procedures for direct care; nurses on Capitol Hill providing the human touch to governmental bureaucracy; and nurses at the bedside who are there when they are needed most. Nurses have been volunteers in communities across the country. Some "buddy programs," programs designed and implemented to provide support services to PWAs, were started by nurses who realized that hospitals and medical centers could not meet many of the PWAs' important needs and that families of PWAs were unable or unwilling to provide for their everyday needs. Nurses started support groups in the community because they realized that a sense of belonging and access to information was essential to empower patients.

What are the future roles for nurses in the treatment of patients with AIDS and HIV infection? Clinical nurse specialists, including nurse practitioners and master's-prepared clinical nurse specialists with a firm background in oncology and infectious diseases, will complement care delivered by physicians. Outpatient care will be coordinated by nurses, and will include a multidisciplinary team of physicians, social workers, nurses, pharmacists, physical therapists, and others. As increasing numbers of PWAs require care in the community, the need for public health nurses will grow. Nursing will need to attract new members, but we do not know yet whether the challenge of AIDS care will deter or encourage applicants to the nation's nursing schools. It is up to those of us who realize and remember why we went into nursing to increase our ranks, to act as advocates for PWAs, to become politically active, and to show by example that in the high-tech world of health care, it is the nurse who remembers the most important reason for our being there: the patient and his or her family. The challenge has been given. As the largest group of health care professionals, we can make a difference.

II. OVERVIEW OF THE USE OF THE NURSING PROCESS

The care of the person with AIDS is complex and involves all areas of functioning: physical, psychological, economic, and spiritual. Use of the nursing process helps organize and coordinate nursing care. The nursing process is a step-by-step analysis of all areas of functioning to solve problems that the nurse encounters when providing patient care. The five components of the nursing process are:

- Assessment: the collection of data, subjective and objective.

- Diagnosis (nursing): identification of the problem as perceived by the nurse and the patient, based on data from the assessment (included are actual, possible, and potential problems).

- Planning: setting of goals, from the perspective of both nurse and patient.

- Implementation: interventions and treatments following nursing orders.

- Evaluation and communication: observation of the effects of nursing intervention and subsequent modification of the nursing plan; oral and written communication of findings.

Each component of the nursing process will be reviewed with specific reference to HIV infection.

A. ASSESSMENT

The assessment component of the nursing process is a systematic method of obtaining information to determine a patient's current needs, status, and perception of health. Past and future coping skills are also assessed. The patient is interviewed and his or her perception of needs is assessed. The nurse must be able to identify needs through conversation, interview, physical examination, direct observation, and chart and record review.[2]

Because needs change, the information obtained in the assessment must be updated and reevaluated frequently to detect and represent changes, new problems, and resolution of problems. To use the assessment to its full potential, the nurse must be able to:

- Communicate with client, family, and other health care providers.

- Observe in a systematic manner.

- Assess the client's physical, psychological, emotional, and spiritual status.

- Develop a partnership with the patient.

- Acknowledge one's own feelings regarding cultural, sexual, behavioral, and economic issues.

The health history is the starting point of the assessment. Much of the health history may be obtained by the physician, in which case the nurse should review the physician's notes rather than obtain a totally separate history.

Special focus on chief complaints and past medical history is indispensable in determining a patient's immune system impairment. Specific questions should be aimed at obtaining information for assessing a history of signs and symptoms of HIV infection and associated risk factors.

1. Signs and Symptoms Specific to HIV Infection. Note the following specific points:

- Fatigue

- Malaise

- Fevers without cause, over 100°F (37.7°C)

- Night sweats

- Swollen or painful lymph nodes

- Unexplained weight loss

- Loss of appetite

- Cough, shortness of breath, chest tightness, orthopnea, tachypnea (not related to smoking or URI)

- Skin blemishes, rashes, lesions, bruising

- Oral thrush (candidiasis) not related to antibiotic therapy

- Changes in central nervous system function, including headaches, changes in mental status, stiff neck, seizures

- Herpes zoster (shingles)

- History of sexually transmitted diseases (STD), including:

  - Gonorrhea
  - Syphilis
  - Venereal warts
  - Hepatitis
  - Herpes simplex
  - Parasite infection
  - Diarrhea with unexplained etiology

2. Risk Factors. It is important to assess the patient's risk for HIV infection. Some patients are comfortable discussing these issues after developing feelings of trust with the interviewer. Others may be reluctant to share this information and need more time to feel comfortable. For many homosexual and bisexual men, having to disclose their sexual identity is very difficult. It is important, however, to ascertain if the patient is:

- Gay or bisexual.

- An IV drug user. If so, does he or she share needles?

- A recipient of blood or blood products before 1985. If yes, where and when?

- Part of an ongoing or previous sexual relationship with a member of any of the above.

3. Patient's Perception of Disease. What is the patient's knowledge of HIV infection? Open-ended questions, rather than questions that can be answered with a simple "yes" or "no," allow the patient to talk freely about issues that are important to him or her. How the patient perceives the implications of HIV affects his or her outlook and perceptions about the future. Appropriate questions include:

- What do you know about HIV infection?

- Do you know or have you known anyone with HIV infection? How well do/did you know them?

- Have you taken care of anyone with AIDS?

- What feelings do you associate with AIDS?

- What do you know about HIV transmission?

4. Physical Exam. The physical exam is critical for identifying HIV-related diseases, progression of HIV infection, and evidence of immune system deterioration. A complete and thorough examination should be performed by the physician. The nurse should be aware of important physical characteristics of HIV infection and its progression (see Table 7.1).

5. Laboratory Findings. A detailed review of laboratory findings is included in other sections of this book. Nurses should be familiar with and know the normal values at their own facility of the following laboratory tests:

- Complete blood count, including platelet count and sedimentation rate

- Chemistry panel (electrolytes, liver, heart, and kidney function)

- RPR (syphilis serology)

- Hepatitis panel

- Cultures of skin lesions

- Chest x-ray

- Lymphocyte study (CD4/CD8 ratio and absolute helper CD4 count)

- Stool cultures for acid-fast bacilli, ova and parasites, and culture and sensitivity, if patient is symptomatic with diarrhea

TABLE 7.1. Physical Signs of HIV Infection

Area of Inspection	Sign	Possible Etiology
Mouth	Whitish coating on tongue, gums, roof of mouth	Oral candidiasis
	Fine lines or ridges on sides of tongue	Hairy leukoplakia
	Purple spots, lesions	Kaposi's sarcoma
	Bleeding gums	ITP
Eyes	Cottonwool spots	CMV retinitis
Neck	Swollen, painful lymph nodes	Lymphadenopathy
	Nuchal rigidity	Cryptococcosis
Lungs	Auscultation for extraneous sounds (rales, wheezes, rhonchi)	PCP
	Cough	Bacterial pneumonia
Abdomen	Tenderness	ITP
	Liver and spleen size	
	Cancers	
GU/Rectal	Warts	Venereal warts
	Whitish coating of membranes	Candidal infection
	Ulcers/lesions	Herpes simplex
Skin	Total body must be inspected for:	
	Purple lesions	Kaposi's sarcoma
	Lesions	Herpes simplex or zoster
	Bruising	ITP
	Dry, flaking skin	Seborrheic dermatitis
	Rashes	Drug reaction
		Disseminated disease
		Syphilis
Neurologic	Memory loss	Cryptococcosis
	Personality changes	Toxoplasmosis
	Decreased cognitive function	CNS lesions
	Decreased or increased reflexes	HIV dementia
	Neuropathies	

6. Psychological Profile. It is essential to assess a patient's psychological state and ability to cope with the disease. The nurse should explore the following issues with the patient:

- AIDS as a life-threatening process

- AIDS as a debilitating and insidious process

- Changes in sexual behaviors (e.g., safer sex)

- Drug use

- The patient's reactions to his or her disease and how he or she is coping with feelings of:

    - Anxiety
    - Fear
    - Denial
    - Anger
    - Guilt
    - Powerlessness
    - Social isolation
    - Geographic isolation
    - Grief
    - Loss
    - Dying, including death as a process and as an event
    - Changes in body image
    - Mental status changes

- Type, quantity, and quality of existing social support systems

- Financial and insurance status

- The patient's concept of "future"

- Perception of the "significant other" and family

- Patient's coping skills

Table 7.2 contains suggested methods of coping that have proven effective.

TABLE 7.2.   Examples of Indirect Coping Patterns (Reproduced by permission from Christensen P, Fayram E. Planning: strategies and nursing orders. In: Griffith-Kenney J, Christensen P, eds. *Nursing Process: Application of Theories, Frameworks and Models.* 2nd ed. St. Louis, MO: CV Mosby; 1986.)

Physical	Psycho/ Intellectual	Social	Spiritual
Exercise	Meditation	Social recreation	Prayer
Smoking	Woodworking,	Avoid others	Attend religious
Eating/drinking	crafts,	Attend social	services
Relaxation	painting	gatherings	Read spiritual
techniques	Fantasy	Talk with	books
	Positive self-talk	friends	Talk with clergy

B. DIAGNOSIS (NURSING)

Nursing diagnosis occurs after the collection of data in the assessment phase is completed. The assessment must be summarized in specific diagnoses in order to plan care. A nursing diagnosis, unlike a physician's diagnosis, is based on the patient's *response* to his or her illness, rather than on the illness itself. Nursing diagnoses also identify the patient's strengths and areas of healthy functioning, not just areas of need. A nursing diagnosis should be specific to the needs of the individual patient and his or her family and community. Knowledge of available resources to assist with the formulation of nursing diagnoses is a great asset to the nurse.

In an attempt to standardize nursing diagnoses, the North American Nursing Diagnosis Association (NANDA) proposed categories of patient needs. The NANDA nursing diagnoses that are relevant in caring for the HIV-infected patient can be categorized in eleven functional health patterns:[3]

- Health perception–health management pattern

- Nutritional and metabolic pattern

- Elimination pattern

- Activity–exercise pattern

- Sleep–rest pattern

- Cognitive–perceptual pattern

- Self-perception–self-concept pattern

- Role–relationship pattern

- Sexuality–reproductive pattern

- Coping–stress tolerance pattern

- Value–belief pattern

C. PLANNING

After thorough assessment and diagnosis have been made, plans to address the needs identified by the nurse, the patient, and the family can be made. Nursing interventions to prevent, reduce, and eliminate problems must be specified and prioritized. The patient should be encouraged to provide input into care planning, based on his or her motivation and ability to identify problems.

There are four phases of the planning component carried out by the nurse and the HIV-infected person.

1. Establish Priorities of Care. Life-threatening situations must be corrected immediately before other problems are addressed. The nurse may direct or assist the patient in focusing on priorities. It is important to remember that the nurse and the patient may rank needs differently. A care plan that does not reflect the patient's perceptions about the importance of certain needs may be doomed to failure.

2. Specify Patient Goals. The outcome (patient's goals) must be realistic, measurable, and specific (e.g., "Patient will demonstrate use of antifungal troches.").

3. Specify Nursing Goals. The process (nursing goals) must be realistic and based on available resources (e.g., "Nurse will instruct patient in use of antifungal troches.").

4. Specify Nursing Orders. The nursing care plan is initiated through nursing orders that are clear, specific to the individual whenever possible, and measurable (e.g.,"Instruct patient in use of antifungal troches and chart patient's progress in nursing notes.").

D. IMPLEMENTATION

The implementation phase of the nursing process is the actual carrying out of the plan by the nurse and the patient. Implementation involves care that is specific to the individual and the problem, is safe, utilizes a multidisciplinary approach, and can be evaluated.

According to Fayram,[4] the important elements for the implementation component of the process include the following:

- The actions performed are consistent with the plan and occur after validation of the plan.

- Interpersonal, intellectual, and technical skills are used competently and efficiently in an appropriate environment.

- The patient's physical and psychological safety are protected.

- Documentation of actions and the patient's response to the plan are evident in the health care record and care plan.

E. EVALUATION

The evaluation component is the final part of the nursing process. There are three parts:[2]

- Establish measurable, observable criteria.

- Assess the present response for evidence.

- Compare the present response with the established criteria.

According to Griffith-Kenney,[5] there are four areas of evaluating a patient's response to a specific plan. They include:

- Physiologic responses (e.g., normal skin condition, wound healing, temperature control)

- Skills (e.g., self-administration of medications, dressing changes)

- Levels of knowledge (e.g., side effects of medications, disease transmission)

- Adaptive behaviors (e.g., ability to perform activities of daily living [ADL], coping)

III. APPLICATION OF THE NURSING PROCESS TO PERSONS WITH AIDS

The nursing process has been described briefly. This section demonstrates the usefulness of the process through case histories and accompanying care plans. Although several potential and probable nursing diagnoses can be identified, only two for each case study will be presented. By studying the examples, it is hoped that nurses will be better able to use the nursing process in their areas of clinical practice.

A. CARE OF THE HOSPITALIZED ADULT WITH AIDS

Initial presentation: Mr. Z. is a 28-year-old man who tested seropositive for HIV in the fall of 1986. He has been asymptomatic and without complaints while being followed at a major medical center. He presents to the ER with complaints of shortness of breath, dyspnea, tachypnea, and orthopnea. He also complains of fever, night sweats, and loss of appetite.

Vital signs:

> temperature: 40°C
> pulse: 120
> respiratory rate: 24
> blood pressure: 100/64

Arterial blood gases (on room air):

> pH: 7.36
> PO_2: 64
> PCO_2: 30

Blood studies:

> CBC: normal
> Chemistries: normal
> Total T helper (CD4) count: 80 cells/mm^3

Chest x-ray: normal

Mr. Z. was admitted to a private room on a busy medical floor. The nurses have asked that HIV-seropositive patients be placed on this particular floor because they feel that they have the knowledge and desire to provide care for them. The patient's presumptive diagnosis is *Pneumocystis carinii* pneumonia; he is scheduled for a bronchoscopy later in the day to confirm it. He is given antipyretics and an IV of D$_5$NS is started. When he returns from bronchoscopy, IV trimethoprim/sulfamethoxazole (Bactrim™, Septra®) is begun. His temperature is checked every four hours and remains high (39–40°C), even with the administration of antipyretics. His mental status is assessed every four hours and he is encouraged to drink fluids. The nurse assigned to this patient begins her care plan.

Assessment

As breathing permits, the patient should be asked questions regarding respiratory history: allergies, asthma, prior respiratory problems, chronic cough, history of TB, shortness of breath, dyspnea on exertion, orthopnea, tachypnea.

The patient should be observed for use of accessory muscles, increased sputum production, gasping, abnormal breath sounds, decreased breath sounds, and fremitus. Laboratory tests should be reviewed, particularly the chest x-ray and arterial blood gas reports.

Diagnosis

- Nursing diagnosis 1: impaired gas exchange.

- Related to: *Pneumocystis carinii* pneumonia.

- Rationale: respiratory rate, dyspnea, and blood gases indicate respiratory difficulties.

Plan

- The patient will demonstrate improved respiratory function.

- The patient will be able to expectorate secretions adequately.

- The patient will have a normal chest x-ray.

- The patient will have blood gases that are within normal limits.

Implementation[6]

- Obtain a baseline assessment of respiratory function, including relevant history, respiratory rate and character, use of accessory muscles, breath sounds, skin color, general appearance, and arterial blood gases.

- Assess patient for signs of impaired gas exchange and hypoxemia such as tachycardia, cool extremities, cyanosis, anxiety, irritability, tachypnea, altered mental status, and changes in orientation.

- Reassess respiratory status every two hours or as necessary for signs and symptoms of respiratory insufficiency/failure (e.g., tachypnea, tachycardia, dyspnea, apprehension, irritability, confusion).

- Monitor CBC for anemia, arterial blood gases for hypoxemia and hypercapnia, and O_2 saturations for decreased saturation of hemoglobin. Alert physician of significant changes; modify ventilatory changes as ordered.

- Suction as indicated; obtain specimens as ordered; carefully monitor lab results.

- Administer antimicrobials as ordered; observe carefully for side effects/toxicity.

- Administer antipyretics to control fevers; note effect on temperature.

- Administer antitussives/expectorants as ordered.

- Monitor use and effectiveness of ordered therapies such as oxygen, mechanical ventilation, humidification, chest tubes, and medications.

- Assist the AIDS patient with clearance of secretions by effective coughing; prevent stasis of secretions by deep breathing, ambulation, and possibly postural drainage.

- Assist patient in finding positions that ease breathing discomfort.

- Encourage fluid intake to prevent dehydration and to promote liquification of secretions.

- Organize nursing care to permit rest periods.

- Administer narcotic analgesics and sedatives cautiously; evaluate response.

- Observe for postbronchoscopy complications such as bleeding, anxiety, drug reactions, and euphoria (if cocaine is used).

Evaluation[6]

The patient:

- Experiences decreased symptoms of dyspnea and air hunger.

- Expectorates secretions.

- Expresses relief from symptoms causing discomfort.

- Has blood gas values within normal limits.

- Demonstrates improved respiratory function.

Assessment

- What was admission/baseline temperature?

- What is temperature now?

- Is patient having chills?

- How many covers (blankets, sweaters, coats) does patient have on?

- What is the thermostat in the room set on?

- Is fever related to specific infection?

- Is patient febrile after medication administration?

- Is patient dehydrated?

- Does the patient have a headache?

- Is the patient drowsy, restless?

- Has the patient had a seizure?

Diagnosis

- Nursing diagnosis 2: ineffective thermoregulation; potential altered body temperature.

- Related to: infection in lungs, *Pneumocystis carinii* pneumonia.

- Rationale: patient is not responding to antipyretics, febrile.

Plan

- The patient will have body temperature return to baseline, or have symptomatic relief and be comfortable.

- The patient will remain well hydrated.

- The patient will alert the staff if he feels his temperature rise/fall.

Implementation

- Monitor temperature every four hours, or more often if needed.

- Assess, document, and report chills, rigors, tachycardia.

- Administer antipyretics as ordered.

- Evaluate effectiveness of medication(s).

- Evaluate need for adjuncts to antipyretics (e.g., sponge baths, ice packs), and implement as ordered and/or necessary.

- Encourage fluid intake; provide water or juice; administer and chart IV fluids; record intake and output.

- Change linens often and avoid heavy covers.

- Keep room cool, and instruct patient to leave thermostat low.

Evaluation

- Patient has returned to his baseline temperature.

- Patient is afebrile.

- Patient verbalizes comfort.

- Skin turgor is normal.

B. CARE OF THE HOSPITALIZED PEDIATRIC AIDS PATIENT

Initial presentation: L.K. is an 8-month-old girl who is brought to the emergency room by her parents. The parents report that L.K. cries all the time, has had high fevers, gasps for breath, and has a whitish coating on her tongue. In the course of interviewing the parents, it is discovered that they are both former IV drug users, having been "clean" for the last three years. The ER physician requests that the parents and L.K. be tested for the presence of HIV antibodies. L.K. is admitted with possible pneumonia and oral candidiasis.

L.K. and her parents test seropositive for HIV. L.K. is diagnosed with lymphoid interstitial pneumonia and recurrent oral candidiasis. L.K.'s brother, age 10, and her sister, age 8, are both tested and found to be HIV seronegative. L.K. responds well to antibiotics for her pneumonia. The admitting pediatrician suggests that L.K. be transferred to a major medical center, over 300 miles away, that has the appropriate staff and technology to give L.K. optimal therapy. The transfer would increase the stress of having a child with AIDS, testing HIV seropositive themselves, taking care of their other children, and telling family and friends. The nurse caring for L.K. requests that a chaplain, social worker, and dietitian visit the K. family before she is transferred to help them handle their feelings, plan for L.K.'s eventual return home, and plan their own health care.

Assessment

- What medications is the patient currently taking?

- What is the consistency and amount of saliva?

- What color are the mucosa? Gums? Tongue?

- Are there ulcers, lesions, bleeding in the mouth?

- Is there exudate?

- Does the patient pull at her ears?

Diagnosis

- Nursing diagnosis 1: altered oral mucous membrane.

- Related to: oral candidiasis.

- Rationale: recurrent white coating on L.K.'s tongue.

Plan

- The patient will have oral mucous membrane integrity.

- The patient will be comfortable.

- The patient will be able to tolerate oral fluids.

- The family will be able to recognize signs and symptoms of oral candidiasis.

- The family will be able to administer appropriate medications and evaluate their effectiveness.

Implementation

- Assess mouth for signs and symptoms of oral candidiasis.

- Administer ordered medications.

- Chart and report effectiveness and side effects of medications.

- Instruct the family in proper technique of mouth care and signs and symptoms of oral candidiasis.

- Teach the family how to administer oral medications.

Evaluation

- The patient will have no evidence of oral candidiasis.

- The patient will appear comfortable and tolerate oral fluids.

- The patient's family will demonstrate their ability to administer appropriate medications and state their dosages and side effects.

- The patient's family will be able to state signs and symptoms of recurrent candidiasis.

Assessment

- Who will provide daily care for the patient?

- What does the family know about HIV/AIDS transmission, infection, treatment, and prognosis?

- How ready are they to learn?

- What is the family's educational level? Literacy level?

- What culturally specific information is necessary to help them learn? (For example, do they need an interpreter?)

- Is the family capable of caring for their child at home?

- What coping skills does the family use?

- What other people (e.g., extended family, friends) can the family depend on for help?

Diagnosis

- Nursing diagnosis 2: knowledge deficit, family.

- Rationale: family has had little preparation regarding HIV; high stress level limits ability to absorb information.

Plan

- The parents will maintain or develop adequate coping skills.

- The parents will help plan their child's care.

- The parents will have an adequate knowledge base (in the form of verbal and written materials).

- The parents will state their knowledge about HIV/AIDS, the appropriate treatment for them and their child, the transmission of the disease, the prognosis for themselves and their children, and the resources that are available to them.

Implementation

- Identify learning needs that are specific to the family's cultural and educational preparedness and language.

- Make a family-centered plan after assessing learning needs and motivation to learn. Have resources available that are specific to the family's situation.

- Use easily understood information, and interpret for the family.

- Teach the family about infection control, disease process, and treatment (including side effects and importance and relevance of therapies).

- Plan for discharge to home; begin long-term planning.

- Give space and time for the family to talk about their feelings, fears, and apprehensions.

- Provide information and referrals for community resources.

Evaluation

The family will be able to:

- State facts about HIV and AIDS and their implications for their family.

- Identify community resources they can use while caring for their child at home.

- Demonstrate proper methods of administering medications while being supervised by the nurse.

C. CARE OF THE AIDS PATIENT IN THE HOME AND COMMUNITY

Initial presentation: P.M., a 23-year-old man, has been hospitalized with cryptococcal meningitis. He has been receiving intravenous amphotericin B for 14 days and has seven days of therapy to complete before being discharged. The discharge planning nurse is preparing him to go home where he will continue receiving IV therapy three times per week, administered by a local home infusion service.

Since admission, P.M. has had very few visits from family and friends. Some of his gay friends are "AIDS-overloaded"—they cannot face another friend with AIDS. P.M.'s parents live in another state, his mother is attempting to be supportive, but his father will not talk to him. P.M.'s parents have asked him to move home with them, but P.M. wants to maintain his independence.

The discharge planning nurse suggests contacting the local AIDS service organization (ASO) to coordinate "buddies" to visit P.M. in the hospital and to help provide for his everyday needs when he is discharged.

P.M.'s apartment is on the third floor of an old building without an elevator. He has running water, appliances, and a clean apartment. His mother has agreed to stay with him for a few weeks until the buddies, the home health infusion nurses, and the local health department coordinate their visits and their respective roles.

Assessment

To obtain the above information, the nurse interviewed the patient to assess the following:

- What social support exists?

- What family support exists?

- Where does the family live?

- Does the patient receive visitors in the hospital?

- Are the feelings of isolation related only to being hospitalized?

- Does the patient feel isolated due to protective clothing worn by the staff?

- Are there issues of homophobia? Does the patient's life-style frighten members of the hospital staff, members of his social support system, and/or family members?

- Does the patient have adequate interpersonal skills?

- Do the patient's family and friends have adequate and current information regarding HIV and AIDS?

- What are the nonverbal clues the patient is giving to the staff?

Diagnosis

- Nursing diagnosis 1: social isolation.

- Related to: absence of social support, friends overloaded with AIDS, and family geographically distanced.

Plan

- Patient will demonstrate coping skills to deal with social isolation.

- Patient will state he is not lonely.

- Staff will provide a caring and supportive atmosphere that will set an example for visitors.

- Staff will be available to answer questions that visitors and family may have without violating the patient's privacy.

- With the patient's permission, the local AIDS service organization will be contacted to provide buddies.

Implementation[6]

- Allow patient to ventilate feelings of isolation. Assist patient in identifying his or her support system and developing a plan to establish supportive relationships with others.

- Involve mental health, social work, and chaplaincy personnel as needed in developing the care plan for emotional support.

- Institute measures to improve patient's self-esteem and interactions with others (e.g., decreasing negative comments about self).

- Communicate nonjudgmental attitudes and acceptance in interactions with patients, family, and significant others.

- Incorporate patient, family, and significant others in planning care.

- Ensure that family learning needs about the transmission of HIV are met to decrease fear and rejection of the patient.

- Conduct conferences for family members and/or the health care team to discuss fears about AIDS and about life-styles.

- Recognize the need for privacy when a significant other or sexual partner is visiting; honor wishes for confidentiality and help others (family, friends, and staff) cope with patient's preference.

- Encourage visiting and modify visiting hours as necessary; avoid unnecessary exaggeration of infection control precautions.

- Give family members permission and encouragement to sit on the bed, and to hug, kiss, and touch the patient with AIDS as desired.

- Be aware that the patient's friends may withdraw out of fear of catching the disease; educate as necessary.

- Involve community AIDS resources in planning patient care as available and appropriate.

Evaluation

The patient will be able to:

- Experience control over feelings of isolation.

- Talk about feelings of isolation.

- Develop new social skills to improve environment.

- Develop skills to find and use community resources.

Assessment

- Where does the patient live?

- Is there an elevator to his apartment?

- Does anyone live with him? Are neighbors available and helpful?

- Is the bathroom accessible and safe?

- Is there hot water?

- Is lighting adequate? Is there sunlight?

- Is there proper heating and air conditioning?

- Is the kitchen functional? Does the refrigerator work properly?

- Are community resources adequate to help the patient live at home?

- Will the patient be able to pay rent and bills?

- Are there pets: dogs, cats, birds, fish?

- Are there vermin: ants, cockroaches, mice, rats?

- Does the patient have an understanding of HIV/AIDS and its transmission?

- Can the patient identify relevant self-care issues?

- Can the patient administer his own medications?

Diagnosis

- Nursing diagnosis 2: impaired home maintenance management.

- Related to: disability due to acute illness, limited resources, third-floor apartment, and weakness.

Plan

- The patient will have a home-care plan before leaving the hospital.

- The patient will know his limitations and identify supports.

- The patient will utilize his community support network.

- The patient will be able to manage most daily activities and know the appropriate method of requesting help.

- The patient will be able to direct his care to meet his needs.

- The patient will preserve his energy by using volunteers and friends.

Implementation

The nurse will:

- Assess the patient's level of HIV knowledge.

- Assess the patient's readiness to learn (e.g., Is he lucid and free from pain?).

- Compare the patient's understanding of what home care means to his or her own perception of home care.

- Work with the patient and the patient's family and support system to develop a home-care plan that is sensitive to their various needs.

- Make referrals that are appropriate to the patient's needs.

- Teach the family and members of the support system pertinent information for home health care.

- Identify structural barriers in the home and recommend modifications.

- Identify roles of the supportive caregivers.

- Be an advocate for the patient in obtaining community resources.

- Review and reiterate the importance of using the nurse as a resource and referral mechanism.

- Assist in implementing "away time" for the caregivers.

- Strive for patient independence.

- Assess the patient's coping skills and teach new skills if necessary.

- Help the patient gain a feeling of control over his or her situation.

Evaluation

The patient, family, friends, support system, and the nurse will have a team conference to clarify goals and objectives of home care.

- The patient will verbalize an understanding of issues about home care.

- The patient will have a realistic view of what the future holds.

- The nurse is used as an advocate and to make referrals.

- Referral services report understanding of home health care needs.

IV. HOW DO NURSES HELP EACH OTHER?

As professional nurses, we are the caregivers at the bedsides working with patients infected with HIV. We are the role models for the ancillary personnel. We are the people the family comes to when they have questions and fears. We have to be comfortable with many issues surrounding HIV infection, including our own mortality, fear of contagion, issues of sexuality and drug use, over-identification, and watching young people suffer and die. These issues are very uncomfortable to many people. The most important strategy for dealing with issues that engender discomfort is to be able to recognize these issues, identify what makes these issues cause discomfort, and develop coping skills to maintain a sense of wellness and a sense of control in dealing with uncomfortable situations.

A. IDENTIFYING THE PROBLEM

The first step is to identify the sources of stress nurses encounter in dealing with patients with AIDS.

1. Mortality. The fact is that all AIDS patients will eventually die. Most of the patients are young and have never had to face illness, hospitalization, or issues of death and dying. As nurses, we have usually dealt with dying in the context of the aging process. We are less prepared to handle death among young people, usually the result of cancer or trauma.

As nurses and as human beings we have to identify and deal with our feelings about death and dying. Many of us feel that death is part of life and have a religious or philosophical perspective that allows us to manage our feelings. But all of us have times when we have difficulty with the losses we are experiencing. When that happens, we must be able to ask for help from our colleagues. We must be able to grieve when our patients die and not hold back our feelings for them. Every time a patient dies, we have to step back and reassess our feelings and attitudes about death. If we don't deal with how we feel, we deny ourselves the opportunity to grow.

An appropriate method for dealing with issues of death and dying would include facilitated discussion groups that address issues as they arise. A planned peer-support group would help those who are having difficulty with these issues. Attending funerals, writing sympathy cards, and keeping in touch with family after the loss of a patient are some other ways to deal with death and dying. Participating in making a quilt panel for the Names Project AIDS Memorial helps to work through feelings of sadness.

2. Fear of Contagion. We can learn the facts about HIV transmission, we can implement the most careful and thoughtful nursing care, and we can assume we are safe from occupational exposure if we follow the Centers for Disease Control's (CDC) guidelines and recommendations. Although these are useful approaches, everything we have ever learned may lose its meaning when fear sets in. When we are confronted with the possibility of our own death due to an occupational exposure, we may be tempted to ask for transfer away from the situation rather than deal with it. The chance of being exposed, however minuscule, prevents us from dealing rationally with the situation as it exists. We are in a much better position to deal with our fears of contagion if we know the facts about HIV transmission and take appropriate action. Universal precautions *must* be adhered to at all times for all patients. You should become thoroughly familiar with the CDC guidelines for preventing HIV transmission reprinted in chapter 1 of this book. Knowing the proper recommendations prevents discrepancies and provides a consistent set of guidelines for all health care providers.

3. Issues of Sexuality. The majority of patients with AIDS are gay and bisexual men. Before the onset of AIDS, it was much easier for gay and bisexual men to hide their sexuality, or not discuss it. AIDS has forced men to "come out of the closet" and divulge their homosexuality. It should be noted that homosexuality is no longer defined as pathological. Both the American Psychiatric Association and the American Psychological Association have removed homosexuality from their lists of psychiatric disorders. Only ego-dysfunctional homosexuality (where the person hates himself for being homosexual) is considered an illness.

Nurses may be more aware than the general population that most homosexuals do not fit the stereotypes of homosexuality. Unfortunately this may raise anxiety levels if the nurse no longer feels confident that he or she can identify "who is and who isn't." Studies have shown that many nurses are not tolerant of homosexuals and actually have an aversion to homosexuality. Research has also shown that nurses who are more tolerant and not judgmental of homosexuals have a friend or relative who is gay or have worked with someone who is gay.

How can nurses help improve attitudes toward homosexuality? Nursing school curricula should include discussion of gay and lesbian life-styles and ways to address special needs of that population. Nurses who are uncomfortable with homosexuality need to examine the issues surrounding homosexuality that make them uncomfortable and have an open forum for their concerns. If possible, a facilitated discussion group would allow issues to be addressed and dealt with. Information on homosexuality should be clear and consistent and should be factual rather than anecdotal.

4. Drug Use. The incidence of intravenous drug use in the United States is staggering. As a nation, we have considered drug use a crime rather than a disease and therefore have responded poorly in providing care and compassion toward drug users. Drug users are often seen as weak people who choose to become dependent on drugs. If we view drug use as anything other than a progressive disease, we avoid treatment for a treatable condition.

5. Overidentification. The majority of persons diagnosed with AIDS are 20 to 49 years old. This is also the age range of most nurses practicing nursing today. We are confronted by a group diagnosed with a devastating illness who are close to their caregivers in age, socioeconomic status, and education. We watch as our patients become sick and then have periods of wellness. We watch the periods of wellness diminish and periods of illness prevail. We feel helpless in the face of adversity.

6. Pain and Suffering. The cumulative losses we experience when caring for persons with AIDS feel manageable next to the amount of pain and suffering that we witness. As our patients suffer, so do we. We feel a sense of helplessness in a desperate situation. As nurses, we have been trained to reduce suffering and to offer consolation to those who are suffering. Our resources are very limited in what we can offer persons with AIDS. Our best method of self-preservation is to know our limitations and to be able to do our best at all times.

B. APPROACHES TO DEALING WITH BURNOUT

Rather than being a single event, burnout is an ongoing process. Sometimes nurses are accused of being "burned out" if we do not show compassion, concern, and caring in our thoughts and our actions. Nurses who are burned out may feel hopeless, helpless, and drained emotionally. They may have negative feelings towards life, career, and other people, including patients, peers, and family members. Burned-out nurses may come to work late or be absent from work. They may be rigid in their approaches to problems or show a decline in their work performance, and even make plans to look for another job.

How can we, as nurses, prevent burnout and deal with the issues that have been discussed? Some nurses that have been in the field of AIDS care have identified the following strategies to maintain a sense of personal wellness while working with persons with AIDS.

1. Use Your Common Sense. It doesn't take an expert to tell you when things are going badly. Recognize the stresses that you are encountering. Step back from the situation that is causing you stress and set priorities. Take time to organize and plan your daily activities. If you know that you will be dealing with a very stressful situation, make plans to get away, or become engaged in activities that are less stressful to balance your workload.

2. Discuss Your Feelings. Talk about your feelings and problems with others rather than withdrawing into yourself. It may take only a minute to let someone you work with know that you are experiencing stress or that you are sad. Share a summary of your daily activities with someone at home.

3. Develop Your Other Interests. Become involved in social and recreational activities. A well-rounded professional is much more effective at work. Hobbies (e.g., gardening, music, art, walking), volunteer work with your favorite charity or civic group, and participation in something completely unrelated to work are invigorating. Some people find that volunteer work in an AIDS service organization is refreshing if you can "wear a different hat" (e.g., be a buddy or work with a support group). This type of volunteerism is also rewarding because you don't have to work within the confines and structure of your job, and you can create your own role.

4. Take Care of Your Physical Needs. Many caregivers use exercise as a personal coping mechanism. Exercising provides a period for unwinding or cooling off. It is much better to leave the problems you encounter at work at the gym, the track, or even the neighborhood where you walk than keeping them to yourself. Find regular exercise that fits your needs and your schedule.

The importance of good nutrition is a concept that we are constantly conveying to our patients. It applies to us as well. Three meals a day that include the four basic food groups is essential to fuel our bodies and to give us the stamina we need.

Vacations are essential. We need to get away to develop an appreciation of how things really are. If our schedules do not permit extended vacations, we can use mini-trips, including day trips, to provide a change of scenery for much-needed revitalization.

5. Learn to Relax. There are many techniques for attaining a high level of relaxation. We all know the value of sleep; make sure that you get enough. Techniques such as the "relaxation response" afford an easy, short, and convenient way to relax. Meditation, prayer, and long walks in the park are all ways we can achieve a state of relaxation.

6. Incorporate Humor. Positive human emotions of humor and joy can move the mind and body in a direction towards good health. Become aware that if you are not having a good time in your life, you need to do something to change the way you look at things. The work we do is not to be taken lightly, but a light-hearted approach may keep us from always being too serious. We should find the videos we know will make us laugh and rent them when we need a good laugh.

7. Support Each Other. Get involved in or initiate staff support groups. The goals of the group should be to become more effective care providers, to build a sense of proficiency and assist group members in feeling good about their work, and to be able to deal with the situations that cause stress.

SUMMARY

Nurses have played a very important role in the delivery of care to persons with HIV infection. There have been nurses since AIDS was first identified who have been advocates, spokespersons, caregivers, administrators, volunteers, and friends to people with AIDS. As the demand and need for professional nurses rises, a challenge to all of the health care system exists to recruit and retain nurses as well as promote job satisfaction. Schools of nursing must design and implement graduate programs that focus on HIV to prepare advanced practitioners to meet the challenges of AIDS care. Schools of nursing at the University of California at San Francisco and Hunter College in New York City have included HIV components in their graduate curricula, and other schools and universities will follow their lead. The Oncology Nursing Society has a position paper on caring for the person with HIV infection, and professional organizations represent nurses caring for patients with HIV infection (e.g., Association of Nurses in AIDS Care).

Because the care of PWAs remains complicated, a standardized method of care delivery is essential. The use of approved and recognized nursing diagnoses affords the nurse some guidelines for care delivery. The five components of the nursing process (assessment, nursing diagnosis, planning, implementation, and evaluation) assist the nurse in solving problems that are encountered in patient care.

Nurses have the most crucial role in the everyday care of the person with AIDS—whether it be by the bedside, in an outpatient setting, or in the home and community. Many issues that engender intense feelings are encountered daily. Nurses must develop coping skills to handle better the myriad feelings that are associated with caring for PWAs. There are ways to cope with death and dying, homophobia, fear of contagion, pain and suffering, and drug use. The most effective coping skill is to be able to recognize that some situations make one feel uncomfortable and then deal with those feelings. To deny our feelings is most dangerous to our mental and physical health. There are strategies available to all of us to increase our coping skills and to help us feel good about what we do. We should feel good: we are there for our patients when they need us most. That is why most of us went into nursing.

The scientific information about HIV infection changes rapidly. As professionals, we must keep up-to-date as best we can. This chapter is just an introduction to some of the resources available through which we can learn more about HIV infection. If your hospital in-service or education department is not able to provide information on HIV infection, learn as much as you can and share the information you obtain with others.

Above all, do not lose your optimism. Maintaining hope that not everybody infected with HIV will die and that new and promising therapies are being pursued may assist you in communicating this to those you care for. Without optimism, you will feel hopeless and become an ineffective caregiver.

REFERENCES

1. Shilts R. *And the Band Played On*. New York, NY: St. Martin's Press; 1987.

2. Carpenito LJ. *Nursing Diagnosis: Application to Clinical Practice*. 3rd ed. Philadelphia, PA: JB Lippincott; 1989.

3. McFarland GK, McFarlane EA. *Nursing Diagnosis and Intervention: Planning for Patient Care*. St. Louis, MO: CV Mosby; 1989.

4. Fayram ES. Implementation. In: Griffith-Kenney JW, Christensen PJ, eds. *Nursing Process: Application of Theories, Frameworks, and Models*. 2nd ed. St. Louis, MO: CV Mosby; 1986.

5. Griffith-Kenney JW. Evaluation. In: Griffith-Kenney JW, Christensen PJ, eds. *Nursing Process: Application of Theories, Frameworks, and Models*. 2nd ed. St. Louis, MO: CV Mosby; 1986.

6. MacIntyre R, Tueller B, Wishon S. Nursing care plans for people with HIV infection. In: Gee G, Moran TA, eds. *AIDS: Concepts in Nursing Practice*. Baltimore, MD: Williams and Wilkins; 1988.

RECOMMENDED FOLLOW-UP

There are many texts and articles that have been published to help the nurse become more effective in providing care to AIDS patients. In addition to the sources in the reference list, the following may be helpful:

Baker L. *You and HIV: A Day at a Time*. Philadelphia, PA: WB Saunders; 1991.

Bartlett JG, Finkbeiner A: *The Guide to Living with HIV Infection*. Baltimore, MD: The Johns Hopkins Press; 1991.

Benson H. *The Relaxation Response*. New York, NY: William Morrow; 1975.

Berry RK. Home care of the child with AIDS. *Pediatr Nurs*. 1988;14:341–344.

Brown M, Kiss M, Outlasw E, Viamontes C. *Standards of Oncology Nursing Practice*. New York, NY: John Wiley and Sons; 1986.

Cousins N. *Anatomy of an Illness*. New York, NY: WW Norton and Co; 1979.

Douglas C, Kalman C, Kalman T. Homophobia among physicians and nurses: an empirical study. *Hosp Community Pharm*. 1985;36:1309–1311.

Eidson T, ed. *The AIDS Caregiver's Handbook*. New York, NY: St. Martin's Press; 1988.

Flaskerud JH, Ungvarski PJ. *HIV/AIDS: A Guide to Nursing Care*. 2nd ed. Philadelphia, PA: WB Saunders; 1992.

Good nursing care for the patient infected with the human immunodeficiency virus (HIV). *HERO*. 101 West Read Street, Suite 812, Baltimore, MD 21201; 1987.

Hughes AM, Martin JP, Franks P. *AIDS Home Care and Hospice Manual*. AIDS Home and Hospice Program, VNA of San Francisco; 1987.

Koop CE. *Surgeon General's Report on Acquired Immune Deficiency Syndrome*. US Public Health Service.

Koop CE. *Understanding AIDS: A Message from the Surgeon General*. US Public Health Service.

Lewis A, ed. *Nursing Care of the Person with AIDS/ARC*. Rockville, MD: Aspen Publishers; 1988.

Martelli L, Peltz F, Messina W. *When Someone You Know Has AIDS: A Practical Guide*. New York, NY: Crown Publishers; 1987.

Meisenholder J, LaCharite C, eds. *Comfort in Caring: Nursing the Person with HIV Infection*. Glenview, IL: Scott-Foreman; 1989.

Miller D. *Living with AIDS and HIV*. London: Macmillan Press Ltd; 1987.

Muldary TW. *Burnout and Health Professionals: Manifestations and Management*. New York, NY: Appleton-Century-Crofts; 1983.

Pines A, Aronson E. *Burnout: From Tedium to Personal Growth*. New York, NY: Free Press; 1981.

NURSING CONTINUING EDUCATION POSTTEST

DIRECTIONS. To receive continuing education credit for this program, read the Test Grading Options section, which follows the Nursing Continuing Education Posttest. Select the posttest submission method you prefer and follow the instructions provided.

1. Which of the following is *not* a documented method of transmission for the virus that causes AIDS?

    a. contamination of food products
    b. cross-placental infection from mother to fetus
    c. heterosexual intercourse
    d. transfusion of infected blood products

2. The cell that suffers the most damage in HIV infection is the

    a. B cell.
    b. macrophage.
    c. T helper/inducer cell.
    d. T suppressor cell.

3. The major function of the immune system that suffers damage in AIDS is the ability to

    a. attach antibodies to antigens.
    b. distinguish "self" from foreign protein.
    c. initiate a cell-mediated immune response.
    d. remove cellular debris.

4. The major action of the cellular immune system is the activation of

    a. B lymphocytes.
    b. plasma cells.
    c. stem cells.
    d. T lymphocytes.

5. The major function of B lymphocytes is the production of

    a. antigens.
    b. antibodies.
    c. lymphokines.
    d. plasma cells.

6. Which of the following is *not* a result of HIV infection of a host cell?

   a. It can cause the functional impairment of CD4 lymphocytes.
   b. It can form buds that break off from the host cell.
   c. It kills the host cell and infects new cells.
   d. It reproduces new virus cells by mitotic division.

7. Cells that express CD4 antigen on their cell surface

   a. are immune to infection by HIV.
   b. are present only during active HIV infection.
   c. include T cells, monocytes, and macrophages.
   d. selectively kill the AIDS virus.

8. Monoclonal antibodies are

   a. a sign of a failing immune system.
   b. less efficient than polyclonal antibodies at combining with their specific antigen.
   c. produced in response to a single epitope.
   d. the most common antibodies produced in HIV infection.

9. All of the following are common side effects of zidovudine *except*

   a. anemia.
   b. granulocytopenia.
   c. macrocytosis.
   d. thrombocytopenia.

10. What is the main advantage of didanosine over zidovudine that we have seen to date?

    a. Didanosine causes less peripheral neuropathy than zidovudine.
    b. Didanosine has been shown to attack the HIV virus *in vitro*.
    c. Didanosine has not caused the hematologic toxicities that have been seen with zidovudine.
    d. Didanosine will probably be much less expensive than zidovudine.

11. A patient's risk of developing clinical AIDS

    a. increases as CD4 cell count decreases.
    b. increases as CD4 cell count increases.
    c. increases only when CD4 cell count drops below 200.
    d. is unrelated to CD4 cell count.

12.   The FDA has approved zidovudine for

       a.   patients with AIDS.
       b.   patients with AIDS and advanced AIDS-related complex.
       c.   HIV-positive patients who have CD4 counts of 500 cells/mm^3 or less.
       d.   any patient with a CD4 count of 500 cells/mm^3 or less.

13.   The toxicities of didanosine include all of the following *except*

       a.   hepatitis.
       b.   peripheral neuropathy.
       c.   pancreatitis.
       d.   thrombocytopenia.

14.   Experimental therapies being investigated for the treatment of HIV infection include

       a.   reverse transcriptase inhibitors.
       b.   inhibitors of other elements in the virus life cycle such as HIV protease.
       c.   immune-based therapies.
       d.   all of the above.

15.   *Pneumocystis carinii* pneumonia

       a.   is caused by a virulent form of bacteria.
       b.   is usually fatal.
       c.   may initially present with mild cough and malaise.
       d.   rarely occurs in conjunction with other infections.

16.   A patient who is seropositive for HIV and presents with retinitis is most probably suffering from

       a.   cytomegalovirus infection.
       b.   diabetic retinopathy.
       c.   toxoplasmosis.
       d.   zidovudine toxicity.

17.   Defining AIDS as a legal handicap implies that

       a.   AIDS-affected employees can be considered handicapped in their ability to perform their jobs.
       b.   AIDS-affected employees may not be fired because of their disease.
       c.   medical care must be given under certain circumstances.
       d.   workers with AIDS must be given a medical leave of absence.

18. Which of the following statements about informed consent is true?

   a. It assumes that the patient has received adequate teaching about the procedure and its possible consequences.
   b. It can be obtained after the test has been performed, but before the results are known.
   c. It implies that the patient gives medical staff permission to disclose results to family members.
   d. It must always be obtained before performing a test for HIV antibodies.

19. Which of the following groups is usually *not* subject to involuntary testing?

   a. applicants for immigration
   b. health care professionals
   c. prison inmates
   d. prostitutes

20. An employer who determines that a health care worker is HIV positive

   a. may terminate employment based on anticipated disability.
   b. must base decisions about transfer on actual risk of HIV transmission.
   c. must transfer other workers away from that worker if they request transfer.
   d. must transfer that worker away from direct patient care.

21. An example of an innovative approach to provide care to persons with AIDS, as demonstrated by the staff of San Francisco General Hospital, is one that includes

   a. community leaders mandating staffing.
   b. a nursing care unit run by nurses and including patient input in decision making.
   c. physicians regulating care decisions.
   d. transferring patients to community hospitals.

22. Nursing care involves all areas of functioning *except*

   a. economic.
   b. ideological.
   c. physical.
   d. spiritual.

23.   Nursing plays all of the following roles in helping AIDS patients *except*

a.   helping establish support services.
b.   helping to set policy for patient care.
c.   providing hands-on care.
d.   researching the cell kinetics of the HIV virus.

24.   The nursing process is essential for patient care in that it incorporates all of the following *except*

a.   assessment.
b.   evaluation.
c.   implementation.
d.   medical diagnosis.

25.   The NANDA taxonomy is useful in developing nursing diagnoses because it

a.   allows nurses to use standardized, approved nursing diagnoses.
b.   prevents patients from making demands.
c.   provides medical information.
d.   specifically addresses only nursing problems.

26.   A young man is admitted to the hospital after an AIDS diagnosis. He has lost 25 pounds due to severe diarrhea. His clothes no longer fit him and he states that he feels "ugly." An appropriate nursing diagnosis category would be

a.   value-belief pattern.
b.   role-relationship pattern.
c.   self-perception–self-concept pattern.
d.   elimination pattern.

27.   An appropriate nursing intervention for this patient's feeling of ugliness would be to

a.   allow the patient to talk freely about his feelings.
b.   encourage the patient not to look in the mirror until he regains weight.
c.   offer high-calorie snacks.
d.   tell the patient he is handsome and not to worry.

28. To evaluate the patient's diarrhea, an appropriate nursing *goal* would be:

    a. Chart frequency and consistency of stools.
    b. Patient will not have diarrhea.
    c. Patient will not lose weight.
    d. Patient will use antidiarrheal medications appropriately.

29. The most appropriate nursing intervention for a patient with cachexia is to

    a. bring the patient home-cooked foods.
    b. meet with the patient and the dietitian to explore options.
    c. recommend supplementary tube feedings.
    d. remind the patient to eat frequently.

30. A 16-month-old child is diagnosed as being HIV seropositive. The child is able to move in the crib, but is unable to perform tasks and activities that you would expect a 16-month-old to do. An appropriate NANDA category of need would be

    a. elimination pattern.
    b. activity-exercise pattern.
    c. role-relationship pattern.
    d. sleep-rest pattern.

31. The child is unable to feed himself. The most appropriate nursing intervention would be to

    a. bottle feed.
    b. observe parent-child interaction for signs of parental neglect.
    c. use combination of spoon feeding and providing "finger foods."
    d. use velcro strap to hold spoon to hand.

32. Which of the following is an appropriate nursing goal for this child?

    a. Child will resume normal neurological development.
    b. Child will show improvement in ability to feed self.
    c. Observe child for improvement in ability to sit up alone.
    d. Spoon feed child q4h.

33. The mother of this child is an IV drug abuser. You feel angry at her because she has infected her child. An appropriate response is to

    a. confront the mother about her behavior.
    b. explore your feelings with a fellow staff member.
    c. remind yourself that anger is not an appropriate response for a professional.
    d. restrict the mother's visits with her child.

34. Essential components of caring for an AIDS patient in the home include all of the following *except*

    a. an interdisciplinary approach to care.
    b. maintenance of the patient's feelings of independence.
    c. mechanisms to provide a clean environment.
    d. strict isolation.

35. On a home visit to this patient, the nurse should check for all of the following *except*

    a. adequate refrigeration and cooking facilities.
    b. adequate written literature on HIV infection.
    c. adequate ventilation throughout the house.
    d. proper safety devices (e.g., siderails on bed).

36. Strategies to maintain a sense of well-being while caring for persons with AIDS include all of the following *except*

    a. avoiding open displays of feeling.
    b. becoming involved in social and recreational activities.
    c. incorporating humor in your daily routines.
    d. taking care of your physical needs.

37. A friend comes to you quite concerned that she might have contracted AIDS from a previous lover. Your counseling should be based on the information that

    a. AIDS could have been contracted only from homosexual contact.
    b. AIDS is associated only with promiscuous behavior.
    c. any sexually active person is at risk of AIDS.
    d. heterosexual women very rarely contract AIDS.

38.   In counseling a family member of a patient with AIDS, you would advise them to do all of the following *except*

   a.   isolate the AIDS patient from the rest of the family.
   b.   keep the kitchen clean and wash utensils in hot, soapy water.
   c.   wash hands carefully.
   d.   wash toilets and bathrooms with a solution of one part household bleach to nine parts water.

39.   A patient who is diagnosed with AIDS is very concerned that his or her diagnosis will become public knowledge. An appropriate strategy for providing confidentiality to this patient would be to

   a.   have a special code for AIDS devised for the hospital that only hospital staff can interpret.
   b.   have the patient isolated for hepatitis B.
   c.   only tell a few health care providers of his diagnosis.
   d.   put the whole unit on universal precautions.

40.   Using community resources is an important component of providing optimal patient care. Of the following resources, the *most* appropriate would be

   a.   community volunteers including local AIDS service organizations.
   b.   the United Fund.
   c.   the World Health Organization.
   d.   the YMCA.

TEST GRADING OPTIONS

To make it as convenient as possible for you to complete this program, Glaxo offers you two choices for having your test graded: **Phone-in Grading and Mail-in Grading.**

To assist you in selecting the type of grading service that best suits your needs, consider the following:

Phone-in Grading:

- Your call is answered by a trained and courteous operator.
- Your certificate is dated the same day as your call.
- You get your test score immediately over the phone. If your score is over 80%, you are informed of the correct answers to any incorrect responses.
- See the instructions on the following page.

Mail-in Grading:

- Your test will be processed promptly upon receipt.
- Simply enclose a check or money order with your completed answer sheet.
- Use the special scannable form contained in the envelope at the end of the book.
- See the instructions on the scannable form.

For your convenience, additional scannable forms are available upon request by calling 516-563-1604, Monday–Friday, 10 a.m. to 5 p.m. (EST).

Phone-in Grading instructions:

To use the **Phone-in Grading** service, call 1-800-327-9263, 10 a.m. to 5 p.m. (EST) Monday–Friday. Please have the following ready when you call:

1) **The posttest answers**
2) **Your Social Security number**
3) **Credit card name, number, and expiration date**

For Phone-in Grading, you can use your **Visa, MasterCard, or American Express** card to pay the $10.00 per test processing fee. Your call will be answered by a trained and courteous operator who will assist you and process your certificate the same day.

You may still complete the program evaluation by returning the special scannable form contained in the envelope at the end of the book.